# RISE OF ROMANTIC HELLENISM IN ENGLISH LITERATURE 1732-1786

# THE RISE OF ROMANTIC HELLENISM IN ENGLISH LITERATURE

1732-1786

BY
BERNARD HERBERT STERN

1969
OCTAGON BOOKS
*New York*

*Reprinted 1969*
*by special arrangement with Bernard Herbert Stern*

OCTAGON BOOKS
A DIVISION OF FARRAR, STRAUS & GIROUX, INC.
19 Union Square West
New York, N. Y. 10003

AM

LIBRARY OF CONGRESS CATALOG CARD NUMBER: 72-86288

*Printed in U.S.A. by*
TAYLOR PUBLISHING COMPANY
DALLAS, TEXAS

## ACKNOWLEDGMENT

The term "romantic hellenism" was first used by Harry Levin in the stimulating little essay, *The Broken Column; A Study in Romantic Hellenism, Bowdoin Undergraduate Prize Essay,* published by the Harvard University Press in 1931. To Mr. Levin's work I wish to acknowledge my indebtedness for the suggestion of many of the ideas developed in this study, particularly in Chapter I.

I wish also to express my thanks to Professor Walter MacKellar of New York University, under whose guidance this study was prepared; to Professors Homer A. Watt and Edwin Berry Burgum of New York University, who read the manuscript and made valuable suggestions; and to Professor Frederic Ewen of Brooklyn College, who first introduced me to the literature of the eighteenth century and its neo-hellenism.

BERNARD H. STERN

Brooklyn College
February, 1940

## CONTENTS

# I

# INTRODUCTION

The latter half of the eighteenth century in England is a transition period rich in manifestations of conflicting artistic forces. Whether one studies its literature or its painting, architecture, gardening, and interior decorating, the same opposing movements are evident.[1] On one side is ranged a group of classical tendencies —Palladianism and the formalism dominating the history of taste since the Renaissance. On the other side, almost equally long-lived, if not so dominant, is another group, generally designated as more or less "romantic"—orientalism, Gothicism, the rococo, and sentimental naturalism. It is in the growth of these tendencies during the eighteenth century that students of literature have found the background of the romantic movement of the nineteenth century. It has been observed,[2] moreover, that while these romantic forces grew more dominant as the century went on, classicism itself, at least in architecture and interior decoration, experienced a "resurgence," but in a new, sentimentalized, and more stimulating guise. Since this romanticized classicism is, in essence, Greek rather than Roman, it may be called romantic hellenism. Its nature, however, must be made clear before it can profitably be studied.

Romanticism is, in essence, a way of life. Its fundamental tenets are liberty and individualism. Its method is that of symbolism.[3] Hence appear its intuitive, mystic, transcendental, and imaginative elements. But it is a mistake to confuse its method with its essence. Romanticism is more than a mode of thought and expression; it is a complete *Weltanschauung* which includes every phase

[1] See B. Sprague Allen, *Tides in English Taste (1619-1800). A Background for the Study of Literature,* Harvard University Press, 1937, 2 Vols.

[2] *Ibid.,* Vol. II, pp. 23, 231-241.

[3] *Cf.* C. S. Lewis, *The Allegory of Love,* Oxford University Press, 1936, Chap. II.

of life as well as art. The romantic ideal is, like the pagan or the Christian, representative of a unique view of God, the world, and man. As such it has immeasurably influenced[4] modern political, social, moral, and aesthetic life.

Traditionally, romanticism in art has been most easily defined by contrast with classicism. According to a recent writer,[5] classicism is, primarily, a moral principle, concerning itself only with noble subject matter and aiming as much at virtuous and moral improvement in life as at beauty and aesthetic pleasure. Secondly, classicism is a representation of the ideal, the abstraction. It imitates nature, but nature idealized and made to conform to a standard. This standard may be deduced from a mathematical calculation, for the ideal is unified, regular, harmonious, symmetrical, and perfectly proportionate, whether this ideal be in an iambic pentameter line, a human figure, or an architectural Order. The most perfect example of this ideal is to be found in the antique, the appeal of which is directed to the intellect rather than to the emotions. Finally, classicism seeks its own enforcement by law and rules; it teaches the suppression of individual "genius" and condemns deviations from its code.

If the concept of romanticism as a way of life is valid, such a view of art would in no wise be compatible with its fundamental tenets of liberty and individualism. Romantic art, therefore, differs basically from classic art in each of these three enumerated principles. Thus, on the whole, romantic art is, primarily, amoral. It is frequently indifferent to any "nobility" or virtuous quality in its subject matter, since it aims to give aesthetic pleasure by creating beauty and not to offer moral instruction. Secondly, romantic art is the representation of reality, not of the ideal. It, too, imitates nature, but concrete nature, not the abstract. It seeks no mathematical standards and often represents that which lacks unity, symmetry, and proportion. It, too, finds its most perfect expression in the antique, but maintains that the appeal of the antique is to the emotions and passions, not the intellect. Finally, romantic

[4] *Cf.* Irving Babbitt, *Rousseau and Romanticism,* Boston and New York, 1919.

[5] F. P. Chambers, *The History of Taste: An Account of the Revolution of Art Criticism and Theory in Europe,* New York, Columbia University Press, 1932, Chap. III.

art scorns the fetters of law and rules and glorifies individual genius. No two views of art could be further apart in essence.

More interesting to the literary scholar, however, is the antithesis of these two views of art in method. Essentially the romantic method is the pursuit of a "true" reality the symbol of which is to be found in the objects of the senses; the classical method is the pursuit of an "ideal" reality, a symbol in itself, which must be deduced logically. The romantic method is thus close to the scientific; the classical method, to the rationalistic. Obviously, then, romanticism begins its expression from observation and experiment rather than theory or abstraction. Obviously, too, observation and experiment are fundamentally sensuous, not logical. Hence the romantic method begins with a sensuous, emotional apprehension of experience which, as the experience is merely symbolic, is interpreted imaginatively, not rationally, in romantic art. Thus, to a Diderot there was not very much interest as such in the façade of a palace, but a palace in ruins was fascinating.[6]

It has long been recognized that the romantic movement of the nineteenth century in England developed out of a complex background in the eighteenth century,[7] both in England and on the continent. Traditionally, such recognition has been based on the study of certain streams in the romantic movement, such as medievalism,[8] naturalism,[9] Miltonianism,[10] sentimentalism,[11] the Celtic revival,[12] and Spenserianism.[13] Little attention has, however, been paid to the development of the widespread interest in

[6] Diderot, *Essai sur la Peinture,* I, quoted *ibid.,* p. 146.

[7] See W. L. Phelps, *The Beginnings of the English Romantic Movement,* Boston, 1893; H. A. Beers, *A History of English Romanticism in the Eighteenth Century,* New York, 1910; Harko G. De Maar, *A History of Modern English Romanticism,* Oxford University Press, 1924, Vol. I.

[8] Kenneth Clark, *The Gothic Revival,* New York, 1929.

[9] Myra Reynolds, *The Treatment of Nature in English Poetry Between Pope and Wordsworth,* 2nd ed., Chicago, 1909.

[10] R. D. Havens, *The Influence of Milton on English Poetry,* Harvard University Press, 1922.

[11] John W. Draper, *The Funeral Elegy and the Rise of English Romanticism,* New York, 1929; Amy L. Reed, *The Background of Gray's Elegy,* Columbia University Press, 1924; Eleanor M. Sickels, *The Gloomy Egoist,* Columbia University Press, 1932.

[12] Edward D. Snyder, *The Celtic Revival in English Literature, 1760-1800,* Harvard University Press, 1923.

[13] W. L. Phelps, *op. cit.;* H. A. Beers, *op. cit.*

things Greek among many of the English romanticists, although the existence of such an hellenic stream has long been noted.[14] The marked hellenism of Byron, Shelley, Keats, and Landor, on the one hand, and of Arnold, Pater, Swinburne, Moore, Henley, and Lang, on the other, was the product of a long and interesting development during the eighteenth century.

Romanticism as a way of life, we have said, differs from classicism in method, rather than in essence. Conceivably, then, the rise of anything "romantic" consists in the transformation of an attitude, although the object of that attitude remains the same. This is precisely the nature of romantic hellenism. The neo-classical attitude toward the antique, with its principles of formalism, moralism, and imitation, is transformed into an attitude equally admiring, but with the different principles of primitivism, symbolism, and individualism. The interest in the antique turns away from books and authority, textual or academic study, to exploration, archaeology, and travel. Classical literary themes are no longer regarded so much as sources of intellectual and moral improvement, but as inspiration for action, moods, art, poetry, and music. Together with an enthusiasm for Greek ruins there is the conception of ancient Greece as an Arcadia where life was ideal because it was primitive, simple, idyllic. Ancient Greece becomes the symbol of liberty and happiness. The outstanding quality of hellenic culture, in this view, was its "repose," its peaceful serenity. Keats finds his Grecian Urn to be:

> Cold Pastoral!
> When old age shall this generation waste,
> Thou shalt remain, in midst of other woe
> Than ours, a friend to man. . .[15]

Byron longs for the paradise that was Greece:

> The isles of Greece, the isles of Greece!
> Where burning Sappho loved and sung,

[14] See, for example, the extraordinary work of Harry Levin, *The Broken Column; a Study in Romantic Hellenism,* Bowdoin undergraduate prize essay, Cambridge, Mass., Harvard University Press, 1931. *Cf.* William Chislett, *The Classical Influence in English Literature in the Nineteenth Century,* Boston, 1918; Frederick E. Pierce, "The Hellenic Current in English 19th Century Poetry," *Journal of English and Germanic Philology,* Vol. XVI, p. 103 (1917); John C. Collins, *Greek Influence on English Poetry,* London, 1910, Lecture II.

[15] "Ode on A Grecian Urn," ll. 45-48.

Where grew the arts of war and peace,
Where Delos rose, and Phoebus sprung!
Eternal summer gilds them yet,
But all, except their sun, is set.[16]

Shelley looks to ancient Greek culture as the goal of human progress:

Another Athens shall arise,
And to remoter time
Bequeath, like sunset to the skies,
The splendor of its prime;
And leave, if nought so bright may live,
All earth can take or Heaven can give.[17]

Such is romantic hellenism, an interesting example of the romantic method of symbolism:

The weakness and final dissolution of the Ancien Régime turned eyes and hearts to those more distant times before its universal rule had been established. Men probed deeper into the classic idea or rejected it altogether; those who had probed into it discovered Greece, those who rejected it discovered the Middle Ages.[18]

When analyzed, the hellenism of the nineteenth century romantic movement shows, in general, two distinguishing characteristics. The first of these is the view of ancient Greece as a symbol of liberty; that is, of social and political perfection. When such a view appears in their poetry, the romanticists invariably identify modern with ancient Greece and express a nostalgia for the old, blissful Grecian days, when man, being free, was happy. They contrast the civilization of the Greeks with that of modern Europe, and mourn the loss of so beautiful a culture. Such poetry is, of course, escapist in nature. It is obvious that the poet uses the alleged freedom of Greece merely as a symbol of his own desire. His lament over the Greece that was gives him pleasure. The idealization of hellenic culture in such poetry is founded not upon study and knowledge, but upon uncritical emotions aroused by the playing of the imagination upon the remains of a past civilization. Byron, apparently addressing modern Britons, looks back to a more perfect age in this fashion:

[16] *Don Juan,* Canto III, song following stanza 86.
[17] Final chorus from *Hellas,* ll. 145-150.
[18] Frank P. Chambers, *op. cit.,* p. 154.

Unhappy Greece! thy sons of ancient days
The Muse may celebrate with perfect praise,
Whose generous children narrowed not their hearts
With Commerce, given alone to Arms and Arts.
Our boys (save those whom public schools compel
To "Long and Short" before they're taught to spell)
From frugal fathers soon imbibe by rote,
"A penny saved, my lad, 's a penny got."[19]

The same Byron, calling upon Pallas to inspire him, apostrophizes her thus:

Ancient of days! august Athena! Where,
Where are thy men of might? thy grand in soul?
Gone—glimmering through the dream of things that were.[20]

He looks about, sees the ruin of a temple, and mourns:

Look on its broken arch, its ruined wall,
Its chambers desolate, and portals foul:
Yes, this was once Ambition's airy hall,
The Dome of Thought, the Palace of the Soul.[21]

In another poem Byron expresses his admiration for the perfection of the Greeks even more clearly:

Blest is the man who dares approach the bower
Where dwelt the Muses at their natal hour;
Whose steps have pressed, whose eye has marked afar,
The clime that nursed the sons of song and war,
The scenes which Glory still must hover o'er,
Her place of birth, her own Achaian shore.
But doubly blest is he whose heart expands
With hallowed feelings for those classic lands;

. . . . . . . . . . . . .

And you associate Bards! who snatched to light
Those gems too long withheld from modern sight;
Whose mingling taste combined to cull the wreath
While Attic flowers Aonian odours breathe,
And all their renovated fragrance flung,
To grace the beauties of your native tongue;
Now let those minds, that nobly could transfuse

[19] "Hints from Horace," ll. 509-516, in Ernest Hartley Coleridge, *The Works of Lord Byron,* London, 1918, Vol. I, p. 424.
[20] *Childe Harolde's Pilgrimage,* Canto II, Stanza II.
[21] *Ibid.,* Stanza VI.

> The glorious Spirit of the Grecian Muse,
> Though soft the echo, scorn a borrowed tone.[22]

In a similar vein, Shelley upbraids the nations of modern Europe for not showing greater interest in the fate of Greece:

> We are all Greeks. Our laws, our literature, our religion, our arts, have their root in Greece. . . .
>
> The human form and human mind attained to a perfection in Greece which has impressed its image on those faultless productions whose very fragments are the despair of modern art, and has propagated impulses which cannot cease, through a thousand channels of manifest or imperceptible operation, to ennoble and delight mankind until the extinction of the race.
>
> The modern Greek is the descendant of those glorious beings whom the imagination almost refuses to figure to itself as belonging to our kind, and he inherits much of their sensibility, their rapidity of conception, their enthusiasm and their courage.[23]

In another preface he says:

> If England were divided into forty republics, each equal in population and extent to Athens, there is no reason to suppose but that, under institutions not more perfect than those of Athens, each would produce philosophers and poets equal to those who (if we except Shakespeare) have never been surpassed.[24]

Here is not only the uncritical idealization of ancient Greece, but its use as a symbol of the ideal of social perfection which constitutes his message. This admiration for Greek perfection is an element in the romantic movement which continues throughout the nineteenth century, both in England and in America.[25]

The other distinguishing characteristic of romantic hellenism is the inspiration which the poet finds in the contemplation of Greece and its remains. This inspiration produces poetic moods

[22] *English Bards and Scotch Reviewers,* ll. 867-889.

[23] Preface to *Hellas,* in George E. Woodberry, *The Complete Poetical Works of Percy Bysshe Shelley,* New York, 1901, p. 319.

[24] Preface to *Prometheus Unbound, ibid.,* p. 163.

[25] *Cf.,* for example, the letter by Charles Eliot Norton to F. A. Tupper, 1885, in the *Harvard Alumni Bulletin,* 1927, p. 258: "I think that a knowledge of Greek thought and life, and of the arts in which the Greeks expressed their thought and sentiment, essential to high culture. A man may know everything else, but without this knowledge he remains ignorant of the best intellectual and moral achievements of his own race."

and lends color to their expression. Frequently the mere sight of a Greek ruin will stimulate in the poet profound emotions. Byron, sitting on the "yet unshaken base" of a marble column, exclaims with evident enjoyment:

> Cold is the heart, fair Greece! that looks on Thee,
> Nor feels as Lovers o'er the dust they loved;
> Dull is the eye that will not weep to see
> Thy walls defaced. . . .[26]

Or, again, upon beholding the shores of Greece, in a narrative poem, he cries:

> 'Tis Greece, but living Greece no more!
> So coldly sweet, so deadly fair,
> We start, for soul is wanting there.
> Hers is the loveliness in death,
> That parts not quite with parting breath.[27]

Shelley has said:

> There is an education peculiarly fitted for a poet, without which genius and sensibility can hardly fill the circle of their capacities. . . . The circumstances of my accidental education have been favorable to this ambition. I have been familiar from boyhood with mountains and lakes, and the sea, and the solitude of forests. . . . I have seen the theatre of the more visible ravages of tyranny and war. . . . The poetry of ancient Greece and Rome, and modern Italy, and our own country, has been to me like external nature, a passion and an enjoyment.[28]

For Keats Greece was a beautiful paradise. "I hope I have not in too late a day touched the beautiful mythology of Greece, and dulled its brightness," he writes in the Preface to *Endymion*.[29] He is profoundly grieved by the loss of the "glory and loveliness" of Greece which "have passed away. . . . Nowadays, under pleasant trees, Pan is no longer sought."[30] As he passes such trees, he recalls with enjoyment

[26] *Childe Harolde's Pilgrimage,* Canto II, Stanza XV.

[27] *The Giaour,* ll. 90-94.

[28] Preface to *The Revolt of Islam,* in George E. Woodberry, *op. cit.,* pp. 46-47.

[29] H. Buxton Forman, *The Poetical Works of John Keats,* Oxford University Press, 1920, p. 56.

[30] "I Stood Tiptoe on a Little Hill," Dedication to Leigh Hunt, *ibid.,* p. 2.

> how fair, trembling Syrinx fled
> Arcadian Pan, with such a fearful dread.
> Poor nymph,—poor Pan,—how he did weep to find,
> Nought but a lovely sighing of the wind
> Along the reedy stream; a half-heard strain,
> Full of sweet desolation—balmy pain.[31]

It will be observed that this sentimental admiration and idealization of Greek antiquity which has been called romantic hellenism differs markedly from the neo-classical admiration of the ancients. The latter is formalistic, pedantic, and predominantly Roman; its primary source is a Latin literary culture. The romantic attitude is, on the contrary, scientific rather than literary. It is much the same as that which has, in the present day, brought about a decline in the study of Greek and Latin in the schools, but has fostered a continued study of Greek art, architecture, music, and athletics. It may be recognized even more clearly when we compare classical studies before the nineteenth century with those of today. Since the Middle Ages knew Rome far better than Greece, education until the late eighteenth century, inherited largely from the Middle Ages, was dominated by the Roman classics. It was a study of Latin texts which was pedantic, humanistic, and authoritarian. The modern method of studying the culture of antiquity is divided into such scientific branches as archaeology, epigraphy, paleography, history, and philology.[32]

The transformation of the neo-classical attitude toward the ancients into romantic hellenism was, like many of the other streams of romanticism, a gradual growth in popularity of an attitude present in the neo-classical period itself. Frequently, for example, many of the characteristics of the romantic attitude are notable in poetry inspired by Rome, rather than Greece. As early as 1741, such a poem was written. The poet tells how, on a trip to Italy, he came to Virgil's tomb, expecting to find it graced by the Muses and decked with such poetic trophies as shields, trumpets, shepherds' pipes, and "never-fading roses":

> And now my bold romantic thought aspires
> To hear the echo of celestial lyres;

[31] *Ibid.*, p. 7.

[32] *Cf.* Harry Levin, *op. cit.*, pp. 25-28.

Then catch some sound to bear delighted home,
And boast I learnt the verse at Virgil's tomb;
Or stretch'd beneath thy myrtle's fragrant shade,
With dreams extatic hov'ring o'er my head,
See forms august, and laurel'd ghosts ascend,
And with thyself, perhaps, the long procession end.
I came—but soon the phantoms disappear'd;
Far other scenes, than wanton Hope had rear'd;
No faery rites, no funeral pomp I found;
No trophied walls with wreaths of laurel round:
A mean unhonour'd ruin faintly show'd
The spot where once thy mausoleum stood:
Hardly the form remain'd; a nodding dome
O'ergrown with moss is now all Virgil's tomb.
'Twas such a scene as gave a kind relief
To memory, in sweetly-pensive grief:
Gloomy, unpleasing images it wrought

. . . . . . . . . .

Health and delight in every balmy gale
Are wafted now in vain: small comfort bring
To weeping eyes the beauties of the spring.
To groaning slaves those fragrant meads belong,
Where Tully dictated, and Maro sung.
Long since, alas! those golden days are flown,
When here each Science wore its proper crown:
Pale Tyranny has laid their altars low,
And rent the laurel from the Muse's brow:
What wonder then 'midst such a scene to see
The Arts expire with bleeding Liberty?

. . . . . . . . . .

Where now are all the nymphs that blest the plains?
Where the full chorus of contented swains?
The songs of love, of liberty and peace,
Are heard no more; the dance and tabor cease:
To the soft oaten pipe, and past'ral reed,
The din of arms, and clarion's blast succeed:
Dire shapes appear in every op'ning glade,
And Furies howl where once the Muses stray'd.
Is this the queen of realms, for arts renown'd?
This captive maid, that weeps upon the ground?
Alas! how chang'd!—dejected and forlorn!
The mistress of the world become the scorn![33]

[33] "Virgil's Tomb. Naples, 1741." This was first published in the fourth edition of *A Collection of Poems in Six Volumes by Several Hands,* London, J. Dodsley,

Here is the mood of romantic hellenism, though in this instance the mood has been aroused by a Latin rather than a Greek monument. Observe the identification of ancient with modern Rome, the use of antiquity as a symbol of liberty, the inspiration which the poet has found in the contemplation of a past culture, and the evident pleasure with which he indulges in his lament. Nothing could show better that the characteristics of romantic hellenism are inherent not in the view of ancient Greece, but in the poet himself. These are precisely the qualities which, stimulated by Greece, appear in the work of Byron, Shelley, and Keats. They are much different from the references to ancient mythology and literature which in neo-classical poetry are used chiefly for ornamentation.

It is conceivable, from what has been said, that this romantic attitude might gradually have developed as romantic Latinism, associated, like the poem cited above, with Rome. To account for the association of this attitude almost exclusively with Greece, however, it is necessary to study three influential forces which developed from 1732 to 1786 and directed the idealization of antiquity to Greece. These forces are, first, the growth of scientific Greek archaeology; secondly, the growth of sentimental accounts of Greece written by travellers; and, finally, the rise of a hellenized body of aesthetics produced by artists, painters, and poets.

It is the purpose of this study to trace the rise of romantic hellenism in England between 1732 and 1786. While our study is limited to England, however, it should be noted that the movement was European. In Italy, under the patronage of Charles VII, King of Naples, the excavation of Herculaneum began in 1738 and that of Pompeii in 1748. 1755 is the year of the foundation of the *Academia Ercolanese,* under the auspices of which there were published the volumes of *Le Antichita di Ercolano,* containing plates of such archaeological treasures as pictures, lamps, and bronzes. The first of these volumes, of which there were seven, appeared in 1757. By 1750 Piranesi had begun to publish

1755. The quotations above are taken from the edition of 1770, Vol. IV, p. 110. The author of this poem is identified by R. W. Chapman, in *Oxford Bibliographical Society, Proceedings and Papers,* Vol. III (1931-1933), p. 284, as Joseph Trapp (1679-1747), a minor poet and pamphleteer.

his etchings of ancient remains, including urns, statues, shattered columns, overturned altars, ruined temples, baths, palaces, and amphitheaters. Some of these, overgrown with leaves and the refuge of beggars and thieves, were well qualified to stimulate both the imagination and the sentimentality of poets.

The discovery of Herculaneum and Pompeii stirred up interest all over Europe. In France one of the earliest of such indications is an anonymous work, published at Dijon in 1750, *Lettres sur l'état actuel de la ville souterraine d'Héraclée.*[34] In 1754 David published his first edition of the *Antiquités d'Herculanum,* and in the same year there appeared Cochin and Bellicard's *Observations sur les antiquités d'Herculanum, avec quelques réflexions sur la peinture et la sculpture des ancients.* The extent of French interest may be inferred from the title of the ambitious work announced by Régnier in 1754, *Recueil général historique et critique de tout ce qui a été publié en Italie sur la ville d'Herculanum.* In addition to these, archaeological stimulus came from the many accounts published by travellers to Greece, such as the *Ruines des plus beaux monuments de la Grèce considérés du côté de l'histoire et du côté de l'architecture,* 1758, by LeRoy.[35] By the seventh decade of the eighteenth century an active group of French hellenists is found associated in the Académie des Inscriptions, offering annual prizes for the best essays in answer to such questions as, "What were the names and attributes of Jupiter among the various peoples of Greece and Italy? Account for the origin and causes of these attributes." In addition, the Académie fostered archaeological study in Italy, Greece, and Asia Minor. The most influential and the most interesting member of this group was the Abbé Barthélémy. In his career one can trace the general steps in the development of romantic hellenism in Europe.

Born in 1716, Barthélémy was early intended for the Church and was sent to the Collège des Oratoriens at Marseilles until

[34] For a detailed discussion of the development of French romantic hellenism see Maurice Badolle, *L'Abbé Jean Jacques Barthélémy et l'héllénisme en France dans la seconde moitié du XVIIIme siècle,* Paris, 1926. *Cf.* Louis Bertrand, *La fin du Classicisme et le retour à l'Antique dans la seconde moitié du XVIIIme siècle,* Paris, 1897; J. Lognon, "Quatre siècles de philhélénisme français," *Revue de France,* 1921, Vol. I, no. 6, pp. 512-542.

[35] For a detailed list see Maurice Badolle, *op. cit.,* p. 157. LeRoy's book, translated into English, was widely read. See *infra,* p. 24.

the age of seventeen, when he entered upon the regular ecclesiastical studies under the Jesuits, including Arabic in his studies. Upon the completion of his course, unable to secure a living, he retired, with financial assistance from his father, to the little town of Aubagne, which was rich both in the remains of ancient monuments and in learned and scholarly men. Here Barthélémy quietly pursued his studies in Greek, Hebrew, and Arabic and cultivated a taste for archaeology. In 1744, having definitely decided to abandon theology as his life work, he left Aubagne for Paris, fortified by letters of recommendation, to seek, as it were, his fortune. In Paris, through the influence of such distinguished men as M. Gros de Boze, a member of the Académie des Inscriptions and Keeper of the Cabinet des Médailles du Roy, Barthélémy rose rapidly in the ranks of French archaeologists and scholars. Appointed Associate Keeper of the Cabinet des Médailles to assist M. de Boze, he was able to devote much of his time to visits to libraries, museums, and other centers of archaeological learning, acquiring the vast knowledge of antiquities which was to earn for him the distinction of having "l'antiquité tout dans la tête."[36] In 1747 he was named to a vacancy in the Académie des Inscriptions. Two months after his appointment he read a dissertation to the academicians, *Réflexions sur une médaille de Xerxes, roi d'Arsamosate,* later printed, which was to be followed by numerous similar monographs.

In 1755 Barthélémy accompanied M. de Stainville, French Ambassador to Rome, on his journey to Italy. Here, like previous travellers, the Abbé devoted his energies for two years to the minute examination of art and monuments in museums and palaces and to discussions with other scholars and archaeologists at Rome. His first hand observation of antiquarian remains convinced him of the futility of studying imperfect copies or reports. Above all, he realized clearly the importance of archaeological study in the clarification and improvement of the texts of antiquity.[37] He returned to Paris in 1757, immediately enriched by

[36] *Ibid.*, p. 16.

[37] *Cf.* Louis Bertrand, *op. cit.*, p. 55: "Une des raisons de la médiocrité de la critique des textes, à l'Académie des Inscriptions, pendant toute la première partie de son existence, c'a été l'ignorance des monuments figurés. Barthélémy, pendant son voyage en Italie, est un des premiers qui s'en soient rendu compte."

his experience. From this year to his death in 1795 Barthélémy was constantly engaged in studying and writing learned dissertations. It is not surprising that the *Voyages du Jeune Anacharsis,* 1789, written against a background so rich and deep, was so successful and influential.

To the planning and preparation of this work, Barthélémy may be said to have devoted almost thirty-two years. While he was at Rome, the idea came to him that it would be an interesting task to condense in a single work all that had been discovered or written about Greek antiquity to his day. He thought first of the possibilities in representing a French traveller in Italy during the Renaissance meeting with the scholars, artists, and authors then abounding in Rome. Later, however, he narrowed his theme to ancient Greece alone, retaining the idea of a traveller, but changing the setting and time of action. In form the work is a novel; in fact it is a critical, comprehensive, and authoritative history of ancient Greek culture, social, political, economic, philosophical, and aesthetic, tinged with all the elements of romantic hellenism.

The fictional framework of the *Voyages du Jeune Anacharsis* concerns the wanderings of a young Scythian philosopher in Greece during the twenty-six years between 363 B.C. and 337 B.C. Eager to learn whatever he can, Anacharsis constantly visits famous places, examines objects of art, and engages in profound discussions with the sages of each city. In the course of these travels he learns about laws, political institutions, customs, and, incidentally, a complete history of Greece before 363 B.C. The voyages of this one traveller present clearly and vividly not only a broad picture of Greece as it was in the fourth century B.C., but also a brilliant summation of all the knowledge available in Europe in 1780 concerning ancient Greece. The popularity and influence of the work were phenomenal. The first edition in 1789 was exhausted in two months and a second appeared in the same year. A third edition in 1790 was followed by a fourth in 1792, a fifth in 1796, and a sixth in 1799. Translations of the work had already appeared in English and German. In the nineteenth century it was also translated into Spanish, Italian, Danish, Dutch, modern Greek, and Armenian. Other editions and abridgements followed in considerable numbers in the nineteenth century. The *Voyages du Jeune Anacharsis* thus occupy a most influential position in the development of romantic hellenism in Europe, helping to spread a love for things Greek, a disdain for modern civilization, and a sentimental admiration for the ruins of Greek antiquity.

Probably the most important reason for the popularity of Barthélémy's work was its glorification of the democratic political theory of the Greeks. Therein consists the outstanding contribution of France to the romantic hellenic movement. Liberty, equality, and fraternity were, for the revolutionists of France, enshrined in the example of Greek antiquity.[38] From Lycurgus, Solon, Aristides, and Epaminondas they learned to esteem before all other peoples the free and brave nation which had fought victoriously against the powerful kings of Persia. With the Greeks as an example, the French revolutionists took courage in their fight.[39] The hellenic spirit thus liberated was to find an echo in other lands where the cause of liberty was to be defended.

In Germany, probably the country most influential in the development of romantic hellenism, the outstanding figure is that of Johann Joachim Winckelmann, whose *Gedanken über die Nachahmung der griechischen Werke in der Mahlerey und Bildhauer-Kunst,* 1755, and the more important *Geschichte der Kunst des Alterthums,* 1764, introduced into Europe a sentimental, scientific, and aesthetic reaction against baroque art and a new insight into classic beauty.[40] The vogue of Greek art and culture in Germany, initiated by Winckelmann, developed rapidly. Lessing published, in 1766, his *Laokoon oder über die Grenzen der Malerei und Poesie,* a brilliant critical investigation of aesthetic laws, inspired by Winckelmann's work. In 1769 appeared Herder's *Sylvae Criticae,* an answer to *Laokoon.* In 1776 Lessing began to edit and annotate the *Geschichte der Kunst des Alterthums.*

[38] It is, of course, well-known that many of the leaders of the French Revolution compared themselves to the ancient Greek heroes. *Cf.* F. P. Chambers, *op. cit.,* Chap. III.

[39] *Cf.* Bertrand, *op. cit.,* Sec. III, "Le goût de l'antiquité grecque et les Assemblées révolutionnaires."

[40] For a detailed discussion of German hellenism, see E. M. Butler, *The Tyranny of Greece over Germany,* New York, 1935. For further discussion of Winckelmann, see *infra,* Chap. IV.

Thereafter, in Schiller, Goethe, Hölderin, and Heine, hellenism becomes a dominant theme.

While it is true that much of the hellenic literature in England during the nineteenth century is influenced by the continental hellenism sketched above, particularly that of Barthélémy and Winckelmann, this influence appears, for the most part, predominantly late. Moreover, romantic hellenism in England had an independent origin, and it is with this that we are here concerned. The following chapters will, then, trace the rise of this English movement from 1732 to 1786. We shall consider, first, the growth of archaeological interest in Greece. Then we shall examine the accounts written by travellers to Greece in order to clarify the origin of the sentimentalism which is so much a part of the movement. We shall then describe the growth of hellenism in English aesthetics. When these three forces have been studied, we shall be ready to examine romantic hellenism in English poetry within our limited period. In all four of these phases, acting and interacting, we shall find the rise of romantic hellenism in England.

# II

# THE SOCIETY OF DILETTANTI AND THE GROWTH OF INTEREST IN GREEK ARCHAEOLOGY AND ANTIQUITIES

The primary force which stimulated the rise of romantic hellenism in England in the eighteenth century was the development of a scientific interest in the archaeological remains of ancient Greece. Such an interest, it is true, existed in the preceding century,[1] and

[1] See the account of seventeenth century English collectors of Greek antiquities, particularly that of the Earl of Arundel, in Adolf Michaelis, *Ancient Marbles in Great Britain,* Cambridge, (Eng.), 1882, pp. 5-54. Greek archaeology may be said to have been founded by the British. In the fifteenth century Poggio Bracciolini had brought a few remains from Greece to Venice, and Ciriaco of Ancona had made observations upon other ruins and had copied some inscriptions. Beyond this, however, very little was done in Greek archaeology until Thomas Howard, Earl of Arundel, having spent some years at Rome collecting marbles and antiquities, took advantage of the appointment of Thomas Roe as Ambassador from James I to the Ottoman Porte in 1621, and through him secured some monuments of Greek art. In 1625 Arundel sent William Petty as special agent to visit Pergamon, Samos, Ephesus, Chios, Smyrna, and Athens, and through him obtained a number of marbles with valuable inscriptions. These were lodged in Arundel House in 1627. John Selden deciphered the inscriptions and published them as *Marmora Arundelliana* in 1628. Additions were made to the collection in that year. Upon Arundel's death in 1646, the marbles were gradually dispersed, although many of them were ultimately reunited at the University of Oxford. Arundel had had a rival collector in George Villiers, Duke of Buckingham, who, being as influential politically as Arundel, had secured monuments for his own collection, and claimed a joint share with Arundel in his discoveries. When Buckingham was assassinated in 1628, Arundel found a new rival in Philip Herbert, Earl of Pembroke and Montgomery. Soon other collectors appeared, including Charles I himself. Among these were the third Earl of Winchelsea, the first Baron Carteret, John Kemp, the first Duke of Devonshire, the second Earl of Oxford, the fourth Earl of Carlisle, the Earl of Burlington, and Sir Andrew Fontaine. While these collectors were primarily interested in portable monuments, some beginning had also been made in the study of monuments *in situ.* About 1674 the Marquis Olier de Nointel, French Ambassador to the Ottoman Porte, passing through Athens, was so struck by the beauties of the remains of Greek sculpture on the Parthenon that he had Jacques Carrey, a pupil of Le Brun, make careful drawings in red chalk of the sculptures than remaining; i.e., prior to the bombardment of the Parthenon sculptures by the Venetians under Morosini in 1687. An account of de Nointel's voyage was published in 1688 by Cornelio Magni of Parma, who had accompanied the French Ambassador, under the title, *Ralazione della Citta d'Athene, colle Provincie dell' Attica, Focia, Beozia, Etc. nei Tempi Che furono passeggiate de Cornelio Magni, Parmegiano, l'anno 1674, e dallo stresso publicate l'anno 1688.* In 1682 the Englishman George Wheler

can be faintly detected as early as the twelfth century.[2] But the most important development of this interest may be traced after 1732, when the introduction of works of ancient Greek art from Rome and Greece passes out of its infancy, and a significant body of literature dealing with Greek archaeology comes into existence. The time of the Stuarts and their immediate successors had been a period of individual collectors of Greek art, who were concerned, for the most part, with smaller objects easy to transport, such as bronzes, coins, and gems.

> Then comes the heyday of dilettantism in England, the last century [the eighteenth] especially in its latter half. In an uninterrupted stream the ancient marbles of Rome poured into the palaces of the aristocracy of Britain, whose wealth in some cases afforded the means of gratifying a real artistic taste by these rare possessions, and in others enabled them at any rate to fall into the new fashion of dilettantism, the furore for antique art. The older Roman collections were bought up; fresh excavations were instituted. Englishmen settled in Rome and dealt in the acquisitions without which *milord* on his travels could not well return home from the 'grand tour.'[3]

The outstanding influence in the development of dilettantism in England in the direction of Greek antiquities comes from the Society of Dilettanti, which was probably founded in 1732,[4] al-

---

published an account in English of his travels in Greece and the Levant in the company of Jacob Spon, a learned antiquary of Lyons, containing descriptions of Greek sculptures. In 1721 Edmund Chishull, Chaplain to the factory of the Turkey company at Smyrna (*cf. infra,* pp. 54-55), published some valuable inscriptions in *Inscriptio Sigea Antiquissima,* and in 1728 he issued the sequel, *Antiquates Asiaticae, Etc.* Chishull owed some of his information to M. Pitton de Tournefort, the French botanist, whose account of travels in the Levant was translated into English in 1718.

[2] *Cf.* the pamphlet by William Miller, *The English in Athens Before 1821, A Lecture delivered before the Anglo-Hellenic League in Athens, February 10, 1926,* published by the Anglo-Hellenic League, 53 and 54 Chancery Lane W.C. 2, 1926.

[3] Adolf Michaelis, *op. cit.,* p. 2.

[4] Traditionally, the date of the foundation of the Society of Dilettanti has been cited as 1734. The reason for such a date is the statement in the preface to the Society's publication, *Antiquities of Ionia,* 1769: "In the year 1734, some gentlemen who had travelled in Italy, desirous of encouraging at home a taste for those objects which had contributed so much to their entertainment abroad, formed themselves into a Society under the name of *The Dilettanti,* and agreed upon such resolutions as they thought necessary to keep up the spirit of the scheme." Professor Michaelis, who had recourse to other documents, maintains (*op. cit.,* p. 62, note 158), that the Society was founded not in 1734, but "towards

though records were not kept before 1736. The Society seems to have been formed originally for social purposes and to have directed its influence to art later. The members were young, rich noblemen who had visited Italy during their grand tours and had there developed an interest in art. A list of these members[5] includes the names of the most distinguished persons in Great Britain. As of 1736 the members of the Society included statesmen, courtiers, soldiers, diplomats, divines, rich merchants, young baronets and peers, and gentlemen of position generally. Among the statesmen were Earl Harcourt, Earl Temple, Sir Francis Dashwood, and William Ponsonby. The courtiers included Lord Robert Montague, Sewallis Shirley, and Daniel Boone. Among the soldiers were George Gray, William Degge, William Denny, and William Strode. Representative diplomats were Andrew Mitchell, Sir James Gray, and Thomas Villiers, Duke of Buckingham. The divines included Arthur Smyth, Robert Hay, and Joseph Spence. There were such merchant princes as William Fauquier, Robert Dingley, Robert Bristow, and Peter Delme. Among the young peers were Sir Lionel Pilkington, Sir Henry Liddell, and Viscount Galway; while the gentlemen of position generally included Simon Luttrell, Thomas Grimston, John Howe, and Henry Harris. Most of the members of the Society had travelled extensively on the continent. Ponsonby travelled in the East until 1749 and became a collector of antique objects of art. Sir James Gray was, in 1754, appointed Envoy Extraordinary to Naples and the Two Sicilies. Although he was, for many years, absent from the meetings of the Society in England, he was able to meet eligible young gentlemen in Naples and

---

the end of the preceding year; probably in December, A.D. 1733." In the definitive work on the Society, *History of the Society of Dilettanti,* compiled by Lionel Cust and edited by Sidney Colvin, London, 1914 (second edition), p. 5, the authors state: "Through their negligence at the outset the actual date of the foundation of the Society remains uncertain. . . . When a separate book was commenced on December 13, 1744, for the minutes of the committee meetings, its date of commencement is *Ann. Soc. Duodec.* From these entries it may be assumed that the first meeting of the Society was held in December, probably on December 5 or 12, 1732." Information concerning the Society is found also in the various publications which it sponsored, discussed below, and in W. R. Hamilton, *Historical Notices of the Society of Dilettanti,* printed for private circulation only, London, 1855. An extract from this work is to be found in *Edinburgh Review,* Vol. CV (1857), pp. 493-517.

[5] Such a list is printed in Lionel Cust and Sidney Colvin, *op. cit.,* Appendix.

Venice whom he proposed for membership in England. Thus the membership of the Society grew. Among the members admitted after 1736, for example, was John Montague, fourth Earl of Sandwich, who, in 1738, toured the Mediterranean and the Greek Archipelago and interested himself in art and antiquities under the tutorship of the Rev. J. Cooke.[6]

The most important achievement of the Society, aside from encouraging fine arts at home, was its sponsorship of classical archaeology in Greece and the Levant and its publication of the results of such scientific projects. By far the most influential of these projects was that undertaken by "Athenian" Stuart and Nicholas Revett between 1748 and 1755. James Stuart (1713-1788)[7] had early in life painted fans for Lewis Goupy, the well-known fan painter in the Strand. Many of these were decorated with views of classical buildings, and it is possible that they stimulated in him an interest in the art of classical antiquity. At the age of thirteen or fourteen he obtained a premium from the Society of Arts for a self-portrait in crayon. He seems also to have had a substantial knowledge of mathematics, and was a good draughtsman. In 1741/2, planning to study art where many other British artists learned their profession, he went to Rome, travelling much of the way on foot and earning what he could as he went. In Rome Stuart met Nicholas Revett (1720-1804),[8] who was studying painting under Cavaliere Benefiale, and Matthew Brettingham and Gavin Hamilton, two other British artists. In April, 1748, these four went to Naples on foot, and during this journey they planned a project to visit Athens in order to obtain accurate measurements of the remains of Greek architecture. Stuart, who had been a student of Latin and Greek in the College of Propaganda at Rome, was enthusiastic over the plan, but the idea seems to have originated with Hamilton and Revett.

Toward the end of 1748 Stuart and Revett published *Proposals for Publishing an Accurate Description of the Antiquities of*

[6] Cooke published an account of this tour in 1799.

[7] A memoir of Stuart is prefixed to Vol. IV of the *Antiquities of Athens Measured and Delineated,* London, 1816.

[8] A memoir of Revett appears *ibid.*

*Athens*. The plan of the young men attracted the attention[9] of the English dilettanti in Rome, especially that of the Earl of Malton, the Earl of Charlemont,[10] James Dawkins,[11] and Robert Wood.[12] With the assistance of these gentlemen, largely financial, Stuart and Revett were able to leave Rome on March 3, 1750. At Venice they were delayed for several months because no ship sailing for Greece was available. Here they met Joseph Smith, the British Consul, and Sir James Gray, who succeeded in having them elected to the Society of Dilettanti. Thereupon Colonel George Gray, brother of Sir James and secretary-treasurer of the Society, issued in London an edition of the *Proposals*. During their detention in Venice, Stuart and Revett spent three months studying the antiquities of Pola in Dalmatia.[13]

On January 19, 1751, Stuart and Revett embarked for Greece, arriving at Athens March 18, after passing Zante, Chiarenza, Patras, Corinth, Cenchrea, Megara, Salamis, and Piraeus. At Athens the two men began their work in earnest, Stuart making drawings of the sculptures and marbles, while Revett made the measurements. They remained in Athens until March 5, 1753, when their work was interrupted by the disturbance which followed the death of the Chief of the Black Eunuchs, Osman.[14] Because of the consequent misrule of the government in Athens, an officer was sent to inquire into political corruption, and a mutinous state of affairs made it dangerous for the artists to remain in the city. Acting on the advice of Sir James Porter, Ambassador in Constantinople, Stuart and Revett left Athens for

[9] Another factor in attracting this attention was Stuart's publication, in 1750, of a Latin treatise on an obelisk found in the Campus Martius, dedicated to Charles Wentworth, Earl of Malton, afterwards Marquis of Rockingham.

[10] James Caulfield, fourth Viscount and first Earl of Charlemont (1728-1799), had gone abroad in 1746 and visited the Greek islands of the Archipelago. He was a friend of Hume, Burke, Johnson, Reynolds, Goldsmith, Beauclerk, and Hogarth, as well as a patron of the arts. He was chairman of the committee of the Society of Dilettanti supervising researches among classical antiquities.

[11] See *infra*, p. 30.

[12] See *infra*, pp. 30ff.

[13] The results of this study were subsequently published in Vol. IV of the *Antiquities of Athens*, 1816.

[14] See William Miller, *The Turkish Restoration in Greece, 1718-1797, Helps for Students of History, No. 38*, London, S.P.C.K., 1921, pp. 8ff. *Cf.* the same author's *The English in Athens Before 1821, op. cit.*, pp. 9ff.

Smyrna, visiting Delos and Scio on the way. They returned to Athens in June, but were again compelled to leave in the following September both by the disturbances[15] and by the plague, without having completed their work of measuring all the buildings on the Acropolis, especially the Propylaea and the Arch of Hadrian. They became involved in a serious dispute with the British Consul, a Greek,[16] and since a new Pasha was appointed to govern the district about the same time, Stuart decided to take advantage of the escort of the retiring Pasha to Constantinople to have his position secured by a firman. The escort proved treacherous and Stuart more than once was in considerable danger of being murdered. He succeeded in escaping, however, and arrived at Salonica, where he was later joined by Revett, and whence the two made their way together again to Smyrna. The continuance of the plague made it impossible for them to return to Athens to complete their measurements and researches, and they arrived in England, after a long quarantine at Marseilles, early in 1755. Here they were welcomed by the Society of Dilettanti and, with the assistance of many of its members, issued a new prospectus of their work.

The fruit of Stuart and Revett's project first appeared in 1762, in the publication of Volume I of *The Antiquities of Athens. Measured and Delineated by James Stuart F.R.S. and F.S.A. and Nicholas Revett, Painters and Architects. London, Printed by John Haberkorn. 1762.* This is a large, beautifully engraved folio. The "Dedication to the King" denotes Athens "the most renowned and magnificent City of Greece, and once the most distinguished seat of Genius and Liberty." The Preface by Stuart[17] states that the world had already been given much knowledge of the edifices of Rome, but not of Greece. "As Greece was the great Mistress

[15] The new Chief of the Black Eunuchs, Bekir, had been executed in Constantinople. His nominee, the *Voivode,* fled and was captured. The new *Voivode* was called a tyrant and was accused of having caused the murder of many leading Athenians who had protested against his autocratic rule. A band of discontented citizens set fire to the *Voivode's* palace, and the *Voivode* himself was carried off in chains by the troops of the Pasha of Negroponte.

[16] His name was Nikolaos Logothetes. The quarrel arose out of Logothetes' demand for 200 Venetian sequins. In the dispute Stuart knocked the Consul down. The Archbishop sided with the Consul, who proceeded to Constantinople to publicize the affair.

[17] This appears on pp. i-viii.

of the Arts, and Rome, in this respect, no more than her disciple, it may be presumed, all the most Admired Buildings which adorned that imperial City, were but imitations of Grecian Originals." He, therefore, emphasizes the importance of knowing Greece rather than Rome:

> Of all the Countries which were embellished by the Ancients with magnificent Buildings, Greece appears principally to merit our Attention; since, if we believe the Ancients themselves, the most beautiful Orders and Dispositions of Columns were invented in that Country, and the most celebrated Works of Architecture were erected there. . . .
>
> The City of Greece most renowned for stately Edifices, for the Genius of its Inhabitants, and for the culture of every Art, was Athens. We therefore resolved to examine that Spot rather than any other; flattering ourselves that the remains we might find there, would excel in true Taste and Elegance every thing hitherto published.

A discussion follows of the "highest perfection of the arts" that took place in Greece after the defeat of Xerxes. This perfection is shown to be a product of their liberty. Stuart then turns to the purpose of his study, which, he says, was "to measure and delineate with all possible diligence" any remains of antiquity which they could find. He describes the origin of their plan, gives a chronicle of their journey, and ends with an expression of glowing admiration for modern Greece, which he, in common with the romantic hellenists of poetry, identifies with ancient Greece:

> The Athenians have perhaps to this day more vivacity, more genius, and a politer address than any other people in the Turkish Dominions. Oppressed as they are at present, they always oppose, with great courage and wonderful sagacity, every addition to their Burden, which an avaricious or cruel Governor may attempt to lay on them. . . . There is great sprightliness and expression, in the countenance of both Sexes, and their Persons are well-proportioned. The men have a due mixture of Strength and Agility, without the least appearance of heaviness. The women have a peculiar elegance of Form, and of Manner; they excel in Embroidery and all kinds of Needle-Work. . . . The air of Athens is extremely healthy.

The book proper is divided into chapters, each concerning a ruin or group of ruins. There are indications of minute observation in the measurements and descriptions. These are accompanied by much literary illustration and footnotes citing ancient and, occasionally, modern authorities. In each chapter is included a series of magnificent full-size plates showing in detail various parts of the ruin under discussion. There are five chapters in all. Chapter I is entitled, "Of a Doric Portico at Athens" and contains six plates. Chapter II is entitled, "Of the Ionic Temple on the Ilissus" and contains eight plates. Chapter III is entitled, "Of the Octogon Tower of Andronicus Cyrrhestes" and contains nineteen plates. Chapter IV, the longest, is entitled, "Of the Choragic Monument of Lysicrates, commonly called the Lanthorn of Demosthenes," and contains twenty-six plates. Chapter V is entitled, "Of a Stoa or Portico, commonly supposed to be the remains of the Temple of Jupiter Olympius," and contains eleven plates.[18]

The book produced an extraordinary effect upon English society. The Society of Dilettanti had for some years been endeavouring to introduce a taste for classical architecture, and the publication of this work caused 'Grecian Gusto' to reign supreme. Under its influence the classical style in architecture was widely adopted both in London and the provinces, and maintained its predominance for the remainder of the century. The publication of Stuart and Revett's work may be said to be the commencement of the serious study of classical art and antiquities throughout Europe. Its publication had been anticipated by a somewhat similar work by a Frenchman, Julian David Le Roy, who had been in Rome in 1748, when the proposals of Stuart and Revett were first issued.[19] Le Roy did not, however, visit Athens until 1754, after Stuart and Revett had completed their work there, and although by royal patronage

[18] A total of 5 volumes of the *Antiquities of Athens* were published as a result of the work of Stuart and Revett, but, except for Vol. I, their dates of publication fall outside the limits of this study. Vol. II, edited by Elizabeth Stuart, appeared in 1787; Vol. III, edited by Willey Reveley, in 1794; Vol. IV, edited by Joseph Woods, in 1816. Volume V is a Supplement entitled, *Antiquities of Athens and Other Places in Greece, Sicily, Etc. Supplementary to the Antiquities of Athens by James Stuart, F.R.S., F.S.A., and Nicholas Revett, Delineated and Illustrated by C. R. Cockerell, A.R.A., F.S.A., W. Kinnard, T. L. Donaldson, W. Jenkins, W. Railton, Architects,* London, 1830. This fifth volume is, in reality, a volume of new matter that Kinnard had added to the reduced size edition of the whole *Antiquities of Athens* which he published between 1825 and 1830. A limited issue was printed on large paper as Vol. V of the old edition. An abridged version, with reduced plates in outline, was published in manual form in 1841. The 3rd edition of this abridgement was issued as one of the volumes in *Bohn's Illustrated Library.*

[19] Le Roy's work was widely read in England. Le Roy had left Rome for Athens in 1753. His book appeared at Paris in 1758, entitled, *Les Ruines des Plus Beaux Monuments de La Grèce, considérées du côté de l'histoire et du côté de*

and other help he succeeded in getting his book . . . published in 1758, it is in every way inferior to the work of Stuart and Revett. The views of Athenian antiquities drawn for Lord Charlemont by Richard Dalton in 1749 and engraved by him, were not done from accurate and scientific measurements, so that Stuart and Revett may fairly claim to have been the pioneers of classical archaeology.[20]

The publication of the *Antiquities of Athens* made Stuart famous, and he was thereafter known as "Athenian" Stuart.[21] He was elected to the Royal Society and the Society of Antiquaries. He found his profession of architect in the new Grecian style very profitable. In 1763 he became official painter to the Society of Dilettanti, while the popularity of his volume called forth rival publications.[22] He died, however, before the second volume of the *Antiquities of Athens* could be published.

In 1764 the members of the Society of Dilettanti decided to continue their sponsorship of Greek researches. In that year they established a fund for the purpose and selected three well qualified men to engage in a further archaeological project. The first

---

*l'architecture; par M. Le Roy, Historiographe de l'Académie Royale d'Architecture et de L'Institut de Bologne.* I have been able to examine only the second edition, 1770. This consists of two volumes, the first dealing with Greek architecture before the reign of Alexander, the second with Greek architecture after the reign of Alexander. Vol. I contains an essay on the history of architecture in which Greece is, of course, eulogized. This is followed by a series of chapters on Athenian ruins, with historical discussions and plates. Vol. II contains an essay on the theory of architecture, followed by similar discussions and plates of Corinthian and Spartan ruins.

[20] Lionel H. Cust, in the *Dictionary of National Biography,* Vol. 19, p. 87 (ed. 1921).

[21] Revett was displeased because most of the credit for the work was given to Stuart. He subsequently sold all of his rights in the succeeding volumes to Stuart, although he continued to be an active member of the Society of Dilettanti.

[22] Cust and Colvin, *op. cit.,* p. 84, mention such a rival publication by Robert Sayer, *The Ruins of Athens,* London, 1749, which I have been unable to examine. Another of these publications was a series of drawings of Athenian antiquities made by the British artist, Richard Dalton, in 1749, when he accompanied Lord Charlemont to Greece. Between 1751 and 1752 he engraved and published these. In *The Manuscripts and Correspondence of James, First Earl of Charlemont, Historical Manuscripts Commission, 12th Report,* Part X, Vol. 28, London, 1891, p. 201, note 2, this publication is cited as *Antiquities and Views in Greece and Egypt, with the Manners and Customs of the Inhabitants. By Richard Dalton.* The Printed Catalogue of the British Museum, however, lists only "Dalton, Richard. [A Series of engravings representing views of places, buildings, antiquities, etc., in Sicily, Greece, Asia Minor, and Egypt. London, 1751-2. 52 plates]." Eyles Irwin (*cf. infra,* pp. 51ff.) mentions (p. 3) Richard Dalton's publication, *Musaeum Graecum et Egyp-*

of these was Richard Chandler (1738-1810),[23] the brilliant classical scholar. Chandler had entered Brasenose College in 1744 and Queen's College in 1755. In 1759 he published *Elegiaca Graeca,* containing his edition in Greek of the fragments of Tyrtaeus, Simonides, Meleager, Theognis, Alcaeus, Sappho, and others, illustrated with succinct notes. In 1763 appeared Chandler's *Marmora Oxoniensiae, Oxonii, E Typographeo Clarendoniano. Impensia Academiae,* a scholarly catalogue of the Oxford or Arundelian marbles, which had been presented to the University by the Earl of Arundel's grandson, Henry Howard, Duke of Norfolk.[24] Chandler examined and collated the inscriptions, rectified previous mistakes, and wrote a full introduction in Latin. This

---

*tarum,* 1752. In the Columbia University Library I have found a volume of Dalton's engravings, undated, entitled, *Antiquatum Graecorum,* some of the plates in which, below Dalton's signature, bear the date 1750, some 1751. The volume, containing 29 beautiful engravings without discussion, is apparently a fragmentary copy of the volume in the British Museum. A list of these engravings, with their titles, follows:

1. Itinerarium Curiosum.

2. The Cupola of the Lanthorn of Demosthenes.

3. A Temple of Hercules commonly called the Lanthorn of Demosthenes.

4. The Frize of the Lanthorn of Demosthenes. On which are Represented certain Labours of Hercules, not to be met with in any other of the Basso Relievos now remaining.

5. The Tower of Andronicus or the Temple of the Winds at Athens.

6. The Basso Relievos on the Frize of the Temple of the Winds. N.B. There are eight winds represented on the Frize of this Temple, but one and a great part of another of the Figures is entirely covered by the wall of an adjoyning Dwelling House.

7-16. 10 engravings of examples of Greek sculpture without titles.

17. An Arch erected by the Emperor Adrian at Athens.

18. The remains of an antient Monument erected by the Athenians, on the hill called Musaeum, in honour of Philopappus.

19. View of the Parthenon or Temple of Minerva on the North Side.

20. The South East Angle of the Temple of Minerva.

21. The Principal Parts of the Temple of Erictheus in Large.

22. The Temple of Erictheus at Athens.

23. One end of the Building contiguous to the Temple of Erictheus.

24. [Another view] The Temple of Erictheus at Athens.

25-29. The Basso Relievos on the Frize of the Inner Portico of the Temple of Minerva.

[23] A memoir of Chandler by Ralph Churton is prefixed to *Travels in Asia Minor and Greece. By the Late Richard Chandler, D.D. A New Edition, with Corrections and Remarks by Nicholas Revett, Esq. . . .* Oxford, 1825, 2 Vols. *Cf. infra,* p. 42n.

[24] The publication of the inscriptions on these marbles by Selden in 1628 appeared in a second edition in 1676, directed by Bishop Fell.

was followed by a series of beautifully engraved plates showing the numerous Greek statues, marbles, busts, and gems. Printed under the imprimatur of the Earl of Litchfield, chancellor of the University, in two volumes, the work was dedicated to George III. A full index to its contents was supplied by John Loveday.[25]

It was on the basis of this scholarly record that, in 1764, the Society of Dilettanti selected Chandler to head another archaeological expedition to Greece. Chandler was to "execute the Classical Part of the Plan,"[26] and was to be accompanied by Revett for "the province of Architecture" and William Pars, a young painter who had just won a medal from the Society of Arts, for "taking Views and copying Bass Relief's." These men were instructed by the Society to be exhaustive in their research:

> . . . That you do procure the exactest measures and plans possible of the buildings you shall find, making accurate drawings of the bas reliefs and ornaments and taking such views as you shall judge proper; copying all the inscriptions you shall meet with, and remarking every circumstance which can contribute towards giving the best idea of the ancient and present state of these places. . . . From this day of your departure from hence to that of your return, you do each of you keep a very minute journal of every day's occurrences and observations, representing things exactly in the light in which they strike you, in the plainest manner and without regard to style or language, except that of being intelligible. . . .[27]

Chandler, Revett, and Pars left England for the Dardanelles on June 9, 1764. They visited the Troad, Tenedos, and Scio, and arrived at Smyrna on September 11. Here they established their headquarters, making two prolonged excursions into the neighboring country. The first of these lasted from September 30 to October 29, 1764; the second, from March 25 to August 8, 1765. They explored the Temple of Apollo Didymaeus near Miletus and the Sacred Way leading up to the Temple from the harbor, with the seated figures of the priestly clan of the Branchidae. They also explored Clazomenae, Erythrae, Teos, Priene, Tralles, Lao-

[25] Chandler also wrote a *History of Ilium or Troy*, London, 1802.

[26] The instructions of the Society to the men are printed by Ralph Churton, *op. cit.*, preface.

[27] *Ibid.* These instructions are dated May 17, 1764.

dicea, Sardis, Philadelphia, and Magnesia. Their work interrupted by the plague, they made their return to Smyrna. On August 20, 1765, they left for Athens, which they reached on August 31, after seeing Sunium and Aegina on the way. They stayed at Athens until June 11, completing some of the work begun by Stuart and Revett. They then visited Marathon, Eleusis, Megara, Epidaurus, Delphi, Salamis, Aegina, Nemea, Corinth, and, in the Peloponnesus, Nauplia, Argos, Mycenae, Patras, Chiarenza, Olympia, and the plain of Elis. Thence they went to Zante, where they embarked for England on September 1, 1766, arriving on November 2.

Upon their return all the marbles, journals, drawings, and inscriptions in their possession were turned over to the Society of Dilettanti. Selecting from this collection such views as would not overlap those scheduled to appear in the forthcoming volume by Stuart and Revett, the Society published these in *Ionian Antiquities,* 1769. Presentation copies of the volume were sent to the King and Queen, the Universities of Oxford, Cambridge, Edinburgh, Glasgow, Dublin, St. Andrews, and Aberdeen, the Royal Society, the Royal Academy, the Society of Antiquaries, the British Museum, and the King of Spain. The remainder of the inscriptions and journals, given by the Society to Chandler to publish, appeared as *Inscriptiones Antiquae, pleraeque nondum editae: in Asia Minori et Graecia praesertim Athenis, collectae. Cum appendice. Oxford, 1774.* Chandler also published a more popular account of this expedition in *Travels in Asia Minor,* 1775, and *Travels in Greece,* 1776.[28]

Churton tells us that Chandler was deeply affected by his voyage to the Levant:

> As he adverted occasionally to the classic scenes, which he had visited in his travels, it was truly delightful, I had almost said enchanting, to my younger ears, to hear him tell, his bright eye beaming with peculiar lustre, how, after a long lapse of ages of ignorance and barbarism, and under the cruel hand of Turkish tyranny and oppression, the lyre, though not now in the hands of a Tyrtaeus or Simonides, was still however cherished on the banks of the Illissus. . . .[29]

[28] See *infra,* p. 42n. [29] Ralph Churton, *op. cit.,* p. vii.

This emotional reaction is reflected in the Society's important publication. The full title of the work is *Ionian Antiquities, Published, with Permission of the Society of Dilettanti, by R. Chandler, M.A., F.S.A.; N. Revett, Architect; W. Pars, Painter. London, printed by T. Spilsbury and W. Haskell, 1769.* It is a beautiful folio volume in three chapters, with a preface "To the Reader." This preface is as full of admiration for Greece as that of Stuart and Revett:

Ionia [is] a Country in many respects curious, and perhaps, after Attica, the most deserving the Attention of a Classical Traveller. . . . The knowledge of Nature was first taught in the Ionic School: And as Geometry, Astronomy, and other Branches of the Mathematics, were cultivated here sooner than in other Parts of Greece, it is not extraordinary that the first Greek Navigators, who passed the Pillars of Hercules, and extended their Commerce to the Ocean, should have been Ionians. Here History had its Birth, and here it acquired a considerable degree of Perfection. The first Writer, who reduced the knowledge of Medicine . . . to an Art, was of this neighborhood: And here the Father of Poetry produced a Standard for Composition, which no age or country have dared to depart from, or have been able to surpass. But Architecture belongs more particularly to this Country than to any other. . . . As to the other Arts which also depend upon Design, they have flourished no where more than in Ionia; nor has any Spot of the same Extent produced more Painters and Sculptors of distinguished Talents.[30]

The chapters which follow consist of historical discussions, descriptions, measurements, and full size plates showing the ancient sculptures. Chapter I is entitled, "The Temple of Bacchus at Teos" and contains six plates. Chapter II is entitled, "The Temple of Minerva Polias at Priene" and contains twelve plates. Chapter III is entitled, "The Temple of Apollo Didymaeus near Miletus" and contains ten plates.

That the Society expected to continue their researches among the antiquities of Ionia is shown by the entries, in their records, of money given to Revett for this purpose in 1771 and 1772, but the project encountered much delay. It was not until 1797 that the second volume appeared.[31]

[30] Pp. iii.

[31] A total of 5 volumes of the *Ionian Antiquities* were ultimately published. Vol. III is dated 1840; Vol. IV, 1881; Vol. V, a supplement to Vol. III, 1915. The

Apart from the work of the Society of Dilettanti, it is possible to trace additional interest in Greek archaeological remains in England between 1732 and 1786. In 1740, for example, Horace Walpole visited the recently excavated Herculaneum with much interest.[32] In 1751 Lady Featherstonhaugh made a similar visit and brought back an account of it to the Royal Society.[33] In 1750 Wickes Skurray translated from the Italian Venuti's description of the remains at Herculaneum, and in 1756 there appeared an English translation of Bellicard's *Observations sur les Antiquités d'Herculaneum*.

More significant than these in the development of romantic hellenism, however, is the work of Robert Wood (1717?-1771).[34] As a young man Wood had travelled through various parts of Europe, and had thus developed a liking for voyages. In May, 1742, he travelled from Venice to Corfu and from Mitylene to Scio. In February, 1743, he sailed from Latakia in Syria to Damietta in Egypt. In the course of these travels he seems to have discovered much pleasure in beholding the sites of antiquity, so that he longed to see the lands of ancient Greece at closer range. About 1749 he made plans with John Bouverie and James Dawkins, two young Oxford graduates with whom he had travelled in France and Italy, to revisit Greece and to study its remains of antiquity. They secured the services of a certain Borra, an Italian artist, who was to accompany them as "architect and draughtsman."

The four men passed the winter of 1749-50 together at Rome, where Bouverie had acquired an extensive knowledge of art and architecture. Here Wood made an effort to learn as much as he

---

records of the Society also mention permission granted, in 1776 and 1777, to Paul Sandby, artist, to publish a series of aquatint engravings from Pars' drawings of Athenian remains.

[32] See his letter to West praising the work in Mrs. Paget Toynbee, *Letters of Horace Walpole*, London, 1903, Vol. I, pp. 71-72.

[33] See Lady Chatterton, *Memorials, personal and historical, of Admiral Lord Gambier*, London, 1861, Vol. I, pp. 16, 43-50. A brief account of the discovery of Herculaneum, translated from the German of the Abbé Winckelmann, appeared also in 1764 in the "Abstract of a Letter concerning Herculaneum . . . ," *Annual Register*, Vol. 8, pp. 182-189 (1765).

[34] An account of Wood appears in Cust and Colvin, *op. cit.*, pp. 60-110.

could about ancient history and geography. They then went to Naples and embarked for Greece on July 25, 1750. They stopped under the Sigean promontory and went on shore at the mouth of the Scamander. On the journey Bouverie died,[35] while the other three men went on to Athens, arriving there in May, 1751. Wood tells us:

When we arrived in Athens, we found Mr. Stewart and Mr. Revet, two English painters, successfully employed in taking measures of all the architecture there, and making drawings of all the bas reliefs, with a view to publishing them, according to a scheme they had communicated to us at Rome. We were much pleased to find that some of the most beautiful work of the Antients were to be preserved by persons so much more equal to the task; and therefore did no more at Athens than satisfy our own curiosity. . . .[36]

Wood, Dawkins, and Borra then very graciously left Athens and proceeded to the ancient site of Palmyra, where they examined ruins from the 14th to the 27th of March, 1751. From this point they went to ancient Balbec on April 1 of the same year, where they engaged in similar work.

The fruits of this voyage are contained in three publications. The first of these is *The Ruins of Palmyra, Otherwise Tedmor, in the Desart,* London, 1753, published without the name of the author. This consists of a preface, "The Publisher to the Reader," evidently by Wood, giving an account of the origin of the project to explore the coast of the Mediterranean "to the most remarkable places of antiquity," the agreement of the four men, and the winter spent in Rome.

We met our ship at Naples in the spring. She brought from London a library, consisting chiefly of all the Greek historians and poets, some books of antiquities, and the best voyage writers. . . .

We visited most of the islands of the Archipelago, part of Greece in Europe; the Asiatic and European coasts of the Hellespont, Propontis, and Bosphorus. . . .

It is impossible to consider with indifference those countries which gave birth to letters and arts, whose soldiers, orators, philosophers,

[35] The date of his death is Sept. 8, 1750. He was buried at Smyrna. See Joseph Foster, *Alumni Oxonienses,* Oxford and London, 1888, Vol. I, p. 140.

[36] Preface to *The Ruins of Palmyra,* 1753.

poets and artists have shewn the boldest and happiest flights of genius, and done the greatest honour to human nature.

Circumstances of climate and situation, otherwise trivial, become interesting from that connection with great men, and great actions, which history and poetry have given them: The life of Miltiades or Leonidas could never be read with so much pleasure, as on the plains of Marathon or at the streights of Thermopylae; the Iliad has new beauties on the banks of the Scamander, and the Odyssey is most pleasing in the countries where Ulysses travelled and Homer sung.

The particular pleasure . . . which an imagination warmed on the spot receives from those scenes of heroick actions, the traveller only can feel, nor is it to be communicated by description.

There follows "An Enquiry into the Antient State of Palmyra," in which an attempt is made to trace the history of the ancient city. Little, Wood says, is known of its ultimate antiquity until it came under the influence of the Greeks and produced the great Longinus:

This people copied after great models in their manners, their vices and their virtues. Their funeral customs were from Egypt, their luxury was Persian, and their letters and arts were from the Greeks. Their situation in the midst of these three great nations makes it reasonable to suppose they adopted several other of their customs and manners. . . .

How much is it to be regretted that we do not know more of a country, which has left such monuments of its magnificence? Where Zenobia was queen, and where Longinus was first Minister?[37]

The remainder of the book, following a section of inscriptions and three pages entitled, "A Journey through the Desart," consists of descriptions and measurements of architectural antiquities and ruins, all of them Greek and in the Corinthian style. The volume, a large folio, contains fifty-seven plates, some of them in several parts.

The second publication is a sequel to the *Ruins of Palmyra* and is entitled, *The Ruins of Balbec, Otherwise Heliopolis in Collosyria,* London, 1757. The preface to this volume, "A Journey from Palmyra to Balbec," is signed "Robert Wood," who acknowledges the editorship of the preceding volume. As he had done with Palmyra, Wood gives a complete historical account of Balbec. He points out that Balbec had formerly been under the

[37] P. 23.

government of Damascus, but was now a minor Turkish possession inhabited by many Greeks and members of other nations. He is much impressed with the architectural remains, which are largely Greek:

When we compare the ruins of Balbec with those of many antient cities which we visited in Italy, Greece, Egypt, and in other parts of Asia, we cannot help thinking them the remains of the boldest plan we ever saw attempted in architecture.[38]

The volume contains discussions and measurements of these ruins, with forty-six full size plates.

These two volumes were greeted in England with much interest[39] and exerted an influence on the rise of romantic hellenism

[38] P. 6.

[39] The esteem in which these works were held is indicated in the remark in *The Adventurer,* No. 139 (Tuesday, March 5, 1754), made by the writer in "an attempt to improve learning and taste," particularly in conversation: "As it is no man's interest to write that which the public is not disposed to read, the productions of the press will always be accommodated to popular taste, and in proportion as the world is inclined to be ignorant little will be taught them. Thus the Greek and Roman architecture are discarded for the novelities of China; the Ruins of Palmyra, and the copies of the capital pictures of Corregio, are neglected for gothic designs, and burlesque political prints; and the tinsel of a Burletta has more admirers than the gold of Shakespeare. . . ." Similarly, "L. M.," writing to "Mr. Fitz-Adam" in *The World,* No. 63 (Thursday, March 14, 1754), says: "I doubt whether, in our most splendid assemblies, the Royal Game of Goose would not have as many eyes fixed upon it, as the lately published curiosity of the ruins of Palmyra. I mention this work, not only to inform such of your readers as do not labour under a total loss of appetite for liberal amusements, what a sumptuous entertainment they may sit down to, but also to give it as a signal instance, how agreeably men of ingenious talents, ample fortune, and great leisure, may amuse themselves, and, laudably employing their leisure time, do honour to their country." *Cf.* the very favorable 7 page review of *The Ruins of Balbec* in *The Monthly Review,* Vol. XVII, pp. 59-66 (1758); and the remark made by Elizabeth Montague in a letter to her husband, July 9, 1754: "We are all going to Vauxhall, where Mr. Tyers has had the ruins of Palmyra painted in the manner of the scenes so as to deceive the eye and appear buildings." See Emily J. Climenson, *Elizabeth Montagu, the Queen of the Blue Stockings. Her Correspondence from 1720 to 1761,* London, 1906, Vol. II, p. 52. As late as 1812 Shelley sang (*Queen Mab,* ll. 109-125);

'Behold,' the fairy cried,
'Palmyra's ruined palaces!
Behold where grandeur frowned!
Behold where pleasure smiled!
What now remains?—the memory
Of senselessness and shame.
What is immortal there?
Nothing—it stands to tell
A melancholy tale, to give
An awful warning; soon
Oblivion will steal silently
The remnant of its fame.
Monarchs and conquerors there
Proud o'er prostrate millions trod—
The earthquakes of the human race;
Like them, forgotten when the ruin
That marks their shock is past.'

by the idealization of Greek ruins which they helped spread. A similar influence was exerted somewhat later by Wood's third publication in 1767, *A Comparative View of the Antient and Present State of the Troade. To which is prefixed an Essay on the Original Genius of Homer.*[40] An enlarged edition of *An Essay on the Original Genius of Homer* appeared in 1769. Both of these works were edited by Jacob Bryant and issued in 1775 under the title, *An Essay on the Original Genius and Writings of Homer, with a Comparative View of the Antient and Present State of the Troade.* In the preface Wood states that his chief object in his eastern voyages was to read "the Iliad and Odyssey in the countries where Achilles fought, where Ulysses travelled, and where Homer sung." The work contains views by Borra of "Antient Troas" and of "Antient Ruins near Troy," and includes many other engravings by Pars. The essay on Homer is an attempt to shed more light on the identity of the Greek poet by considering the geography of modern Greece and comparing it with Homer's accounts. Wood considers in turn Homer's place of birth, which he identifies as Ionia, Homer's geography and navigation, his religion and mythology, his accounts of local customs and habits, his historical allusions, his chronological computations, and his language and learning. The work was very popular, being pirated at Dublin in 1776[41] and translated into French, German, Italian, and Spanish before the end of the century.

To the work of Dawkins and Wood should be added the volume, *Ruins of the Palace of the Emperor Diocletian at Spalatro in Dalmatia, by R.* [*obert*] *Adam, F.R.S., F.S.A., Architect to the King and to the Queen. Printed for the Author, 1763.* Adam (1728-1792), the most famous of the four celebrated Adam brothers, architects, had, in 1754, visited Italy with Clérisseau, a French architect. Of this visit the work we are considering was the result. On his return to England in 1762, Adam was appointed Royal Architect. In the four page introduction, Adam gives a colorful account of the origin of the project:

Nor could I help considering my knowledge of Architecture as imperfect, unless I should be able to add the observation of a private edifice of the

[40] No copies of this edition are probably extant at present.
[41] It was also reissued in 1824.

Ancients to my study of their public works. This led me to form the scheme of visiting the Ruins of the Emperor Dioclesian's [*sic*] Palace at Spalatro, in Dalmatia. . . . I was convinced, notwithstanding the visible decline of Architecture, as well as of the other arts, before the reign of Dioclesian, that his munificence had revived a taste in Architecture superior to that of his own times, and had formed artists capable of imitating, with no inconsiderable success, the stile and manner of a purer age. . . . We set sail from Venice on the 11th of July 1757, and on the 22d of that month arrived at Spalatro.

This city, though of no great extent, is so happily situated that it appears, when viewed from the sea, not only picturesque but magnificent. As we entered a grand bay, and sailed slowly towards the harbour, the Marine Wall, and long Arcades of the Palace, one of the ancient Temples, and other parts of that building which was the object of our voyage, presented themselves to our view, and flattered me, from this first prospect, that my labor in visiting it would be amply rewarded. . . . By unwearied application during five weeks, we compleated, with an accuracy that afforded me great satisfaction, those parts of our work which it was necessary to execute on the spot.

Encouraged by the favorable reception which has been given of late to work of this kind, particularly to the Ruins of Palmyra and Balbec, I now present the fruits of my labor to the public. I am far from comparing my undertaking with that of Messieurs Dawkins, Bouverie, and Wood, one of the most splendid and liberal that was ever attempted by private persons. I was not, like these gentlemen, obliged to traverse desarts, or to expose myself to the insults of barbarians; nor can the remains of a single Palace vie with those surprizing and almost unknown monuments of sequestered grandeur which they have brought to light; but at a time when the admiration of the Grecian and Roman Architecture has risen to such a height in Britain, as to banish in a great measure all fantastic and frivolous tastes, and to make it necessary for every Architect to study and to imitate the ancient manner, I flatter myself that this work, executed at considerable expence, the effect of great labor, and perseverance, and which contains the only full and accurate Designs that have hitherto been published of any private Edifice of the Ancients, will be received with indulgence, and may, perhaps, be esteemed an acquisition of some importance.

There follows "A Description of the General Plan of Dioclesian's Palace as Restored, Explaining the Manner of disposing the Apartments in the Houses of the Ancients," including measurements. The remainder of the book is made up of sixty-one magnificent full-size plates showing various parts of the ruins in detail. Many of these plates are signed by F. Bartolozzi.

In addition to the work of the Society of Dilettanti and of Wood, Dawkins, and Adam, mention should be made of the numerous private collections of Greek sculpture and art made in England between 1732 and 1786,[42] such as those of Mr. Perry at Penhurst and Sir Robert Walpole at Houghton Hall.[43] Between 1748 and 1761 a collection of Greek marbles was made by Thomas Hollis and Thomas Brand and placed in the Hyde, the country seat of Hollis. Similar collections were those of Lord Anson at Shugborough; Lord Malton at Wentworth House; Sir Richard Hoare at Stourhead; Wellbore Ellis, afterwards Lord Mendip, at Twickenham; and Mr. Fox, afterwards Lord Holland, at Kingsgate, Isle of Thanet.

A more significant collection was that of Thomas Coke, Earl of Leicester, a member of the Society of Dilettanti after 1740. Coke had engaged Matthew Brettingham about 1755 to bring from Italy eleven Greek statues, eight busts, a relief, and some mosaic slabs to adorn his estate in Norfolk. The same Brettingham bought for Charles Wyndham, second Earl of Egremont, the most extensive aggregate of antique sculptures in the whole country to adorn the Earl's Petworth estate. This collection consisted of twenty-four statues and nearly forty-eight busts.

The role of Brettingham as a purchasing agent in Italy is a significant one because to him was given the charge of selecting the type of sculpture to be bought. Brettingham was one of a group of such individuals, including Gavin Hamilton and Thomas Jenkins, an artist and dealer in sculptures, who was frequently associated with the sale of marbles to Englishmen. About 1761 Jenkins made some excavations in Corneto which yielded many fine sculptures.[44] From about 1769 to 1775 James Byres joined Hamilton and Jenkins in a series of excavations at Tivoli, on the Via Appia, Prima Porta, Monte Cognuolo, Castel di Guido, and Ostia, which produced results in scores of statues and marbles. Many of these ultimately came to England.

1760 is the year of accession to the throne of England of

[42] A detailed account of these will be found in Adolf Michaelis, *op. cit.*, pp. 55-128 and 92ff.

[43] This collection was catalogued by Horace Walpole in *Aedes Walpolianae*, 1747.

[44] See P. Paciaudi, *Lettres au Comte de Caylus*, Paris, 1802, p. 248.

George III, who was very much interested in ancient art. Through James and Robert Adam, the latter of whom was Royal Architect, he purchased from Cardinal Albani[45] in 1762 a collection of drawings and prints of classic art. In the same year the King also procured a collection of gems and additional drawings belonging to Mr. Smith, Consul at Venice. Another such collection of gems was formed by George Spencer, third Duke of Marlborough, by adding to the Arundel gems, which he obtained from his sister-in-law, the collection of Lord Bessborough and a selection of unusual specimens belonging to the Venetian Count Antonio Maria Zanetti, together with other occasional purchases. The Duke had the choicest of these specimens of art engraved and published in sumptuous style.[46] The King's love for collecting was frequently used by Roman dealers, such as Jenkins, as a means of procuring under the British flag unhindered conveyance to England of works purchased by private individuals, their exportation from the Papal States being ordinarily forbidden.

A collection of ancient sculptures for his house at Wimbledon was also formed, over a period of thirty years, by Lyde Browne, a member of the Society of Dilettanti who was frequently in Rome during the latter half of the eighteenth century. In 1768 Browne issued a catalogue of this collection, *Catalogus veteris aevi varii generis monumentorum, quae Cimeliarchio Lyde Browne Arm. apud Wimbledon asservantur.* To this collection Browne added many works resulting from the excavations of Hamilton and Jenkins, and the increase was noted in a new catalogue, *Catalogo dei piu scelti e preziosi marmi, che si conservano nella Galleria del Sigr. Lyde Browne, Cavaliere Inglese, a Wimbledon, nella Contea di Surry, raccolti con gran spesa nel corso di trent'anni, molti dei quali si ammiravano prima nelle piu celebri Gallerie di Roma,* London, 1779. Another collector who dealt with Hamilton and Jenkins was Charles Townley, who came to London from Italy in 1772, and bought a house in Westminster. For twenty years thereafter he adorned it with sculptures which he procured from the

[45] The influential German hellenist, Johann Joachim Winckelmann, was librarian to the Cardinal at the time.

[46] See Story Maskelyne, *The Marlborough Gems,* London, 1870, p. vi.

two dealers.[47] Similarly, Henry Blundell of Ince, a friend of Townley, bought from Jenkins some of the Ince marbles collected between 1777 and the end of the century.[48] Still other collectors of ancient art in England were William Locke, Charles Lennox, third Duke of Richmond, Charles Dunscombe, H. Constantine Jennings, the Earls of Exeter, Yarborough, and Bessborough, the Duke of Devonshire, and the Marquis of Monthermer.

The work of the Society of Dilettanti, of Wood, Dawkins, and Borra, and of the numerous private collectors of ancient sculpture in England may be said to have spread an interest in and admiration for the remains of ancient Greece. The publications of the Society, the volumes by Wood, and the printed catalogues of the collectors constitute a record of widespread idealization of Greek ruins as well as of Greek architecture and sculpture. When this archaeological stimulus is added to the antiquarian worship of Greece already present in the age,[49] there emerges a distinct force in the rise of romantic hellenism in England.

[47] See James Dallaway, *Statuary and Sculpture Among the Ancients, with some Account of Specimens Preserved in England,* London, 1816, p. 324.

[48] See James Dallaway, *Anecdotes of the Arts in England, or Comparative Remarks on Architecture, Sculpture, and Painting, chiefly illustrated by Specimens at Oxford,* London, 1800, p. 352.

[49] The antiquarian idealization of ancient Greece is attested by the *Archaeologia Graeca, or the Antiquities of Greece, by John Potter, D.D., late Archbishop of Canterbury. To which is added an Appendix, containing a concise history of the Grecian states, and a short account of the lives and writings of the most celebrated authors.* The first edition of this work appeared in 1697; the seventh, in 1751. I have examined an American edition, New York, 1825. Aside from the appendix, the work consists of four books, the first two of which contain 26 chapters each. The third book contains 22 chapters and the fourth 20 chapters. Book I deals with the early history of Athens, its political and social organization, and, especially, its laws. Book II deals with the Greek religion and contains full discussions of gods, temples, games, music, and festivals. Book III deals with Greek military and naval supremacy and describes in detail the knowledge of these activities possessed by the Greeks. Book IV describes miscellaneous customs among the Greeks on such occasions as birth, marriage, and death. In addition to its exhaustiveness, the work is also highly appreciative. It contains such statements as these: "Greece became the celebrated mother of the bravest and most experienced soldiers in the world" (p. 404). "Most of the arts and inventions which are necessary to the management of human life, owe their first originals to the Athenians, from whom they were derived into the other parts of Greece, and thence carried into foreign countries for the common benefit of mankind" (p. 124). In 1772 appeared the successor to Potter's work, *Antiquities of Greece. By Lambert Bos . . . Translated from the original Latin by Percival Stockdale.* This is, in essence, a concise outline of Potter's work, brought up to date. Shorter than its predecessor, it includes, nevertheless, discussions of the natural history and geography of the Greeks, as well as more precise statements concerning temples and other edifices which the age had learned.

## III

## ROMANTIC HELLENISM IN THE LITERATURE OF TRAVEL TO THE EAST

The awakening of interest in the archaeological remains of ancient Greece which we have traced in the preceding chapter was partly the cause of the growth in travel to the East notable between 1735 and 1786. But even before the beginning of the eighteenth century English travels had almost ceased to be adventurous and had become more scientific and educational in purpose.

> By 1660 the heroic age of English exploration and discovery had run its course. The English voyager no longer sailed recklessly into remote waters lured by the strange and the unknown. . . . Ardor for the wholesome conversion of savages had also cooled. The glitter of gold . . . was no longer an important factor in determining the course English expansion was to run.[1]

The interest of the English traveller after 1660 was directed more toward ideas and cultural forces than toward the discovery of new lands for commercial or other practical gain. In the literature of these travels one senses an awareness of a "scheme, fostered by the Virtuosi, whereby man's intellectual horizon was to be widened and his condition improved."[2] The traveller sought to enlighten the world and was, therefore, open to enlightenment from the culture of the lands which he visited.

By the middle of the eighteenth century the accounts written by English travellers to lands distant and near are preoccupied largely with ideas current in the age, to which they lend validity and conviction. In these accounts there is, for example, much emphasis on the "State of Nature," the "Inspired Peasant," on

[1] R. W. Frantz, *The English Traveller and the Movement of Ideas, 1660-1732,* in *University of Nebraska Studies,* Vol. 32/33 (1932-1933), p. 7.
[2] *Ibid.,* p. 13.

"Genius," primitivism, liberty, and equality.[3] As this chapter will demonstrate, moreover, such travel literature is also influential in the development of the idea of romantic hellenism.

One reason for the preoccupation of eighteenth century travellers with current ideas is, of course, the vogue of the Grand Tour. For the average young man in the higher ranks of society travel was an indispensable form of education and culture. Consequently, most of the travel literature of the age is of a non-commercial and non-utilitarian nature, reflecting the spirit in which the voyages were undertaken. The Grand Tour in the eighteenth century, it is true, did not normally extend to such lands as Greece and Turkey, being limited usually to France, Italy, Germany, and the Low Countries.[4] There is, however, a body of literature dealing with voyages to Greece either directly or incidentally, most of which is written with aims similar to those of the Grand Tour.[5] As the century goes on, this literature increases in bulk until, after 1786, it assumes major proportions.

It should be observed that the earlier accounts of Greece generally appear in travel literature dealing with the Levant as a whole or with the Ottoman empire. It is not until the eighth decade of the century that romantic hellenism becomes sufficiently pervasive an idea to stimulate wide travel to Greece alone. Where

[3] *Cf.* Chauncey B. Tinker, *Nature's Simple Plan. A Phase of Radical Thought in the Mid-Eighteenth Century. The Louis Clark Vanuxem Lectures,* Princeton University Press, 1922.

[4] *Cf.* William Edward Mead, *The Grand Tour in the Eighteenth Century,* Boston and New York, 1914.

[5] There is contemporary evidence that hellenic antiquarianism among travellers was sufficiently in vogue to be the subject of satire. In Thomas Warton's *Newmarket: A Satire,* London, 1751, occur these lines (ll. 11-14):

> Convinc'd too late that modern strains can move,
> Like those of ancient Greece, th' obedient grove:
> In headless statues rich, and useless urns,
> Marmoreo from the classic tour returns.

Thirty-one years later William Cowper utters a similar complaint in *The Progress of Errour,* 1782:

> We give some Latin and a smatch of Greek;
> Teach him to fence and figure twice a week
> And having done, we think the best we can,
> Praise his proficiency, and dub him man.
> From school to Cam or Isis, and thence home

Greece is discussed in these earlier accounts, however, definite elements of romantic hellenism appear.[6]

---

And thence with all convenient speed to Rome,
With rev'rend tutor clad in habit lay
To tease for cash, and quarrel with all day;
With memorandum-book for ev'ry town
And ev'ry post, and where the chaise broke down.
. . . . . . . . . .
Surpris'd at all they meet, the gosling pair,
With awkward gait, stretch'd neck, and silly stare,
Discover huge cathedrals built with stone,
And steeples tow'ring high much like our own.
. . . . . . . . . .
Ere long some bowing, smirking, smart abbé
Remarks two loit'rers, that have lost their way;
And being always prim'd with *politesse*
For men of their appearance and address,
With much compassion undertakes the task,
To tell them more than they have wit to ask;
Points to inscriptions wheresoe'er they tread,
Such as, when legible, were never read,
But, being canker'd now and half worn out,
Craze antiquarian brains with endless doubt;
Some headless hero, or some Caesar shows—
Defective only in his Roman nose;
Exhibits elevations, drawings, plans,
Models of Herculanean pots and pans;
And sells them medals, which, if neither rare
Nor ancient, will be so, preserv'd with care.

See Alexander Chalmers, *The Works of the English Poets from Chaucer to Cowper,* London, 1810, Vol. 18, pp. 613-614.

[6] There had, of course, appeared accounts of travel to Greece before 1735, but these do not, in general, display so much romantic hellenism as those published after 1735. Among the most significant of these earlier accounts are Paul Rycant, *The Present State of the Ottoman Empire,* London, 1668; George Wheler and Dr. Spon, *A Journey into Greece,* London, 1682; Ellis Veryard, *An Account of Divers Choice Remarks, as Well Geographical, as Historical, Political, Mathematical, Physical and Moral: Taken in A Journey Through the Low Countries . . . As Also a Voyage to the Levant,* Exeter, 1701; Henry Maundrell, *A Journey from Aleppo to Jerusalem,* Oxford, 1703; and Aaron Hill, *A Just Account of the Ottoman Empire . . .,* London, 1709. Bibliographies of travel literature dealing with various parts of the world appear in John Pinkerton, *A General Collection of the Best and Most Interesting Voyages and Travels in All Parts of the World,* London, 1814, Vol. 17. The bibliography of books dealing with Greece and its vicinity appears on pp. 61ff. Some of the accounts mentioned by Pinkerton are not easily available in America. Pinkerton lists, for instance, an anonymous *Journey from Aleppo to Damascus; To Which is Added, An Account of the Maronites Inhabiting Mount-Lebanon,* London, 1736, which I have been unable to examine. It probably would not, however, add much to our general conclusions. While this study is limited to romantic hellenism in English literature, it should be observed that between 1780 and 1786 there appeared two French publications which were read and reviewed in England

Upon analyzing that portion of the travel literature which deals with Greece, one is immediately struck with the fact that, in almost all of these accounts, the authors tend to sentimentalize what they see, reading into the lands what is not necessarily there. Richard Chandler, one of the most scholarly of the travellers,[7] admits that being objective in such literature is difficult:

---

and, therefore, exerted further influence in the development of romantic hellenism in English literature. The first of these is by Marie Gabriel Auguste Florent, Comte de Choiseul-Gouffier, *Voyage Pittoresque de la Grèce,* Paris, 1782. The second is by M. Guys, *Voyage Littéraire de la Grèce, ou lettres sur les Grecs anciennes et modernes avec un parallèle de leurs moeurs,* Paris, 1783. The edition of Choiseul-Gouffier's work that I have examined, which may be a facsimile, contains a "Notice sur la vie et les ouvrages de M. le Comte de Choiseul-Gouffier. Par M. Dacier, Sécrétaire Perpetuel de l'Académie Royale des Inscriptions et belles-lettres." The Count was born in 1752 and died in 1817. Dacier says of him: "Il était surtout tellement épris de l'antique Grèce, qu'à peine sorti de l'enfance il montrait le plus vif désir de voir cette contrée rendue si célèbre par les arts, par les talents, et par les grands hommes dans tous les genres auxquels elle a donné le jour, et dont le nom seul commande le respect et l'admiration. . . . Ce n'était pas la Grèce opprimée par le farouche et orgueilleux Musulman qu'il brûlait de visiter; il n'aurait en qu'à gémir sur de hautes et accablantes infortunes; il demandait à la Grèce captive et humiliée des impressions plus douces, quelques traces non entièrement effacées, quelques faibles restes de sa splendour passée; il y cherchait la Gréce d'Homère et d'Hérodote, et, remontant de trois mille ans dans l'espace des ages, il voulait retrouver les vieux peuples, les vieilles divinités. . . ." The book contains 126 plates, with discussions and descriptions of ruins and monuments, as well as of the social and political life of the modern Greeks. For English reviews of these French publications see *Annual Register,* Vol. 14, p. 184 (1771); Vol. 30, p. 23 (1788). Between 1780 and 1786 there also appeared a book by a certain McIntosh, *Travels in Europe, Asia, and Africa, from 1777 to 1781,* London, 1782, which I have not been able to examine. In the same year there was published a bitter political attack on McIntosh by Joseph Price, *Some Observations and Remarks on the Late Publication, entitled "Travels in Europe, Asia, and Africa,"* London, 1782.

[7] See *supra,* pp. 26ff. Chandler (1738-1810) had been instructed by the Society of Dilettanti to keep an accurate journal of his travels when he was sent to Greece to do research among Greek antiquities. The fruits of this research, as we have seen, were *Ionian Antiquities,* 1769, and *Inscriptiones Antiquae, pleraeque nondum editae: in Asia Minori et Graecia, praesertim Athenis, Collectae, Cum Appendice,* 1774. In 1775 appeared Chandler's *Travels in Asia Minor.* This is reprinted in the third edition, *Travels in Asia Minor and Greece. By the Late Richard Chandler, D.D. A New Edition, with Corrections and Remarks by Nicholas Revett, Esq. To which is prefixed an Introductory Account of the Author, by Ralph Churton, M.A., Archdeacon of St. Davids.* Oxford, Clarendon Press, 1825, Vol. I. There was also a second edition, including Revett's corrections, in 1817. Revett's own copy of the first edition, with his corrections in manuscript, is now in the British Museum. The 1775 volume of travels was followed in 1776 by *Travels in Greece; or, An Account of a Tour Made at the Expense of the Society of Dilettanti.* The copy which I have used bears the imprint, "Dublin, 1776." It is in 319 pages octavo and contains 79 chapters and six plates. These two volumes of travels constitute the

And here it may be remarked, that the poets who celebrate the Ilissus as a stream laving the fields, cool, lucid, and the like, have both conceived and conveyed a false idea of this renowned water-course. They may bestow a willow fringe on its naked banks, amber waves on the muddy Meander, and hanging woods on the bare steep of Delphi, if they please; but the foundation in nature will be wanting; nor indeed is it easy for a descriptive writer, when he exceeds the sphere of its own observation to avoid falling into local absurdities and untruth.[8]

---

publication of Chandler's journal. While the *Ionian Antiquities* and the *Inscriptiones Antiquae* are scientific, scholarly, and objective, the *Travels* are much more imaginative and absorbing. Chandler's accounts are highly detailed, including interesting histories, legends, traditions, and various literary associations, as well as vivid descriptions of ruins, people, manners, and customs. Because of his rich knowledge Chandler was able to write a very thorough account of Greece, so that it served to acquaint readers who were not university trained with the beauties of the mythology, history, and literature of ancient Greece, as well as with its monuments and its "present state." Constant reference to these associated matters is made wherever Chandler finds an opportunity to do so. The *Travels in Asia Minor* includes discussions of the islands in the Archipelago, Smyrna, Hellespont, Tenedos, Troas, Scio, Ionia, Ephesus, Miletus, Myus, Laodicea, Hierapolis, Chonos, Sardis, and Magnesia. This volume contains 84 chapters. The *Travels to Greece* contains discussions of Aegina, Athens and its surrounding territory, Megara, Corinth, Salamis, Argos, Epidauria, Delphi, Patrae, Olympia, and many lesser places in Greece. An example of the educational quality of Chandler's work may be found in Chap. 7, which includes a detailed summary of the history and significance of the city of Cecrops, from its origin through the tyranny of Pisistratus, the expulsion of Hippias, the invasion of Darius, the battle of Marathon, the sieges of Xerxes and Mardonius, the victories of Plataea and Salamis, the Peloponnesian War, Philip of Macedonia and his son, Alexander, and the conquest by Alaric, King of the Goths, to the conquest by the Venetians in 1464. There then follows a list of important references to Cecrops since that date. When writing of the Propylea in the Acropolis, he narrates the myth of Minerva's assistance to the architect, Mnesicles, who, having been mortally hurt by a fall, was revived by the plant called Parthenium, "a remedy," which grew near the Acropolis and of which Minerva had informed Pericles. Similarly, he explains the meaning of part of the Propylea thus (p. 42): "The right wing of the propylea was a temple of victory. They related that Aegeus had stood there, viewing the sea, and anxious for the return of his son Theseus, who was gone to Crete with the tributary children to be delivered to the Minotaur. The vessel which carried them, had black sails suiting the occasion of its voyage; and it was agreed, that, if Theseus overcame the enemy, their colour should be changed to white. The neglect of this signal was fatal to Aegeus, who, on seeing the sails unaltered, threw himself down headlong from the rock, and perished. The idol was named *Victory without wings;* it was said, because the news of the success of Theseus did not arrive, but with the conqueror. It had a pomegranate in the right hand, and an helmet in the left. As the statue was without pinions, it was hoped the goddess would remain forever on the spot." Similar historical and mythological accounts throughout the work make the book alive, imaginative, stimulating, and interesting to the ordinary reader.

[8] *Ibid.*, p. 83.

Dr. Charles Perry, indeed, says outright:

Some modern Writers have expatiated egregiously upon this Piece of Antiquity [the Theatre of Bacchus]; and have discovered in it (at least, so they pretend) all that ever existed in it, and perhaps more too. Hence we may conjecture, that these industrious and obliging travellers have ransack'd all those Records of Antiquity that relate to it; and fancying they actually saw (and the Power of Fancy is very delusive) everything that has been reported of it (right or wrong) by antient Historians; so they have related them as things really existing at this Time.[9]

It is because of this tendency of the writers of books of travel to Greece to permit their emotions somewhat to distort their view that romantic hellenism appears in full bloom in their pages.

Analysis of this romantic hellenism into its component parts reveals six elements. The first of these is the expression of a sweeping admiration for ancient Greek art and sculpture. Thus Perry approaches Athens with rapture:

When we came in sight of Athens, the once famous and celebrated city which is situate in a spacious and beautiful Plain, we were charm'd with the distant view of its antient Edifices, which rise conspicuous above the modern Buildings. But afterwards, when we came to have a near View of them, our Pleasure and Delight were not only continued, but much augmented, from observing with what Neatness, Harmony, and Symmetry they were form'd and finish'd.[10]

[9] *A View of the Levant: Particularly of Constantinople, Syria, Egypt, and Greece. In Which Their Antiquities, Government, Politics, Maxims, Manners, and Customs, (With Many Other Circumstances and Contingencies) Are Attempted To Be Described and Treated On. In Four Parts. By Charles Perry, M.D.*, London, 1743, pp. 504-505. Charles Perry (1698-1780) had received his medical degree from Cambridge in 1727, and, between 1739 and 1742, had travelled in France, Italy, and the East, visiting the lands mentioned in the title of his book. While Perry is primarily interested in diseases, he displays fondness for the expression of sentimental remarks on what he meets in his travels. For this reason considerable romantic hellenism is to be found in the fourth part of his book, "Containing an Account of a Voyage from Alexandria to Athens, with Some other Parts of Greece; and of such Remains as that famous City at present exhibits to View." This part appears on pp. 479-519. The book is a large folio volume, illustrated with 33 beautiful plates. Its popularity is shown in the fact that it was twice translated into German, once in a three-volume edition at Erlangen in 1754, and again in a two-volume edition at Rostock in 1765. A second impression of the original work appeared in 1770, dedicated to John Montague, Earl of Sandwich. Perry is also the author of many medical treatises. See the account of him given in Francis Blomefield, *History of the County of Norfolk*, London, 1805-10, Vol. IV, p. 197.

[10] Charles Perry, *op. cit.*, p. 488.

In Athens, he looks at the Temple of Olympian Jove and says:

This Temple is, or was, built in the Corinthian Order; in which Taste it was a Master-piece; for, as 'tis commonly thought and said, this best and most perfectly expressed the Beauty and Dignity of that Order. Indeed we can't see what Remains are yet extant of this noble Edifice, to any Advantage; because they are greatly eclipsed, and choaked up, with Houses that are built about them. However, what we can discover of it, strikes the Eye with great Pleasure, and the Mind with Delight and Admiration.[11]

He is even more pleased with the Temple of Theseus:

This precious morsel of antiquity has withstood the Injuries of Time, and the Malice of Men, beyond most others; for the Body of this Temple, with the Colonade that incloses it, are yet perfect and intire. This Edifice is, as to its Figure, a long Square; being 27 Yards in Length, 13 Yards in Width, and near as much in Height. . . . [Here follow detailed measurements.] This beautiful Colonade consists of 34 Pillars of the Doric Order, besides Two others, of the same Order and Dimensions, which are situate within at the North End, and join to the Nave of the Temple. The Frize of the Temple is adorned with a Range of Figures, in a very bold Demi-relief, representing that Hero's Battles with the Amazons, the Centaurs, and the Minotaur. This Sculpture is so beautiful and perfect, that one who had not seen Minerva's Temple would imagine nothing of the kind could equal, much less excell it.[12]

In a similar manner Richard Pococke[13] describes the wonders which are visible on the island of Samos:

The Temple of Juno was another of the wonders of Samos; and it was a very extraordinary building, both with regard to its size, and the manner of its architecture. . . . The pillars were built of several round stones laid one on another; they are of white marble, and the bases of grey. . . . About one-half mile to the west of the Temple there is a rivulet . . . on which, they say, Juno was born, under a white willow. . . . The river runs below by a ruinous village called Milo, which is

[11] *Ibid.*, p. 497. [12] *Ibid.*, p. 495.

[13] Richard Pococke (1704-1765), having received the degree of D.C.L. from Oxford in 1733, spent the ensuing three years in tours to France, Italy, and other parts of Europe. From these experiences he seems to have developed a passion for travel. Planning an extended visit to the East in 1737, he went to Alexandria and toured upper Egypt, including Thebes and Cairo. Thence he travelled to Palestine and Balbec, Cyprus, Candia, parts of Asia Minor, and Greece. He was at Messina in

almost forsaken by reason of the injuries they have received from the corsairs.[14]

J. Aegidius Van Egmont and John Heyman are similarly enthusiastic about the beauties of Greek art.[15] They look upon the ruins of Smyrna and recall that of old:

All the streets were broad, straight, well-paved, and decorated on each

---

1740. After visiting Italy, Germany, and Switzerland, he returned to England in 1742, having spent five years abroad. The fruit of this voyage was the voluminous *A Description of the East, And Some Other Countries,* London, printed for the author by W. Bowyer. The first folio volume, dealing with Egypt, contains five books and appeared in 1743. The second volume, containing discussions of Palestine, Syria, Mesopotamia, Cyprus, Candia, Asia Minor, Greece, and parts of Europe, appeared in 1745, dedicated to the Earl of Chesterfield. This second volume is in six books, the first two of which deal with the Holy Land and Syria. The third, fourth, fifth, sixth, and seventh books are concerned with Cyprus (six chapters); Candia (eight chapters); the Greek islands of the Archipelago, such as Scio, Ipsara, Mytilene, Tenedos, Lemnos, Samos, and Patmos (eight chapters); Asia Minor (twenty-three chapters); and Thrace and Greece (seventeen chapters). Pococke's account of these lands includes detailed descriptions and measurements of ruins and accounts of governments, customs, revenue, trade, education, religion, dress, architecture, climate, soil, vegetables, and animals. The work was widely read and brought Pococke advancement in the Church. It was translated into French in 1772-3 (at Paris, 7 Vols.), German in 1754-5 (at Erlangen), and Dutch in 1776-86 (at Utrecht). Later in life Pococke made additional tours in England, Ireland, and Scotland. His collection of Greek, Roman, and English coins was sold in London at auction by Langford on May 27-8, 1766. Pococke is also the author of *Inscriptionum Antiquarum Graec. et Lat. liber. Accedit numismatum . . . in Aegypto cursorum . . . Catalogus, Etc.,* [London], 1752. A memoir of Pococke appears in John Nichols, *Literary Anecdotes of the Eighteenth Century,* London, 1812-16, Vol. II, p. 157. In addition to the original edition, *A Description of the East* is also printed in John Pinkerton, *op. cit.,* Vol. X. My quotations are taken from the original first edition.

[14] Richard Pococke, *op. cit.,* Vol. II, Part II, pp. 27-28.

[15] A scientific account of Greek islands became available in 1759, in the translation, *Travels Through Part of Europe, Asia Minor, The Islands of the Archipelago, Syria, Palestine, Egypt, Mount Sinai, Etc. Giving a particular account of the most remarkable Places, Structures, Ruins, Inscriptions, Etc. in these Countries. Together with the Customs, Manners, Religion, Trade, Commerce, Tempers, and Manner of Living of the Inhabitants. By the Honourable J. Aegidius Van Egmont, Envoy Extraordinary from the United Provinces to the Court of Naples; and John Heyman, Professor of the oriental languages in the university of Leyden. Translated from the Low Dutch. In Two Volumes. London, Printed for L. David and C. Reymers, Printers to the Royal Society. 1759.* In the Preface it is stated that the authors visited the lands enumerated on two different occasions, their first visit lasting nine years, their second, four. Among the places described are Smyrna, Ephesus, Tmolus, Sardis, Myteline, Tenedos, Troy, Scio, Rhodes, Cyprus, Damascus, Balbec, Laodicaea, and Aleppo. Pinkerton, *op. cit.,* Vol. 17, p. 61, also mentions an account by Russell, *The Natural History of Aleppo, and Ports Adjacent; Containing a Description of the City and the Principal Natural Productions in its Neighborhood,* London, 1756, which indicates the presence of a scientific interest in the East.

side with stately palaces, and colonnades: and besides the temple of Cybele, it had others of great magnificence; a publick library, and an excellent harbour, which could be shut up in case of necessity; but what the inhabitants of Smyrna most glory'd in, is the circumstance of it's [*sic*] giving birth to the divine Homer.[16]

After describing the Temple of Diana at Ephesus, they say:

Such are the remains of that vast and celebrated temple; formerly one of those structures termed the wonders of Asia. The first temple was reckoned a work of the Amazons, and was so magnificent and superb a structure, that when Xerxes ordered all the temples of Asia to be burnt, this alone was spared. But afterwards, the wretch Herostratus, whose name ought to have been condemned to oblivion, set it on fire, instigated by the vain ambition of perpetuating his name, and thus destroyed the finest structure in the world.[17]

The scholarly Chandler finds the sight of Greek sculpture a source of aesthetic pleasure:

We kept on in the plain, and crossed the dry bed of Ilissus. On our left were the door-ways of antient sepulchres hewn out in the rock; the Museum, and on it the marble monument of Philopappus; and then the lofty Acropolis, beneath which we passed. Before us was a temple standing on the farther bank of the Ilissus; and some tall columns, of vast size, the remains of the temple of Jupiter Olympus. We arrived at the French convent, which is at this extremity of the town, infinitely delighted and awed by the majesty of the situation, the solemnity and grandeur of ruin, which had met us.[18]

After he has described the Acropolis and told of Phidias and other artists employed by Pericles, he says, by way of summary:

The artificers in the various branches were emulous to excel the materials by their workmanship. To grandeur of proportion were added inimitable form and grace. . . . Plutarch affirms, that, in his time, the structures of Pericles alone demonstrated the relations of the ancient power and wealth of Hellas not to be romantic. In their character was an excellence peculiar and unparallelled. Even then they retained all their original beauty. A certain freshness bloomed upon them, and preserved their faces uninjured; as if they possessed a never-fading spirit, and had a soul insensible to age. The remains of some of these edifices, still extant in the Acropolis, cannot be beheld without admiration.[19]

[16] J. Aegidius Van Egmont and John Heyman, *op. cit.*, pp. 75-6.
[17] *Ibid.*, p. 108. [18] Richard Chandler, *Travels in Greece, op. cit.*, p. 27.
[19] *Ibid.*, p. 40.

The second element in the romantic hellenism of the literature of travel to the East is the expression of profound admiration for ancient Greek culture in general, its valor, its government, its love of liberty, its Arcadian nature. Perry, for example, having given a brief history of Athens, turns to the famed Athenian valor and love of liberty with these words:

Indeed the Athens we are speaking of, was so far superior, in Fame and Renown, to all the other Cities which went by the same Name, (on account of its Polity, Literature, the Culture of Arts and Sciences in general, and the great Figure it made in the World) that it eclipsed them all, as it were: So that in past Ages, as well as the present, whenever Athens was spoken of, without any explanatory Epithet, this was always understood.[20]

When he beholds the remains of the Athenian Academy, he gives a tribute to Athenian Wisdom:

This was a wise, well-judged Politic of the Athenians (and what they were very punctual and constant in the practice of) to decree and erect Monuments in Honour, and to the Memory of their deceas'd Heroes and Sages, and to such others (of whatsoever Order, or Class, they might be) as had signalized themselves in the interest and Benefit of the Republic. For these posthumous Recompences and Honours would necessarily inspire every one with Sentiments of Emulation, and with an Ambition to appear deserving, in their respective Spheres. 'Tis certain, the antient Greeks (and especially the Athenians) had that, which at this Day is styled the universal Passion, very strongly implanted in them. . . .[21]

In the *Travels of Charles Thompson,*[22] an account is given of

[20] Charles Perry, *op. cit.*, p. 491. [21] *Ibid.*, p. 502.

[22] In the year following the publication of Perry's book there appeared a sumptuous three-volume octavo work entitled, *The Travels of the Late Charles Thompson, Esq.; containing His Observations on France, Italy, Turkey in Europe, The Holy Land, Arabia, Egypt, and many other parts of the World: Giving a particular and faithful account of what is most remarkable in the Manners, Religion, Polity, Antiquities, and Natural History of those countries: With a curious description of Jerusalem, as it now appears, and other places mentioned in the Holy Scriptures. The whole forming a compleat View of the ancient and modern state of great part of Europe, Asia, and Africa: Publish'd from the Author's Original Manuscript, interspers'd with the Remarks of Several other Modern Travellers, and Illustrated with Historical, Geographical, and Miscellaneous Notes by the Editor. Adorn'd with Maps and Prints. In Three Volumes. Reading, Printed by J. Newbery and C. Micklewright, at the Bible and Crown in the Market-Place. 1744.* That "Charles Thompson, Esq." was a fictitious traveller was evident, it seems, to many of the

the social customs, natural history, trade, and religion of modern Athens. Then, in the words of the author:

> After this short Account of what Athens is at present, it cannot but be agreeable to look back into its ancient History, and, instead of the melancholy Scene it now affords us, to view it in its flourishing Condition, when it was universally renowned for Valour, Power, Learning, and whatever else could make its name illustrious.[23]

Then follows a detailed history of Athens from its foundation by Cecrops to its subjugation by the Turks, in which much emphasis is laid upon the Greek love of liberty. The author concludes his account with this eulogy, tempered with a bit of puritanical moralizing:

> To this Summary of the History of Athens from its Origin to the present Time, give me leave to subjoin a short Character of its ancient Inhabitants, to which that of the modern Greeks in many Particulars may be look'd upon as quite the Reverse. The darling Passion and most active Principle of the Athenians was their ardent Love of Liberty, which appear'd in all their Actions and Enterprizes. The least Shadow of Servitude, and sometimes even a lawful and reasonable subjection, sat heavy upon their Shoulders, and made them restless and uneasy. The Democracy was their favourite Form of Government, and whoever endeavor'd to wrest the supreme Power out of the Hands of the

---

reading public even of 1744. In the "Preface by the Editor," occupying not quite five unnumbered pages, it is said that when proposals for the work had been first issued, "some persons" maintained that both the author and the travels were fictitious because nothing at all was known about Charles Thompson. The editor insists, however, that he can say no more about the author than that, when he died, he had left the editor his manuscripts to edit and publish, issuing a "dying injunction" forbidding him to disclose the full identity of their author. He further insists, citing the example of Homer, that it is not necessary to be familiar with the details of a writer's career in order to appreciate his work. He openly admits that he has "interwoven additions from the writings of other travellers, such as Sandys, Wheeler [*sic*], Burnet, Addison, Maundrell, Shaw, Pococke, Thevenot, Tournefort, and many others." The book, then, is really a compendium of all available knowledge at that date of the lands which are discussed in it, placed within a framework of a fictitious traveller who meets with fictitious adventures. The portion of this work dealing with Greece is in Volume I (pp. 277-448), and is entitled, "Turkey in Europe." The author supposedly visits the Island of Candia, Mount Ida, the rich ruins of Gortyna, Siphnos, Naxos, Paros, Delos, Athens, Mount Hymettus, Salamis, Eleusis, Megara, Corinth, Mount Parnassus, Delphos, and Thebes. To each of these he devotes pages of description and explanation historical, antiquarian, and sentimental. His observations include remarks not only on ruins and the climate, but also on customs, natural history, trade, and religious sects.

[23] *Ibid.*, Vol. I, p. 333.

People, were sure to be the Object of the publick Odium and Resentment. They were easily provoked to Anger, and as easily induced to resume their Sentiments of Compassion. Even their Enemies they treated with Humanity, and never made such an insolent Use of Victory, as to exercise Cruelty towards the Vanquish'd. They had naturally an amazing Penetration, Vivacity, and Delicacy of Wit; were passionately fond of theatrical Entertainments, and delighted in Pleasantry, Humour, and Raillery. They were strict Observers of the Rules of Politness [*sic*], and even scrupulous in point of just Behaviour; and this too upon Occasions when Forms of Complaisance are usually forgotten or neglected. It is remarkable, that though they lov'd to hear themselves prais'd, and were much better pleas'd with Flattery than Censure from their Orators; yet, in Affairs of Importance, and Emergencies of State, they generally gave ear to the Advice of those who had made it their Practice to oppose their unreasonable Measures and Desires. Popularity, even if it arose from Merit, was a Crime in the Eyes of the Athenians, who were not only suspicious of the Rich and Great, but of those who distinguish'd themselves by superior Talents and Abilities. They were ready enough to grant Exemptions and Immunities to those who had render'd any considerable Services to their Country; but sometimes, however, they have shewn themselves ungrateful to their Generals, and such as have deserv'd their highest Honours and Rewards. They excell'd in the Arts of War and Government, in Philosophy, Eloquence, Poetry, Painting, Sculpture, and Architecture: Nor was their Delicacy of Taste confined to those of a more exalted Condition and liberal Education, but was visible even among their Artificers, Husbandmen, Soldiers, and Mariners, from whom it is least expected. Athens, in short, may in some Sense be said to have been the School of the Universe, to which Rome herself stands indebted for her Arts and Learning and whose Lessons cannot fail of refining our Taste, and filling our Minds with generous and exalted Sentiments. I shall only add, that the love of Liberty, the Characteristick of the Athenians, seems frequently to have inclined them to Licentiousness; and that their great Qualities were mix'd with great Defects, such as must naturally flow from a jealous turbulent Spirit, and a fluctuating, inconstant, capricious Disposition.[24]

Similar admiration is expressed by Chandler when he speaks of certain engraved marbles which he sees on the hill of the Acropolis:

Religion furnished Athens with a great variety of spectacles and amusements. The festivals were celebrated with gymnic exercises, music, and plays. The public sometimes defrayed the expense of the choruses; but

[24] *Ibid.*, Vol. I, pp. 349-351.

that burthen was commonly laid upon rich citizens, who had attained to the age of forty years. Rewards were proposed for superior excellence, and the victory was eagerly desired. The glory of individuals reflected lustre on the community, to which they belonged; and the tribes were emulous to surpass each other. It was a splendid contention, the parties vying in the display of spirit and generosity. The conquerors were distinguished and applauded, and their names registered on marble.[25]

Eyles Irwin[26] is filled with inspiration at the valor of ancient Crete, which he identifies with modern Candia:

As I contemplated the outlines of this celebrated land, my memory was not wanting to fill up the sketch, with the remarkable circumstances, which the history of Crete has afforded to the admiration of mankind. Ida, which then burst on our sight, teemed with the idea of the youthful Jove; while the city of Minos, and the labyrinth of Dedalus, were still visible in the ruins, which are scattered along the shore! But, at no period, did she give birth to such splendid action, as occurred in the in-

[25] Richard Chandler, *Travels in Greece, op. cit.*, p. 64.

[26] In 1780 appeared *A Series of Adventures in the Course of a Voyage up the Red-Sea, on the coasts of Arabia and Egypt; and of a route through the Desarts of Thebais, in the year 1777. In Letters to a Lady. By Eyles Irwin, Esq. In the Service of the Honourable The East India Company. Illustrated with Maps and Cuts.* Another edition of this book appeared in the same year. A third edition, containing "A Supplement of a Voyage from Venice to Latichea; and of a route through the Desarts of Arabia, By Aleppo, Bagdad, and the Tygris, to Busrah in the years 1780 and 1781," appeared in 1787. This third edition, which I have used, bears the imprint, "London, Printed for R. Dodsley." Irwin (1751-1817) had been appointed, in 1766, to a writership in the East India Company's service in the Madras Presidency. In 1768 he went to India, his birthplace. In 1771 he was appointed Superintendent of the Company's grounds within the bounds of Madras. Upon the deposition of Lord Pigot in 1776, Irwin signed a protest against the revolution in the Madras government. When he refused to accept the post of Assistant at Vizagapatan, to which he had been appointed by the Council of the Company in 1776, he was suspended from the Company's service. In order to seek redress for this unjust treatment, he sailed for England early in 1777. This journey of eleven months forms the basis of the first part of his book. When he returned to England, however, Irwin found that he had already been reinstated in the service of the Company. He, therefore, returned to India by another route in 1780, the account of which constitutes the Supplement published in the third edition. Irwin's work consists of a series of four sentimental and verbose letters, supposedly written by the author as a kind of diary while on his voyages with three companions, Major Henry Alexander, Mr. Anthony Hammond, and one other, not named, who died in the course of the journey. Part of the book is concerned with the unscheduled adventures of these gentlemen in various parts of Greece (Letters III and IV), the narrative of which displays elements of romantic hellenism. Irwin's *Adventures* were translated into French at Paris in 1792. He went to China for almost two years in 1792, and is the author of some oriental poetry. A memoir of Irwin, together with a portrait of him, appears in the *European Magazine,* Vol. XV, pp. 179-181 (1789), and Vol. LXXII, p. 277 (1817).

vasion of the Turks, while the Venetians were her masters. The blockade and the siege of the city of Candia, which lasted without intermission for twenty-four years, and cost the Turks near 200,000 men, will suffice to carry her name down with honor to the latest posterity.[27]

The third and, perhaps, most abundant element in this romantic hellenism is the sentimental lamentation over the decay and ruin of the magnificent culture that was ancient Greece. Invariably the traveller to Greece has expected to see the land which he imagined in reading Greek literature, so that the sight of ruins and a far different scene is the occasion of expressions of disappointment which, in some cases, border on tears. Such, for instance, are the feelings of Alexander Drummond:[28]

> When we landed at Delos, mine eye was struck with the immense quantities of broken marbles, and my heart pierced with real concern, to see the devastations which had been made among such glorious edifices, and which I considered as the ruins of some friend's habitation. I therefore walked on with a kind of sullen pensiveness. . . .[29]

At Zante Drummond sees a picture done "in the modern Greek manner," and is bitterly disappointed:

> What a melancholy reflection it is to think that those people, who once

[27] Eyles Irwin, *op. cit.*, pp. 230-231.

[28] A rather emotional treatment of Greece appears in *Travels through Different Cities of Germany, Italy, Greece, and Several Parts of Asia, as far as the Banks of the Euphrates; In a series of letters. Containing an Account of what is most Remarkable in their present State, as well as in their Monuments of Antiquity. By Alexander Drummond, Esq. His Majesty's Consul at Aleppo. London, 1754.* Drummond (d. 1769), British Consul at Aleppo from 1754-1756, had commenced his travels in May, 1744. He reached Venice in August, Smyrna in December, and Cyprus in March, 1745. His book consists largely of observations by the way and in excursions made in intervals of what appear to be commercial activities during a residence in Cyprus and Asia Minor between 1745 and 1750. It is a beautiful quarto volume, adorned with plates, and is in the form of thirteen long letters, most of them addressed to Drummond's brother. The fourth, fifth, sixth, seventh, eighth, and thirteenth of these letters deal with various Greek islands, especially Cyprus, Zante, and Delos. Drummond had an eye for the dramatic, and his detailed accounts of life in these islands is both interesting and moving. He is much attracted to "natural curiosities," such as an "extraordinary attachment of two men eighty years old." Because of the absence of the customary erudition and scholarship found in most accounts of such voyages, this volume is rich in sentiment and popular interest. Very little information concerning Drummond is extant. The facts which I have stated are based partly on Henry Manners Chichester's account in the *Dictionary of National Biography* (ed. 1921/2), Vol. VI, p. 22.

[29] Alexander Drummond, *op. cit.*, p. 107.

excelled all the world in those liberal arts, are now sunk to such a degeneracy of taste and execution! Painting had arrived at such perfection in Greece, that the different stiles of this art were distinguished by the cities of that country in which they severally prevailed. The Bolognian taste, conspicuous for strength and boldness, was imported from Athens; the softness and effeminacy of the French, was borrowed from Corinth; the graceful and tender, the Venetians had from Rhodes; the stile of Rome and Florence, said to be easy and correct, is supposed to have been derived from the Sicyonians.[30]

Writing of the Temple of Apollo at Delos, he is even more bitter:

. . . It was adorned and resorted to by all those who were under his [Apollo's] influence and protection; that the ground was deemed sacred, the structures were magnificent, and that the contributions, levied from the votaries, were sufficient to maintain the priests in all the pomp of luxury and pride. Hence arose those noble piles of antiquity, those animated statues, and breathing pictures, that decorated this hallowed spot; that were afterwards exposed to the blind zeal and superstitious fury which prevailed in the first ages of Christianity, and afterwards totally ruined by the avarice and barbarity of Turkish conquerors. I reflect upon these ravages with the spirit of a mason, and bitterly curse the effects of ignorance, bigottry [*sic*], and priestcraft.[31]

Perry is less emotional, but equally disappointed, in his expression of regret at the state of modern Greece:

'Tis well known that Greece, in ancient Times, was divided and distinguished into a great many distinct Republics—that each of these Republics was populous and rich, and that the Whole formed a very powerful and great People.

The Country in general (however) appears so mountainous and desolate, and unfit for Culture, that one seems astonished at the Report of its former Strength, Power, and Grandeur. . . . At this day, on the contrary, we see the whole Country a Desert, as it were, void of Culture, and destitute of People.[32]

At Gortyna, near Mount Ida, the author of the *Travels of Charles Thompson* is dejected among the ruins:

Among these unregarded Ruins we saw Sheep feeding; and the Shepherds have built themselves Huts, or Places for Shelter, out of huge Pieces of antique Marble, which would be an Ornament to the Palaces

[30] *Ibid.*, p. 96. [31] *Ibid.*, p. 112.
[32] Charles Perry, *op. cit.*, p. 511.

of Princes. Such is the present face of Gortyna, which was once the principal city and chief Bishoprick of the Island.[33]

At Delos his mood is no happier:

> Its ancient Glory is now quite obscured, but may be guess'd at by the Heaps of Ruins that are found upon the Island, which at present is utterly deserted, and only serves as a Retreat for Pirates.[34]

Edmund Chishull[35] sadly finds desolation where once there was magnificence:

> Instead of that Sardis, which antiently was the seat of kings of Lydia, afterwards in great renown . . . we now find in the same place, at the foot of Mount Tmolus, a small Turkish village by the name of Sart. . . .
>
> Before the cool of the evening we visited the ruins of this once flourishing city; and towards the western part observed the standing walls of two or three spatious and lofty rooms, not unworthy the palace of the antient kings of Lydia. . . . From hence we passed thro heaps of rubbish, and tracks of continued foundations, to the eastern part of the city. . . . [Here we observed] a fair and magnificent portal, the pilasters of which, being about twenty feet high and twelve feet distant from each other, are joined at the top by one entire stone, which, by what art or force it was there erected, is difficult to conceive. . . .[36]

[33] *Travels of Charles Thompson, op. cit.*, p. 282.

[34] *Ibid.*, pp. 316-317.

[35] In 1747 there appeared the interesting *Travels in Turkey and Back to England. By the Late Reverend and Learned Edmund Chishull, B.D., Chaplain to the Factory of the Worshipful Turkey Company at Smyrna,* London, 1747. Chishull (1671-1733) had received the "traveller's place" from Corpus Christi College, of which he was a fellow, and was appointed chaplain to the factory in 1698. He set sail September 12 in that year, arriving at Smyrna on November 19. He stayed with the factory until February 10, 1701, making several tours to nearby lands and keeping a journal of all that he saw and did. It is this journal which was published posthumously by his son, Edmund, in quarto, in 1747, with a preface by Dr. Mead, the antiquary. The journal consists of five parts. Part One (pp. 1-31) is entitled, "An account of a journey round the antient Ionia, from Smyrna, thro St. George's, Magnesia, Durguthli, Sardis, Birghee, Tyria, Ephesus, and back to Smyrna, in the Year MDCXCIX." Part Two (pp. 32-54) is "An account of a voyage from Smyrna to Constantinople, and a journey back from thence to Smyrna, in the Year MDCCI." Part Three (pp. 55-71) is "An account of a journey from Smyrna to Adrianople, at the end of the Year MDCCI, and begining [*sic*] of MDCCII." Part Four (pp. 72-169) is "An account of a journey from Adrianople, thro Bulgaria, Walachia, Transylvania, Hungary, Germany, Flanders, Holland, and thence to England, in the Years MDCCII and MDCCIII." Part Five (pp. 170-177) consists of "A Letter to the Reverend Dr. Thomas Turner." This is dated June 13, 1700, and tells of Cadiz, Messina, and Milo. Parts One, Two, and Five relate in part to Greece. They manifest a striking sentimental interest in hellenic ruins.

[36] *Ibid.*, pp. 15-16.

At Ephesus this sadness has become dejection:

> The once glorious and renowned Ephesus was seated in a fruitful vale, encompassed almost round with mountains, at a small distance from the Cayster, and about five miles eastward from Cape Trogilium; where, at the common charge of all Ionia, the Panionia, or common councils of Ionia, were formerly celebrated. This vale rises advantageously in the middle with two or three little hills, on which the several parts of the antient city lay extended. The same spot of ground is still covered with the rich remains of its former glory. Such are the massy walls, the portals, the arches, the aqueducts, the marble chests, together with the dejected cornishes, shafts, and capitals of many lofty pillars. But the face of the whole yeilds [*sic*] a melancholy and disagreable [*sic*] prospect, being overrun with an incredible quantity of rank and luxuriant weeds, which serve only to corrupt the air, and to conceal the curiosities of the place.[37]

And when he sees the remains of the Temple of Diana, the dejection becomes a lament:

> Of the temple of Diana there are extant no considerable ruins, nor anything that is lofty and beautiful enough to bespeak it the remains of that famous structure. But in a marshy ground . . . there stand two broken pieces of a massy wall . . . surrounded with heaps . . . among which occur some lofty dejected pillars of beautiful and splendid marble. . . . Returning . . . the traveler has nothing else in view, but venerable heaps of rubbish, and uncertain traces of foundation; and must be forced to supply his curiosity with considering, that this was the place, where once stood and flourished that renowned wonder of the world.[38]

Frederick Hasselquist[39] reports similar desolation in Cyprus:

[37] *Ibid.*, p. 23. [38] *Ibid.*, pp. 26-27.

[39] In 1766 appeared the English translation of the brilliant *Voyages and Travels in the Levant; In the Years 1749, 50, 51, 52. Containing observations in Natural History, Physick, Agriculture, and Commerce: Particularly on the Holy Land and the Natural History of the Scriptures. Written Originally in the Swedish Language, By the Late Frederick Hasselquist, M.D. Fellow of the Royal Societies of Upsal and Stockholm. Published, by order of her Present Majesty the Queen of Sweden, by Charles Linnaeus, Physician to the King of Sweden, Professor of Botany at Upsal, and Member of all the Learned Societies in Europe. London, Printed for L. Davis and C. Reymers, 1766.* The account of the life of Hasselquist by the famous Linnaeus occupies the preface (pp. i-viii). Hasselquist (1722-1752) was one of Linnaeus' most brilliant disciples. One day, having heard a lecture in which Linnaeus explained that very little was known concerning the natural history of the Holy Land, he became intensely interested in investigating this void in the scientific knowledge of the age. Suffering from tuberculosis and in the face of much other discouragement, Hasselquist completed his journey to the East, making a remarkable

The town of Famagusta is now in a worse condition than the fort. All the houses . . . are either entirely demolished or uninhabitable. There are now no more than 300 inhabitants in the town, most of them Turks, who possess the miserable remains which are left of the once fine and famous Famagusta.[40]

Patrick Brydone[41] is likewise affected by the contrast between the mighty ancient and the petty present:

Many of the places on this coast [near Mt. Aetna] still retain their antient names; but the properties ascribed to them by the antients are now no more. The river Acis, which is now so poisonous, was celebrated for the sweetness and salubrity of its waters; which Theocritus says, were ever held sacred by the Sicilian shepherds.[42]

Thus he beholds a statue of Jupiter in Cattania:

But what do I behold!—Jupiter,—the sovereign of gods and men, with a ragged cloak over his shoulders!—What a humiliating spectacle!—Well do I remember, with what awe we bent before that once respectable image.—But what has become of the thunderbolt, which he held in his hand to chastise the world; and what is that he has got in its place?—

---

collection of specimens from plant and animal life, drugs, Arabian manuscripts, and mummies, but died before he could return to Sweden. Through the influence of Linnaeus and the Queen of Sweden, Hasselquist's debts were paid and his collection brought back to his native land. His manuscripts, containing observations on the life and manners of the peoples whom he visited, as well as discussions of their natural history, are the basis of the published volume. Hasselquist included Smyrna, Cyprus, Rhodes, and Chios in his travels, and his remarks frequently partake of the nature of romantic hellenism.

[40] *Ibid.*, p. 174.

[41] See *A Tour through Sicily and Malta. In a Series of Letters to William Beckford, Esq. of Somerly in Suffolk; from P.* [*atrick*] *Brydone, F.R.S. In Two Volumes.* London, 1773. Brydone (1736-1818) was a traveller early interested in scientific experiments with electricity. Early in life he travelled through Switzerland for this purpose. See *Gentleman's Magazine*, Vol. 88, Part I, p. 643. In 1767, he had become travelling preceptor to Mr. Beckford of Somerly and two other gentlemen. In 1770 he toured Sicily and Malta. Elected a fellow of the Royal Society in 1772, he published the account of his tour in 1773. On his tour Brydone passed such places as Calabria, Messina, Taurominum, Naumachia, Mount Aetna, Cattania, Hybla, Syracuse, Melita, and Agrigentum. At each of these points Brydone frequently indulges in the expression of emotional reactions to the remains of Greek antiquity. Rich in imagination, as well as scientific observations, the work also abounds in anecdotes. The work was extremely popular, passing through nine editions in Brydone's lifetime, and being translated into French and German. The editions appeared in the following years: 1773, 1774, 1774 (another edition), 1776, 1780, 1799, 1807, 1809, 1817. See also the favorable review of the book in the *Monthly Review*, Vol. XLIX, pp. 22, 115. The French translation appeared at Amsterdam in 1776; the German, at Leipsig in 1777 and again in 1831.

[42] *Ibid.*, Vol. I, p. 121.

His conductor would tell him, that it was only a piece of rope, with knots upon it, to chastise himself;—adding, that he was now doing penance for his long usurpation;—and that the thunder had long ago been put into much better hands.[43]

He is most deeply affected, however, at Syracuse:

Soon after this, the remains of the great Syracuse appeared; the remembrance of whose glory and magnificence, and illustrious deeds both in arts and arms, made us for some time forget our turtle. But alas! how are the mighty fallen! This proud city, that vied with Rome itself, is now reduced to a heap of rubbish; for what remains of it does not deserve the name of a city. We rowed round the greatest part of its walls without seeing a human creature; those very walls that were the terror of the Roman arms; from whence Archimedes battered their fleets, and with his engines lifted up their vessels out of the sea, and dashed them against the rocks.[44]

There is grimness in the humor of his remark when he sees what was formerly Diana's fountain:

The fountain of Arethusa was dedicated to Diana, who had a magnificent temple near its banks, where great festivals were annually celebrated in honour of the goddess. We found a number of nymphs, up to the knees in the fountain, busy washing their garments, and we dreaded the fate of Actaeon and Alphaeus: but if these were of Diana's train, they are by no means so coy as they were of old; and a man would hardly chuse to run the risk of being changed either into a stag or a river for the best of them.[45]

As he leaves Syracuse, he looks back fondly on its former splendor:

It is truly melancholy to think of the dismal contrast that its former magnificence makes with its present meanness. The mighty Syracuse, the most opulent and powerful of all the Grecian cities, which, by its own proper strength alone, was able, at different times, to contend against all the power of Carthage and of Rome:—Which is recorded, (what the force of united nations is now incapable of) to have repulsed fleets of two thousand sail, and armies of two hundred thousand men; and contained within its own walls, what no city ever did before or since, fleets and armies that were the terror of the world. This haughty and magnificent city, reduced even below the consequence of the most insignificant burgh.—"Sic transit gloria mundi."[46]

[43] *Ibid.*, p. 145.
[44] *Ibid.*, p. 265.
[45] *Ibid.*, pp. 276-277.
[46] *Ibid.*, p. 285.

Even the scholarly Chandler is deeply moved at the sight of the modern Ephesus:

The Ephesians are now a few Greek peasants, living in extreme wretchedness, dependence, and insensibility; the representatives of an illustrious people, and inhabiting the wreck of their greatness; some, the substructions of the glorious edifices which they raised; some, beneath the vaults of the stadium, once the crowded scene of their diversions; and some, by the abrupt precipice, in the sepulchres, which received their ashes. We employed a couple of them to pile stones, to serve instead of a ladder, at the arch of the stadium, and to clear a pedestal of the portico by the theatre from rubbish. We had occasion for another to dig at the Corinthian temple; and sending to the stadium, the whole tribe, ten or twelve, followed; one playing all the way before them on a rude lyre; and at times striking the sounding-board with the fingers of his left hand in concert with the strings. One of them had on a pair of sandals of goat-skin, laced with thongs, and not uncommon. After gratifying their curiosity, they returned back as they came, with their musician in front.

Such are the present citizens of Ephesus, and such is the condition to which that renowned city has been gradually reduced. . . . Its streets are obscured and overgrown. . . . The glorious pomp of its heathen worship is no longer remembered. . . .[47]

His descriptions of the ruined monuments of ancient Greece are a study in contrast. At Piraeus he describes the Temple of Jupiter:

This fabric was then adorned with wonderful pictures, the works of illustrious artists; and on the outside, with statues. In the second century, besides houses for triremes, the temple of Jupiter and Minerva remained, with their images in brass; and a temple of Venus, a portico, and the tomb of Themistocles. By Munychia was then a temple of Diana. By Phalerum was a temple of Ceres, of Minerva, and, at a distance, of Jupiter; with Altars of the unknown gods and of the heroes.

We found by Phalerum and Munychia a few fragments, with rubbish. Some pieces of columns and a ruined church probably mark the sight of one of the temples. In many places the rock, which is naked, has been cut away.[48]

In Athens and its vicinity he points to similar contrasts:

The acropolis furnished a very ample field to the antient virtuosi. It was filled with monuments of Athenian glory, and exhibited an amazing display of beauty, of opulence, and of art; each contending, as it were,

[47] Richard Chandler, *Travels in Asia Minor, op. cit.*, p. 160.
[48] Richard Chandler, *Travels in Greece, op. cit.*, p. 23.

for the superiority. It appeared as one entire offering to the deity, surpassing in excellence, and astonishing in richness. . . . But this banquet, as it were, of the senses, has long been withdrawn; and is now become like the tale of a vision. The spectator views with concern the marble ruins intermixed with mean flat-roofed cottages, and extant amid rubbish; the sad memorials of a nobler people; which, however, as visible from the sea, should have introduced modern Athens to more early notice. . . . Atticus is represented by Cicero as receiving more pleasure from the eminent men it had produced, than from the stately edifices and exquisite works of antient art, with which it then abounded. The traveller needs not to be so refined in order to derive satisfaction, even now, from seeing Athens.[49]

. . . The mansions of the illustrious dead, like the bodies which they covered, are consumed, and have disappeared. Time, violence, and the plough, have levelled all, without distinction; equally inattentive to the meritorious statesman, the patriot, the orator, and philosopher, the soldier, the artist, and physician. Atticus is described by Cicero as pleased with recollecting where the renowned Athenians had lived, or been accustomed to sit or dispute; and as studiously contemplating even their sepulchres. The traveller will regret, that desolation interferes, and by the uncertainty it has produced, deprives him of the like satisfaction. . . .[50]

The reader will recollect the account we have given of the god Pan, and his prowess at the battle of Marathon. It is likely, the mountain owed its name and the cave to his supposed merit in that transaction. He became a favourite deity, and, it seems, was provided with a habitation near the spot, where he had acquired so much renown. But now Pan with his terrors is forgotten. His goat-stand is possessed by an ideal woman; and the old fable concerning it, whatever it was, is supplanted by a modern fiction, ingenious as capable of moral application. . . .[51]

Irwin is less restrained in his bitterness at the decay of ancient Greece:

The island of Cyprus, so renowned of old for its beautiful aspect and fertile soil, exhibits at present, little but dreary and uncultivated tracts of land. This extraordinary change appears to be, as much owing to the want of inhabitants, as to the oppression of the Turks. . . . The capital, from neglect of commerce, and being chiefly inhabited by Turks, is become poor and wretched; and the once impregnable Famagusta, is now

[49] *Ibid.*, pp. 38-39.
[50] *Ibid.*, p. 115.
[51] *Ibid.*, p. 177.

dismantled, and untenanted, except by about seven families, who have built themselves huts among the ruins![52]

They [the natives of Montagna Negro] are, in all probability, the aborigines of the country; and when Greece declined from her former greatness, mouldered by degrees from the Roman hands, and became a prey to the barbarous nations, these wretched remains of a celebrated people, forsook their fertile plains and vallies, and took refuge amidst barren and almost inaccessible mountains. They preserved, indeed, their liberty by this desperate step; but lost, what is, perhaps, of more consequence to the happiness of mankind—the manners, the morals, the laws, which form and preserve, unbroken, the bonds of society. The Montanegrines have returned to the state of nature; and in a few ages have undone a system, which their forefathers could not accomplish, during the revolution of a thousand years.[53]

We were now about to round the peninsula of Peloponnesus, which made so conspicuous a figure during the ages of Greece; and if the character of its inhabitants, the magnificence of its cities, or the various produce of its soil be considered, stood, perhaps, without a rival in the antient world. And yet, nothing can be more desart and bleak, than the coast we were then approaching; which the tyrrany of the Turks, and the indolence of the oppressed natives, may have in some measure occasioned. . . . Modon was the antient Methone, and one of the seven cities, which Agamemnon promised to Achilles. . . . With the rest of the continent of Greece, it now groans under the Ottoman dominion.[54]

But perhaps the most romantic expression of lamentation over the fallen magnificence of ancient Greece is found in the preface to the account of Van Egmont and Heyman. Here is an approach to the mood which one finds in Shelley:

Many of the above cities, so celebrated by the Ancients for their wealth and splendor, are now reduced to a mere heap of ruins; the palaces once inhabited by the powerful and voluptuous princes of Asia, are razed to their foundations, and levelled with the ground. And the superb temples, once the wonder of the world, and whose ruins still astonish the traveller, are become a retreat for bats and owls, and their grand pavements, so often swept by the embroidered robes of the superb ladies of the east, are now the haunts of venomous serpents, and retreats for the savage inhabitants of the desert. An affecting lesson! and should teach us to value the liberty and religion we enjoy in this happy island, and stimulate us to transmit those invaluable blessings to our posterity; for

[52] Eyles Irwin, *op. cit.*, Vol. II, pp. 238-241.

[53] *Ibid.*, p. 215.

[54] *Ibid.*, pp. 227-228.

the iron hand of tyranny, and the insatiable sword of superstitious bigotry, destroyed these ancient cities, reduced their celebrated temples and palaces to heaps of rubbish, and laid the pride and splendor of the inhabitants in the dust.[55]

The fourth element in the romantic hellenism of the literature of travel to the East is the expression of a sentimental admiration for the scenery, culture, and inhabitants of modern Greece. In this view there is frequently an identification of the modern Greeks with what the travellers call their ancient forbears, while the modern scene is described as beautiful and serene. It is often possible to detect in this idealization of modern Greece the same strain of primitivism apparent in other manifestations of eighteenth century attitudes. Thus Pococke describes the inhabitants of Candia, the ancient Crete:

The people of the island do by no means want parts. . . . They are sharp and sagacious, which they discover in their countenances; the young people are very fair and handsome, and have fine eyes. . . . The Greek women do not cover their faces, but wear a muslin veil upon their heads, and bind up the hair in ribbands, and roll it round their heads, so as to make it a high dress; they tye their petticoats and aprons near as high as their armpits; and, when in high dress, they wear a sort of short stays, adorned before with gold lace.[56]

In the villages the men and women dance together in the public squares, and the mothers and the virgins sit round till midnight, and enjoy the conversations of their neighbours; it seems to be a custom continued from the antient Greeks, among whom dancing was looked on as a great perfection. . . .[57]

Chishull is delighted with the scenic beauties of Greece:

Every other tack brought us near to the Thracian shore, and entertained us with a fair view of the most green and fertile campaign I ever yet beheld. By the same means we enjoyed the opportunity of seeing the famous port and city of Heraclea, built behind a small eminence, which protends itself into the sea, and forms an haven on each side of the city. Not far from hence stands on the same shore the fair town of Selymbria; near which the night now overtakes us, and deprives us of that delicious prospect, which the whole day afforded us, of the fields of Thrace.[58]

[55] Van Egmont and Heyman, *op. cit.*, pp. vii-viii.
[56] Richard Pococke, *op. cit.*, Vol. II, part I, p. 266.
[57] *Ibid.*, p. 267.
[58] Edmund Chishull, *op. cit.*, p. 38.

The author of the *Travels of Charles Thompson* is enamored of the climate and the inhabitants:

The air of Athens is exceedingly healthful, and undoubtedly contributes to that Wit and Sprightliness which is observable in the Inhabitants, notwithstanding they are so far degenerated from their famous Ancestors. Though Learning is at a low Ebb amongst the Athenians, they are still more polite and civiliz'd than their Neighbours; and the natural Brightness of their Parts shows itself whenever an Opportunity offers. Their old jealous Humour, with regard to their Liberties and Privileges, will also sometimes appear, though they have little hopes of ever getting rid of the Turkish Tyranny, and therefore wisely refrain from running into Rebellion, or fomenting Factions in the State; but now and then venture to complain of their Injuries, and in some instances have obtain'd Redress; which few of the Greeks, especially in the Isles of the Archipelago, dare to attempt, be their Oppressions ever so notorious.[59]

Van Egmont and Heyman are also admiring:

The air of Rhodes excels that of any other place in the Archipelago. It has an affluence of all kinds of provisions. . . . It's [*sic*] wine is still excellent, and proper for the table, when a little diluted. . . .[60]

Lady Mary Wortley Montague,[61] writing from Belgrade, says:

This stiffness and formality of manners are peculiar to the Turkish

[59] *Travels of Charles Thompson, op. cit.*, p. 329.

[60] Van Egmont and Heyman, *op. cit.*, p. 270.

[61] To the body of travel literature dealing with Greece was added a feminine point of view when, in 1763, there appeared in print the three volumes of *Letters of Lady M[ar]y W[ortle]y M[ontague]*, edited, perhaps, by John Cleland. The facts concerning Lady Mary's letters have been stated by W. Moy Thomas in *The Letters and Works of Lady Mary Wortley Montague; edited by her great grandson, Lord Wharncliffe. With . . . A Memoir by W. Moy Thomas*, London, 1887. On June 5, 1716, Lord Montague had been appointed British Ambassador to the Ottoman Porte, then at war with Austria. The embassy was intended to reconcile the Turks and the Emperor. Montague left England with his wife and child in July, and arrived at Vienna in September. Having spent four months there, the family travelled to Adrianople, where, again, two months were spent. At the end of May they reached Constantinople and remained there until June 6, 1718. The record of this voyage is contained in the letters written by Lady Mary to friends in England and elsewhere in the East. These letters were originally given by Lady Mary at Rotterdam, in 1761, to a Mr. Sowden, minister of the English church there, with a note authorizing him to use them as he pleased. He is said to have sold them to her daughter for 500 pounds. Another copy, given by Lady Mary to Mr. Molesworth, came into the possession of Lord Bute. The letters circulated in manuscript before they appeared in print in 1764. They contain vivid accounts of life among the Turks, but, incidentally, they often deal with the Greeks, displaying elements of romantic hellenism. In the letter to the Abbé Conti from Constantinople, May 29, 1717, for instance, she speaks

ladies; for the Grecian belles are of quite another character and complexion; with them pleasure appears in more engaging forms, and their persons, manners, conversation, and amusements, are very far from being destitute of elegance and ease.[62]

Writing from Adrianople, she is more detailed:

. . . [There is not] one instrument of music among the Greek or Roman statues, that is not to be found in the hands of the people of this country. The young lads generally divert themselves with making garlands for their favourite lambs, which I have often seen painted and adorned with flowers, lying at their feet while they sung or played. . . . These are the ancient amusements here, . . . the softness and warmth of the climate forbidding all rough exercises, . . . and naturally inspiring a laziness and aversion to labour, which the great plenty indulges. These gardeners are the only happy race of country people in Turkey. . . . They are most of them Greeks, and have little houses in the midst of their gardens. . . .

I no longer look upon Theocritus as a romantic writer; he has only given a plain image of the way of life amongst the peasants of his country; who, before oppression had reduced them to want, were, I suppose, all employed as the better sort of them are now.[63]

She tells Mr. Pope that she has just read his translation of Homer with "infinite pleasure," for she finds many passages in it clarified by what she sees in her present location:

. . . Many of the customs, and much of the dress then in fashion [are] yet retained, and I don't wonder to find more remains here of an age so distant, than is to be found in any other country. . . . The snowy veil that Helen throws over her face, is still fashionable. . . . Their manner of dancing is certainly the same that Diana is sung to have danced on the banks of the Eurotas. The great lady still leads the dance, and is followed by a troop of young girls, who imitate her steps, and, if she sings, make up the chorus. The tunes are extremely gay and lively, yet with some-

---

of making some progress in a collection of Greek medals, and expresses admiration for "the true Greek sculpture" which they display. See *Letters of the Right Honourable Lady Mary Wortley Montague. Written during her Travels in Europe, Asia, and Africa. Which Contain, Among other Curious Relations, Accounts Of The Policy And Manners Of The Turks; Drawn From Sources That Have Been Inaccessible To Other Travellers. A New Edition. In Two Volumes.* Paris, 1793, Vol. II, p. 37. Wherever possible, my quotations are taken from this edition, a copy of which is in my own possession.

[62] "Letter to Mr. P——, Sept. 1, 1717," in *Letters, op. cit.* This letter is lacking in the edition cited above, and is, therefore, quoted from the edition by R. Brimley Johnson, New York, 1925, p. 147.

[63] "Letter to Mr. Pope," April 1, 1717, *Letters, op. cit.*, Vol. II, p. 14.

thing in them wonderfully soft. The steps are varied according to the time, and infinitely more agreeable than any of our dances, at least in my opinion. . . . These are Grecian dances, the Turkish being very different.[64]

Lord Baltimore[65] admires the feminine Greeks:

The Greek women have fine features, and beautiful complexions; they have very engaging countenances much like what we see of them in their statues. The Greeks certainly have excelled in sculpture all other nations. . . .[66]

But he is also sensitive to the romantic beauty of the scenery:

I think I never beheld so entertaining a sight; the sun casting its rays on the greatest variety of objects I ever saw; the different light and shade, the prismatic tints which this fountain of all colours at its first appearance in the horizon gave them, is impossible to be expressed. The prospects in this neighbourhood are exceeding beautiful; whichever way a landscape painter turns his eye, he is struck with a charming picture. Rocks, seas, mountains, volcanos, ruins of cities, baths, bridges, porticos, temples, and palaces, are elegantly, by accident, here alone found mingled with ships, boats, castles, stately cities, men, women, children, cattle, villages, vines, country seats, trees, and pasture.[67]

Brydone is moved by the beauty of Calabria's landscape:

From this spot we had a very good opportunity of observing a pretty

[64] *Ibid.*

[65] See the curious little 16mo volume of 176 pages, entitled, *A Tour to the East, in the Years 1763 and 1764. With Remarks on the City of Constantinople and the Turks. With Select Pieces of Oriental Wit, Poetry and Wisdom. By F. Lord Baltimore. London, Printed by W. Richardson and S. Clark, 1767.* Frederick Calvert, sixth Lord Baltimore (1731-1771) is the author. Baltimore was not in any sense a person of literary ability, his claim to literary fame resting more on his unsavory reputation as a rake than on this specimen of his writing. See the illuminating 74 page pamphlet, *The Trial of Frederick Calvert, Esq., Baron of Baltimore . . . for a Rape on the Body of Sarah Woodcock, and of Eliz. Griffinburg, and Ann Harvey, otherwise Darby, as Accessaries before the Fact . . . at the Assizes held at Kingston, for the County of Surry, on Saturday, the 26th of March, 1768, before the Hon. Sir Sydney Stafford Smythe,* London, Owen, 1768. Baltimore's book is neither vivid nor profound. It shows, however, a strikingly sentimental view of Greece in those portions of the book which deal (very superficially) with the cavern of old Eolus, Messina, Mount Aetna, Corfu, Cephalonia, Zante, Morea, Zea, Andros, Tinos, Scio, Myteline, and Tenedos. This sentimentality is produced by the constant association by the author of well-known events and figures of antiquity with the sights of modern Greece. Very frequently the emotional effects thus produced are enhanced by Baltimore's evident sensitiveness to romantic beauty.

[66] Lord Baltimore, *op. cit.*, p. 29.

[67] *Ibid.*, pp. 5-6.

large portion of Calabria, which formerly constituted a considerable part of that celebrated country, known by the name of Great Greece, and looked upon as one of the most fertile in the empire. These beautiful hills and mountains are covered over with trees and brush-wood to the very summit; and appear pretty much in the same state as some of the wilds of America that are just beginning to be cultivated. . . . This country (like many others) from the highest state of culture and civilization, became a wild and barren wilderness, overgrown with thickets and forests; and, indeed, since the revival of arts and agriculture, perhaps of all Europe this is the spot that has profited the least;—retaining still, both in the wildness of its fields and ferocity of its inhabitants, more of the Gothic barbarity than is to be met with any where else. Some of these forests are of a vast extent, and absolutely impenetrable; and no doubt conceal in their thickets many valuable monuments of its ancient magnificence. Of this indeed we have a very recent proof in the discovery of Pestum, a Grecian city, that had not been heard of for a vast number of ages; till of late, some of its magnificent temples were seen, peeping over the tops of the woods; upbraiding mankind for their shameful neglect; and calling upon them to bring it once more to light.[68]

Johann Hermann Riedesel[69] reads gentleness into the inhabitants of Mount Aetna:

Die Einwohner um den Aetna sind nicht, wie Fazellus sie beschreibet, rauh und wild von Gitten, *horridi aspectu.* Ich habe hier, wie aller Orten wo wenig Fremde hinkommen, die Menschen nicht durch die Menschen verdorben sind, wohl natürliche Menschen wohnen, gute, willfahrige und wahrhafte Leute gefunden; sie sind wohl gebildet, und die reine und heitere Luft des Berges macht sie munter, lustig und frölichen herzens; die Weiber sind schön, von weisser haut und lebhaften Augen; die Manner von der Sonne verbrannt, aber gros, gesund und leutseliger Art; sie sind

[68] Patrick Brydone, *op. cit.,* Vol. I, p. 42.

[69] The influence of German romantic hellenism in England may be observed in the very significant English translation, *Travels through Sicily and That Part of Italy formerly called Magna Graecia. And A Tour through Egypt. Translated by J. R. Forster,* London, 1773. The original of this work is *Reise durch Sicilien und Grossgreichenland,* Zurich, 1771. This is a little book of 272 pages by Johann Hermann Riedesel zu Eisenbach, the well-known friend of the great German hellenist, Johann Joachim Winckelmann. The book is in the form of two letters written to Winckelmann, containing Riedesel's reactions to the ruins of Greek art and culture. While the patent purpose of these letters is to inform Winckelmann of the location, measurements, and general appearance of various monuments in Sicily and Greece, they are, as would be expected, steeped in emotional expressions of romantic hellenism, and contributed much to the development in England of a sentimental attitude to the remains of ancient Greece. The English title which I have cited is taken from the Printed Catalogue of the British Museum. I have used the original work in German.

aufrichtig, dienstfertig, und man findet sich unter ganz guten Leuten in diesen Dörfern, welche wohl bevölkert sind.[70]

Chandler is full of admiration for both the people and the beauties of the landscape:

Their [the Greeks] ladies wear the oriental dress, consisting of large trowsers or breeches, which reach to the ancle; long vests of rich silk, or of velvet, lined in winter with costly furs; and round their waist an embroidered zone, with clasps of silver or gold. Their hair is platted, and descends down the back, often in great profusion. The girls have sometimes above twenty thick tresses, besides two or three encircling the head, as a coronet, and set off with flowers, and plumes of feathers, pearls, or jewels. They commonly stain it of a chestnut colour, which is the most desired. Their apparel and carriage are alike antique. It is remarkable that the trowsers are mentioned in a fragment of Sappho. The habit is light, loose, and cool, adapted to the climate. . . . Girls of inferior rank from the islands, especially Tino, abound; and are many of them as beautiful in person, as picturesque in their appearance. They excel in a glow of colour, which seems the effect of a warm sun, ripening the human body as it were into uncommon perfection.[71]

Early in the morning we steered with a favourable breeze toward Sunium, a promontory of Attica fronting the islands called Cyclades and the Aegean sea. . . . The sun arose burnishing the silver deep, skirted by the Attic and Peloponnesian coasts. We had capes, mountains, and islands in view; and among the latter, the Hydriotes soon discovered their native rock, which they beheld, though bare and producing nothing, with the same partiality of affection, as if it were adorned with the golden fruits, and perfumed by the aromatic gales of Scio; pointing it out, and expatiating on the liberty they possessed there.[72]

Some Greeks, to whom the captain had notified his arrival, came on board early in the morning. The wine circulated briskly, and their meeting was celebrated, as usual among this lively people, with singing, fiddling, and dancing.[73]

The evening was hazy, and the mountain-tops on the west and northwest enveloped in clouds; from which proceeded lightning, pale and forky, or resembling the expansion of a ball of fire. We were becalmed for a few minutes; but the breeze returned, and we moved pleasantly along;

[70] *Ibid.*, pp. 139-40.
[71] Richard Chandler, *Travels in Asia Minor, op. cit.*, pp. 81-82.
[72] Richard Chandler, *Travels in Greece, op. cit.*, pp. 5-6.
[73] *Ibid.*, p. 19.

the splendid moon disclosing the solemn hills, and the sea as bright as placid.[74]

To Irwin Greece is a blissful Arcadia:

We encountered a large flock of sheep in our walk, of the black kind; small, and much resembling the Welch mutton. Indeed, the fragrant shrubs, with which the hills are cloathed, render them excellent pasture for the mutton, which is fat and well-flavored, and very reasonable. The primitive lives of the shepherds of Greece, seem to continue here without deviation. The lad, who looks after the flock, sits on a stone or beneath a tree, and sings or whistles, while the sheep crop the heath or shrubs; the only verdure that the mountain affords. Should a lamb idly stray, his keeper searches every crevice of the rocks to reclaim it; and, like Maro's swain, chides the little run-away for the trouble it has given him. . . . Ragusa is the capital of the small republic of that name, and is built near the site of the antient Epidaurus. It is a populous, though small, city; strong by nature. . . . Her weakness and insignificancy induced the republic, to put herself early, under the protection of the Turks, her most powerful neighbors. . . . The republic boasts of antiquity beyond Venice itself; and, like her, is governed by a doge; though so jealous are the Ragusans of their liberty, that he, and the governor of the castle, are changed monthly.[75]

When he comes to Castel Nuova, he is stirred by its beauty:

Little did I dream when we left London, of visiting so celebrated a part of the continent of Greece. . . . Ceres and Bacchus, and every rural deity, who made a garden of the antient territory, have disclaimed the homage of the present race, and denied their smiles to the labors of the peasant. . . . But, in spite of poverty and discord, the charms of nature cannot be wholly obliterated. The rosebushes even at this season blush with unnumbered flowers; and, while the mountains above Castel Nuova are white with snow, the vallies beneath, produce the orange and citron, whose fruit is now of a golden tint.[76]

He comes to the country near the canal of Catarro:

This canal is at once, the most pleasing, romantic and savage, which the world can afford.[77]

We found ourselves on the point of a rock, rent, as it were, from the magnific mountain behind it. We had left the city and canal some hundreds of fathoms below; we seemed to breathe another air, and were ar-

[74] *Ibid.*, pp. 14-15.
[75] Eyles Irwin, *op. cit.*, Vol. II, pp. 198-199.
[76] *Ibid.*, pp. 200-202.
[77] *Ibid.*, p. 206.

rived at the middle regions, where the thunder is heard to roll, and the lightning plays. We thought ourselves cut off from the society of mankind, and yet we looked up, and lo! Montagna Negro, the residence of a multitude of human beings, shot up his aspiring head, and made us fancy ourselves in the bottom again! . . . The extravagance of nature could not afford a *coup-d'oeil,* more fantastic, terrible and sublime.[78]

The fifth element in the romantic hellenism of the literature of travel to the East is the expression of sympathy for the modern Greeks who have been subjected to near-slavery by the Turks. To most of the travellers such treatment of a nation possessed of so illustrious a history is unjust and lamentable in the extreme. Their feelings are particularly intense when they recall the remarkable love of liberty associated with Greece. After describing the political corruption which he has seen, for example, Drummond remarks:

. . . Every man in power is a despotic tyrant by the nature of his office, and all the subjects are miserable slaves; though the Greeks, as a conquered people, are more specially exposed to their cruelty and extortion: they are now become familiarised to oppression, which hath likewise disposed them for villainy, as it were in their own defense; insomuch that they are reconciled to all manner of crimes; and mean dejection, wretchedness, or deceit, is to be read in every countenance. In a word, notwithstanding their silk, cotton, oil, and rich wines, these people will ever be poor and despondent.

While proud ambition in their valleys reigns,
And tyranny usurps their happy plains.[79]

Pococke describes this sight:

Coming into the open country, we passed by the house of the Aga of the territory of Sfachia, who invited us to go in, but we pursued our journey; we saw here six or seven Greeks with a heavy chain about their necks, a punishment inflicted on them for not paying a tax of about the value of half a crown, demanded on their guns, though they affirmed that they had none. . . .[80]

The author of the *Travels of Charles Thompson* is embittered at the Turks because of this treatment of the Greeks:

[78] *Ibid.*, p. 213.
[79] Alexander Drummond, *op. cit.*, p. 150.
[80] Richard Pococke, *op. cit.*, Vol. II, part I, p. 241.

The Inhabitants of Milo are all Greeks, there being hardly a Turk in the Island, except the *Cadi,* or Judge and the *Waywode,* whose principal Business is to levy the Land-Tax, to punish Offenders, and to take care that the Sultan is not defrauded of his Tribute: At the same Time he does not forget to fill his own Pockets, the poor Greeks suffering much by his Extortions.[81]

Chishull's feelings at Milo are similar:

This isle, known to the antients by the name of Melos, and esteemed the largest of all the Cyclades, is deservedly famous for its fair and commodious harbour. . . . I went ashore at this place with the greater satisfaction, considering that among other antiquities it lays claim to Socrates and Aristophanes. It has a city of the same name, inhabited at present, like the other island of the Archipelago, by Greek Christians, who have been burthened in the late war, by a cruel tax of fifteen thousand dollars to the Venetians, as well as to the Turks. . . .[82]

He cannot forgive the Turks for their neglect of Greek ruins:

I made a visit to the Seven Towers, now a prison for persons of quality, since by the fate of war it has fallen into the hands of the Turks, but antiently the Porta Janicula of Constantinople. The beautiful remains of this gate are still admirable, tho by the Turks suffered to be almost concealed by a dead wall, and the shade of the neighboring trees.[83]

Van Egmont and Heyman report:

The Greeks here [Salamis], as in Rhodes, are not permitted to live in the town, and the shops which they have in it must be all locked-up at sunset, and every one retire to their dwellings.[84]

They narrate this vivid instance of the mistreatment of the Greeks:

Though the nobility of the Greeks is at present of no manner of consequence, so that it may truly be said of them, that their wisdom is changed into ignorance, and their freedom into slavery, yet whenever they imagine themselves of noble descent, they still retain that vain pride, of not suffering their children to marry into an inferior family. . . .

But notwithstanding all this pride, the following instance will shew in what light they are considered by the Turks. One evening while I was in

[81] *Travels of Charles Thompson, op. cit.,* p. 297.
[82] Edmund Chishull, *op. cit.,* p. 176.
[83] *Ibid.,* p. 48.
[84] Van Egmont and Heyman, *op. cit.,* Vol. I, pp. 291-292.

Scio, the Muselhim, or governor of the city, coming into the house of a certain Latin, who gave an entertainment, obliged several Greek women, and even some of the best fashion in the country, to dance with their husbands before him. But however indecent this order was, there was no remonstrating against it. And, not being satisfied with this mark of his power, he ordered, at his going away, some handful of paras to be thrown among the company, and presented the handsomest of them with sequins.[85]

Lady Mary Wortley Montague is indignant at the thought of considering a Greek a slave:

You desire me to buy you a Greek slave. . . . The Greeks are subjects, not slaves. Those who are to be bought in that manner, are either such as are taken in war, or stolen by the Tartars from Russia, Circassia, or Georgia, and are such miserable, awkward, poor wretches, you would not think any of them worthy to be your housemaids. 'Tis true that many thousands were taken in the Morea, but they have been, most of them, redeemed by the charitable contributions of the Christians, or ransomed by their own relatives at Venice. The fine slaves that wait upon the great ladies, or serve the pleasures of the great men, are all bought at the age of eight or nine years old, and educated with great care, to accomplish them in singing, dancing, embroidery, etc. . . . Those that are exposed to sale at the markets are always either guilty of some crime, or so entirely worthless that they are of no use at all. I am afraid you will doubt the truth of this account, which I own is very different from our common notions in England; but it is no less truth for all that.[86]

Brydone at Agrigentum is deeply moved by the subjection of the Greeks:

The sight of these poor people has filled me with indignation. This village is surrounded by the finest country in the world, yet there was neither bread nor wine to be found in it, and the poor inhabitants appear more than half-starved.

"'Mongst Ceres' richest gifts with want oppres'd,
"And 'midst the flowing vineyard, die of thirst."

Sacred liberty! thy blessings alone are the blessings of the soul, and however small our portion, with thee it is ever sweet; but without thee, the richest gifts of nature are but so many curses.—Accursed be those that made them so.[87]

[85] *Ibid.*, p. 241.
[86] "Letter to Lady ——— from Belgrade Village, June 17, 1717," in *Letters, op. cit.*, Vol. II, pp. 42-43.
[87] Patrick Brydone, *op. cit.*, Vol. II, pp. 21-22.

Chandler echoes this pity for a subjected people:

> The old Athenian had a multitude of deities, but relied chiefly on Minerva; the modern has a similar troop, headed by his favourite Panagia. He listens with devout humility to fanciful tales of nightly visions, and of miracles vouchsafed on the most trivial occasions. . . . By such arts as these are the wretched Greeks preserved from despondency, roused to expectation, and consoled beneath the yoke of bondage. The traveller, who is versed in antiquity may be agreeably and universally employed in studying the people of Athens.[88]

> The Turks of Athens are in general more polite, social, and affable, than is common in that stately race; living on more equal terms with their fellow citizens, and partaking, in some degree, of the Greek character. . . .
>
> The Greeks may be regarded as the representatives of the old Athenians. . . . The Archons are now mere names, except a tall fur-cap, and a fuller and better dress than is worn by the inferior classes. . . . By following the lower occupations, they [the meaner citizens] procure, not without difficulty, a pittance of profit to subsist them, to pay their tribute-money, and to purchase garments for the festivals, when they mutually vie in appearing well-clothed, their pride even exceeding their poverty. . . . They are conscious of their subjection to the Turk, and as supple as depressed, from the memory of the blows on the feet, and indignities, which they have experienced or seen inflicted, and from the terror of the penalty annexed to resistance, which is the forfeiture of the hand uplifted; but their disposition, as antiently, is unquiet; their repose disturbed by factious intrigues and private animosities; the body politic weakened by division, and often impelled in a direction opposite to its true interest.[89]

Perhaps the most interesting element in the romantic hellenism of the literature of travel to the East is the sixth, the expression of moods and sensations aroused or inspired by various parts of Greece. These moods, frequently poetic in nature, arise from a combination of the other five elements which we have examined. One frequently feels while reading them an underlying nostalgia for the glories of ancient Greece produced by the associations which the travellers weave around the lands they visit. In these passages the unconscious identification of ancient with modern Greece approaches most closely to the moods of Byron, Shelley, and Keats.

[88] Richard Chandler, *Travels in Greece, op. cit.*, pp. 144-145.
[89] *Ibid.*, pp. 124-127.

A typical passage of this nature is to be found in one of Lady Montague's letters:

We saw very plainly from this promontory the river Simois rolling from Mount Ida, and running through a very spacious valley. . . . This was Xanthus among the gods, as Homer tells us; and 'tis by that heavenly name the nymph Oenone invokes it in her epistle to Paris. . . .

All that is now left of Troy is the ground in which it stood. . . . However, there is some pleasure in seeing the valley where I imagined the famous duel of Menelaus and Paris had been fought, and where the greatest city in the world was situate; and 'tis certainly the noblest situation that can be found for the head of a great empire. . . . We passed that evening the Isle of Tenedos, once under the patronage of Apollo, as he gave it in himself in the particulars of his estate when he courted Daphne. It is but ten miles in circuit, but in those days very rich and well-peopled, still famous for its excellent wine. I say nothing of Tennes, from whom it was called; but naming Mytilene, where we passed next, I cannot forbear mentioning that Lesbos, where Sappho sung, and Pittacus reigned, famous for the birth of Alcaeus, Theophrastus, and Arion, those masters in poetry, philosophy, and music. This was one of the last islands that remained in the Christian dominion after the conquest of Constantinople by the Turks. . . . 'Twas with regret I saw us sail swift from this island into the Aegean sea, now the Archipelago, leaving Scio (the ancient Chios) on the left, which is the richest and most populous of these islands, fruitful in cotton, corn, and silk, planted with groves of orange and lemon trees; and the Arvisian mountain, still celebrated for the nectar that Virgil mentions. Here is the best manufacture of silk in all Turkey. The town is well built, the women famous for their beauty, and shew their faces as in Christendom. There are many rich families, though they confine their magnificence to the inside of their houses, to avoid the jealousy of the Turks, who have a pasha here: however, they enjoy a reasonable liberty, and indulge the genius of their country;

And eat, and sing, and dance away their time,
Fresh as their groves, and happy as their clime.

Their chains hang lightly on them, though 'tis not long since they were imposed, not being under the Turk till 1566. . . . Passing the strait between the islands of Andros and Achaia, now Libadia, we saw the promontory of Sunium, now called Cape Colonna, where are yet standing the vast pillars of a temple of Minerva. This venerable sight made me think, with double regret, on a beautiful temple of Theseus, which, I am assured, was almost entire at Athens till the last campaign in the Morea, that the Turks filled it with powder, and it was accidentally blown up. You may believe I had a great mind to land on the famed Peloponnesus, though it were only to look on the rivers of Aesopus, Peneus, Inachus, and Eurotas, the fields of Arcadia, and other scenes of ancient mythology. But instead of demi-gods and heroes, I am credibly informed 'tis now overrun by robbers. . . . 'Tis impossible to imagine anything more agreeable than this journey would have been between two or three thousand years since, when, after drinking a dish of tea with Sappho, I might have gone the same evening to visit the temple of Homer in Chios, and have passed this voyage in taking plans of magnificent temples, delineating the miracles of statuaries, and conversing with the most polite and most gay of human kind. Alas! Art is extinct here; the wonders of nature alone remain; and it was with vast pleasure I observed those of Mount Etna, whose flame appears very bright in the night many leagues off at sea, and fills the head with a thousand conjectures.[90]

Observe how, in this passage, Lady Mary finds great pleasure in musing on the beauty of ancient Greece as she passes its modern sites. She is obviously reading into what she sees that which is really within herself; these lands are to her a symbol of something which in reality is not there. In this sense she here anticipates the hellenism of the romantic poets of the nineteenth century.

Lord Baltimore betrays a similar tendency when he says:

The next day we came into the harbour of Corfu, which is a beautiful island. . . . I enquired after, but could hear no tidings of, those delightful gardens of king Alcinous, which were said formerly to have been here, and wherein he entertained Ulysses after his shipwreck.[91]

Brydone finds the same kind of pleasure in a garden in Ortygia, Syracuse:

There is a variety of wild and romantic scenes in this curious garden; in the midst of which we were surprised by the appearance of a figure under one of the caverns, that added greatly to the dignity and solemnity of the place.—It was that of an aged man, with a long flowing white beard that reached down to his middle. His old wrinkled face and scanty grey locks pronounced him a member of some former age as well as of this. His hands, which were shook by the palsy, held a sort of pilgrim's staff; and about his neck there was a string of large beads with a crucifix hanging to its end.—Had it not been for these marks of his later existence, I don't know but I should have asked him, whether, in his

[90] "Letter to the Abbé Conti, Tunis, July 31, 1718," in *Letters, op. cit.*, Vol. II, pp. 101-107.

[91] Lord Baltimore, *op. cit.*, p. 20.

youth, he had not been acquainted with Theocritus and Archimedes, and if he did not remember the reign of Dionysius the Tyrant.[92]

This tendency to identify the ancient with the modern Greeks is clearly seen in Hasselquist's account of life at Smyrna:

The 15th, Easter-day, the festival of the Armenians and Greeks began. The manner in which it was celebrated by the latter was worth notice, as it testified how much this nation retains of its former inclinations for dissolute diversions at festivals. He that knows what is related about Bachanals, etc. of their ancestors, may here see the remains of them in their offspring. They purchase from their masters the Turks, the liberty of pursuing their pleasures uncontrouled; for which they pay to their Muselem in Smyrna one purse (500 pieces of eight); but in Constantinople they give five or six purses. In consideration of this, they are at liberty, in their houses and in the streets, to get drunk, fight, dance, play, and do every thing their hearts desire. An Easter seldom passes in Constantinople, without some persons being murdered.[93]

This noble art is now no more to be found, in a country where it once had arrived to the highest perfection. In vain may we now look for an Orpheus among the Greeks; but a dance, a remain of the Grecian age, performed by the Greek women, afforded me infinite pleasure. They were about fifteen in number, the foremost of which conducted the dance, by making signs with a garment she held in her hand. The art consisted in keeping an equal half-circle, to be observed under all their different turnings. They likewise several times made a labyrinth, but immediately reassumed their former station. There was something particular in their dance, which at first sight, convinced me it was ancient. My conjectures were confirmed by Mr. Peysonell, the French Consul, who hath much knowledge in what relates to Grecian antiquities. He told me, that some monuments of marble had been found, on which this dance was sculptured. It is so agreeable when danced by Greeks, dressed in the ancient manner and conformable to the dance, that no modern invention of this kind seems to equal it.[94]

We had now time to pay adorations in a silent contemplation of the sublime objects of nature. The sky was perfectly clear, and the immense vault of the heavens appeared in awful majesty and splendour. . . . The number of the stars seemed to be infinitely increased, and . . . the light of each of them appeared brighter than usual. The whiteness of the milky way was like a pure flame that shot across the heavens; and with

[92] Patrick Brydone, *op. cit.,* Vol. I, pp. 268-269.
[93] Frederick Hasselquist, *op. cit.,* p. 49.
[94] *Ibid.,* pp. 22-23.

the naked eye we could observe clusters of stars that were totally invisible in the regions below. . . . Had Empedocles had the eyes of Gallileo what discoveries must he not have made! . . . No imagination has dared to form an idea of so glorious and so magnificent a scene. Neither is there on the surface of this globe, any one point that unites so many awful and sublime objects.—The immense elevation, from the surface of the earth, drawn as it were to a single point, without any neighboring mountain for the senses and imagination to rest upon; and recover from their astonishment in their way down to the world. This point or pinnacle, raised on the brink of a bottomless gulph, as old as the world, often discharging rivers of fire, and throwing out burning rocks, with a noise that shakes the whole island. Add to this, the unbounded extent of the prospect, comprehending the greatest diversity and the most beautiful scenery in nature; with the rising sun, advancing in the east, to illuminate the wondrous scene.[95]

A different mood, but a similar spirit appears in Irwin's account:

It would be unpardonable in me to quit Cyprus, without saying a word on the subject, for which that island was celebrated of old. The supposed residence of Venus, and the land on which numerous temples were raised to her honor, could not but have produced objects, the most worthy of human idolatry. Beauty and Love went hand in hand in this rendezvous of pleasure; and the votaries of the goddess paid her closer adoration, in the persons of her unrivalled daughters. Though beauty be but an annual flower, its species, like those of Nature's humbler growth, is successive and imperishable. The cities of Greece exhibit nothing at present, but heaps of ruins. Her glory is eclipsed; her very language has failed! But the beauty of her women still affords a gleam of splendor, like the softened light of the setting sun. An Italian gentleman carried our company to visit a Greek damsel, whose beauty was much spoken of. I must confess, that I should have regretted to have missed a sight, so worthy of observation. We look at fine pictures and statues, with an enthusiasm, that is encreased, in proportion to their merit. Here the finest model of art—the boast of Phidias' or Titian's hand—was outdone. The figure breathed: the nicest proportions received new grace from motion; and the most regular and finished set of features imaginable, were animated with spirit and sensibility. The first view of this fair Greek recalled to memory, those spirited lines of Waller:

> "Such Helen was—and who can blame the boy,
> Who in so bright a flame consum'd his Troy!"

[95] Patrick Brydone, *op. cit.*, Vol. I, pp. 184-188.

. . . I would advise my friend Romney, when he wants a new model for a Venus, to visit Cyprus, in order to improve on the Venus of Medicis.[96]

But perhaps the most perfect expression of the tendency in romantic hellenism to read into modern Greece what is really within the author is found in Riedesel's remarks on Greece in general:

Die alte Wollust und Unmässigkeit in Essen und Trinken ist gänzlich verschwunden: Sie leben so massig als möglich; und die Trunkenheit ist das grösseste Laster, welches sie mehr als alle andere verabscheuen. . . . In der Viehzucht findet man deu Theocrit und viele Beschreibungen desselben; die hausigen Ziegen, welche in denen hugeln Kräuter zu ihrer Nährung suchen, die grossen Schaafe und Widder, an dem Bauche eines derselben Ulysses sich aus der hole Polyphems gefluchtet; das häusige rothe wiewol kleine hornvieh, zeichnen die Gemahlde seiner Eclogen vor Augen in der Natur und Wahrheit; die hirten singen noch mit einander um die Wette und stellen einen Stab order Tasche zum Preiss aus; das gelinde und gluckliche Clima erlaubt denselben, das ganze Jahr auf dem Felde zu wohnen; sonst wohnen sie in Strohhutten, welche sie sich selbsten erbauen, und die Thiere bleiben Tag und Nacht unter freyem Himmel. . . .

Kurz zu zagen: Das Clima, der Boden des Landes, und die Fruchte desselben sind noch so vollkommen als sie iemals gewesen; die Griechische goldene Freyheit aber, die Bevölkerung, die Macht, die Pracht und der gute Geschmack sind nicht mehr in derselben, so wir vor Zeiten, zu finden; die ietzigen Einwohner mussen sagen: Fuimus Troes.[97]

Stellen Sie sich, mein werther Freund, einen allmähligen abhängigen Hügel, unter meinem Fenster, vier Miglie lang, welcher ins Meer endigt, und sich von beyden Seiten sechs bis sieben Miglie in die breite erstrekt, vor, der mit Weinstocken, Oelbaumen, Mandelbaumen, dem herrlichsten, Getraide, welches den 7ten Aprill in volliger Blute, mit dem schmakbastesten Gartengewachsen und allen moglichen Fruchten der Erde bepflanzet und wechselsweise bebauet war; die Besiszungen der Eigentumer sind mit Zaunen von Alpe und Indianishen Feigenpflanzen unterschieden; hundert und mehr Nachtigallen erfullen die Luft mit ihren Gesangen; und in diesen entzuckenden Feldern endeckte ich den wohlerhaltenen so genannten Tempel der Juno Lacinia, den unversehrten der Concordia, die Ueberbleibsel des dem Hercules gewiedmeten, und die Trummer des riesenformigen Tempels des Jupiters. Hier rief ich aus:

[96] Eyles Irwin, *op. cit.*, pp. 250-252.
[97] Johann Hermann Riedesel zu Eisenbach, *op. cit.*, pp. 174-178.

——— Hic vivere vellem,
Oblitusque meorum, obliviscendus et illis.
Neptunum procul e terra spectare furentem.[98]

From this analysis of the literature of travel to the East, then, we can make three generalizations. In the first place, because travel books are usually more widely read than scientific books of archaeology or erudite volumes of Greek antiquities, these books helped spread a knowledge of Greece, both ancient and modern, particularly among those readers who were not university trained. In the second place, because of their colorful and emotional nature, these books of travel intensified attitudes of sympathy with, and idealization of, Greece. Finally, these books contributed six specific elements to romantic hellenism: the sentimental admiration of the remains of ancient Greek art; the sentimental admiration of ancient Greek culture in general, particularly its government and its bravery; mournful laments over the decay of ancient Greek civilization; the sentimental admiration of the scenery of modern Greece and the primitive attractiveness of the modern Greeks; expressions of sympathy for the subjection of the modern Greeks to the Turks; and pleasurable moods inspired by the identification of ancient with modern Greece.

[98] *Ibid.*, pp. 31-32.

## IV

## WINCKELMANN AND THE BEGINNINGS OF ROMANTIC HELLENISM IN AESTHETICS

We have observed in the preceding chapters how the archaeological discoveries in Greece between 1732 and 1786 were sentimentalized by travellers to the East who brought back to England emotional accounts of Greece, its ruins, and its inhabitants. The third force in the rise of romantic hellenism was the development of a hellenized aesthetics; i.e., theories of art based in large measure upon subjective interpretations and analyses of the art of the ancient Greeks. Such theories invariably display the tendency of the romantic hellenist to read into Greek art that which is not necessarily there, but which resides either in himself or in the age. To such an aesthetician Greek art is merely a symbol of an idea which he explains and elaborates. Frequently, for example, he will use Greek art to bolster the validity of an idea already current, such as primitivism, genius, or liberty and equality. At other times he will wax ecstatic over the delight afforded by Greek art and its ennobling, inspirational effects on the beholder. At such times the aesthetic theory is escapist in nature. That these elaborations of the meaning of Greek art are almost wholly subjective, however, appears in the fact that other aestheticians will find the reverse of these ideas in similar interpretations of Greek art. To one it is a heaven; to another, a hell. To one it is eloquent testimony to the divine effects of liberty and equality; to another, a symbol of licentiousness, anarchy, and immorality.

It is obvious that the aesthetic literature which we are to examine in this chapter arises from deeper causes than the growth of Greek archaeology. Aesthetics was one of the main currents in eighteenth century thought:

> The eighteenth century, especially in its latter decades, teemed with discussion of artistic theories: even in England, it was an age of theories; and the cultivation of the fine arts and an effort to find an easy road to

culture, seem especially to have engaged the attention of the rising bourgeoisie.[1]

The stream of aesthetics in these discussions with which we are concerned takes the form of a philosophical reaction to the picturesque baroque and rococo,[2] fashionable in the middle of the eighteenth century:

> Rococo was a belated baroque, by means of which freedom of imagination made its rights valid even in the face of classicism.
>
> But towards the middle of the eighteenth century there came a reaction against the pictorial and the rococo. It was moral and intellectual. Moral, because the rococo was too much associated with the aristocratic classes and the artificial life that the French Revolution was soon to destroy. Therefore artists like Greuze interested themselves in sentimental expression, with a didactical pretense. It was an intellectual reaction, because the new excavations at Pompeii and Herculaneum, and the more intense interest in Greco-Roman art, brought an understanding of the seriousness and greatness of antique masterpieces. Then arose the type of philosophical painter, and it arose in Germany where there was preparing a very lofty philosophical civilisation, without, however, a close and beneficial relation between artistic ideas and the best aesthetic of the time: this type was incarnated in Mengs. Precisely because it was regarded as a "philosophical" reaction rather than artistic, and was conducted on principles, prevailing over modes of feeling, it created a detachment from tradition so great that it is difficult to find the like again in the remaining history of art.[3]

It is from Germany, the source of this sentimental-philosophical reaction, that the strongest influence in the rise of romantic hellenism in aesthetics comes to England. It is true, of course, that, as early as 1740 and for much of the remainder of the century, one can trace an aesthetic admiration of Greek art in England, but this admiration is rarely philosophical and utterly conven-

[1] John W. Draper, *Eighteenth Century Aesthetics, A Bibliography, Anglistische Forschungen*, Heft 71, Heidelburg, 1931, p. 5, note. *Cf.* William D. Templeman, *Contributions to the Bibliography of Eighteenth Century Aesthetics, Modern Philology*, Vol. XXX, pp. 309-316 (1932-1933).

[2] Detailed discussions of the history of baroque and rococo art, together with many beautiful illustrations, will be found in Sacheverell Sitwell, *German Baroque Art,* New York, 1928. *Cf.* Hermann Popp, *Die Architektur der Barock- und Rokokozeit in Deutschland und der Schweiz,* Stuttgart, 1913.

[3] Lionello Venturi, *History of Art Criticism, Translated from the Italian by Charles Marriott,* New York, 1936, p. 137.

tional. It is more akin to the neo-classical than to the romantic hellenic. Representative of this attitude is *A Treatise on Ancient Painting, Containing Observations on the Rise, Progress, and Decline of that Art amongst the Greeks and Romans. By George Turnbull, LL.D. London, 1740.* This large folio volume contains eight long chapters of discussion and analysis, together with fifty plates "of ancient painting discovered at different times in the Ruins of old Rome, accurately engraved from drawings of Camillo Paderni a Roman, lately done from the Originals with great Exactness and Elegance." Turnbull, in Chapter IV, finds the characteristics of ancient painting to be "Truth, Beauty, Unity, Greatness, and Grace in Composition," and comes to the conclusion that "Painting then had arrived to such a pitch of Perfection and Excellence amongst the Greeks in Apelles, that none hath ever been able to come near him but Raphael, who had the same Temper, Genius, and Turn of Mind."[4] In the *Analysis of Beauty. Written with a view to fixing the fluctuating Ideas of Taste. By William Hogarth. London, 1753,* there is expressed much the same kind of conventional view of Greek art as eminently worthy of imitation. Hogarth finds the characteristics of Greek art to be "Fitness, Symmetry, Simplicity, and Grace." Similar discussions appear in the translation by J. H. Muentz, *Encaustic: or Count Caylus' method of painting in the manner of the ancients,* London, 1760,[5] and in the anonymous *A Letter to his*

[4] P. 20. Scattered references to ancient Greek art of a similar nature appear in Joseph Spence, *Polymetis, or an Enquiry concerning the Agreement between the works of the Roman Poets and the Remains of the ancient Artists. Being an attempt to illustrate them mutually from each other,* London, 1747.

[5] Anne-Claude-Philippe de Tubières, de Grimoard, de Pestels, de Lévy, Compte de Caylus, etc. (1692-1765) spent the greater part of his life in engraving prints and discussing questions of painting and sculpture based on his research among Egyptian, Etruscan, Greek, and Roman antiquities. Influenced by the French painter Watteau, he made a voyage to Italy in 1714, learning art. In 1716 he visited Constantinople, Smyrna, and Ephesus, and developed a passion for archaeology. In 1729 he became Honorary Amateur in the Académie Royale de Peinture et de Sculpture. Later he became a member of the Académie des Inscriptions. During his life he patronized artists and published many works dealing with ancient art. The most significant of these are *Receuil d'Antiquités égyptiennes, étrusques, grecques et romaines,* Paris, 1752-1767, 7 Vols., and *Mémoir sur la peinture à l'encaustique et sur la peinture et de sculpture,* Paris, 1755. See the memoir of Caylus by André Fontaine, *Comte de Caylus' Vies d'Artistes du XVIIIme siècle. Discours sur la Peinture et la Sculpture,* Paris, 1910, pp. xi-xliv.

*Excellency Count* [*Caylus?*] *on poetry, painting, and Sculpture,* London, 1768.

The aesthetic treatment of Greek art which constitutes a force in the rise of romantic hellenism is to be found not in these discussions, but in the influence of Johann Joachim Winckelmann, whose *Geschichte der Kunst des Alterthums,* 1764, constitutes one of the masterworks of romantic hellenism in Europe during the eighteenth century. Born in 1717 of a cobbler in dire poverty, Winckelmann, even as a boy, displayed a keen interest in books which gave some account of the monuments of antiquity.[6] At the age of seventeen he was studying under Christian Tobias Damm, a lover of Greek scholarship. At nineteen he begged his way to Hamburg in order to acquire some of the famous classical texts in the collection of Johann Albert Fabricius. For three years he studied antiquity enthusiastically at Stendal, Berlin, Salzwedel, Halle, and Jena. In 1742 he became tutor in the home of the Lamprechts in Hadmersleben, where he made a lasting and influential friendship. In 1743 he began a term of five years as a village schoolmaster at Seehausen:

> Wrapped in an old fur coat in the winter months and huddled in an arm chair by the fire, Winckelmann read his beloved Greek until the clock struck twelve. He then slept in his chair from midnight until four in the morning, when he had another two hours at Greek, resuming school work at six. In the summer he slept on a bench; and for fear he should not wake in time, he tied a block of wood to his feet which fell down at the slightest movement. The thudding noise awakened him. Someone was knocking at the door. Banished for over a century from Europe, Greek literature was seeking admittance again. It was next to impossible to procure the texts; and yet in a dreary little provincial town in the Altmark a wretchedly shabby and mortally unhappy young schoolmaster was reading Homer, Aeschylus, Sophocles, Xenophon, Plato, and Herodotus in the original and seeing midnight visions of Greece.[7]

During the next seven years Winckelmann, as librarian to Count Bunan at Castle Nothnitz near Dresden, became intimately familiar with both baroque and ancient art and came to associate his

[6] For a detailed discussion of Winckelmann and his influence in Germany, see E. M. Butler, *The Tyranny of Greece over Germany,* New York, 1935.

[7] *Ibid.,* p. 14.

ruling passion with Rome, which was then considered the unique repository of ancient art. In 1754, having become a convert to Catholicism, he was received into the Church. The next year, having produced his anti-baroque pamphlet, *Gedanken über die Nachahmung der griechischen Wercke in der Mahlerey und Bilderhauer-Kunst,* he left Dresden for Rome.

At Rome Winckelmann lived first with the painter, Raphael Mengs, and began his lifelong friendship with Philip and Muzel Stosch, his patrons. Later he lived with the famed Cardinal Albani. Through these friends and others he was able to win the favor of the great and the noble, in whose palaces and castles were to be found the treasures of antiquity. He visited Florence and Naples, attempting almost stealthily to examine the ruins of Pompeii and Herculaneum. By the end of 1763, after years of intense archaeological study, he was made President of Antiquities in Rome.

It was, however, really to Greece, rather than Rome, that Winckelmann longed to go. He had had many offers from distinquished travellers to accompany them to Greece. In the winter of 1758-9 the Scottish painter, Morison; in 1760 Lady Oxford; in 1762 the Englishman Adam; in 1763 Edward Wortley Montague; in 1764 a German traveller and a rich Englishman—all had made offers to Winckelmann to accompany them to Greece. But in each instance something interfered with his acceptance. Finally, however, in 1767, an offer to travel to Greece came from his intimate friend, Riedesel, which tempted Winckelmann strongly. In order to decide definitely whether or not to accept, he decided, in 1768, upon a brief visit to Germany. In the midst of this journey he changed his mind and while waiting at Trieste for a boat to return him to Venice, he was murdered by a thief who sought his gold medals.

Winckelmann's masterpiece, the *Geschichte der Kunst des Alterthums,* 1764, is romantic in three senses: its sentimentalism, its scientific method, and its aesthetic reaction against baroque art. Winckelmann's theory of aesthetics, contained in embryo in his *Gedancken über die Nachahmung der griechischen Wercke in der Mahlerey und Bildhauer-Kunst,* 1755, was remarkably influential on his literary successors. Its tenets are diametrically opposite to the principles of baroque technique:

Baroque sculptors aim at picturesqueness and complexity in grouping, at the expression of movement in stone and marble, and of passion as the soul of movement. The artists of the seventeenth and eighteenth centuries, and in particular Bernini, attained this end by means of a technical mastery of their medium which has rarely been equalled and perhaps never excelled. Against this miraculous achievement Winckelmann violently rebelled. He knew by instinct that it was not Greek; and turned away from the racing, dancing, rippling statues in the 'Grosser Garten' at Dresden to peer through the lattice-work in the pavilions at the motionless figures glimmering in the semi-darkness.[8]

As was pointed out long ago by Pater,[9] Winckelmann had seen nothing of Greek sculpture of the best period, because this had not yet been discovered, and his knowledge was based on inferior plaster cast copies, though he was aware of this. Yet despite these obstacles he succeeded in characterizing the essential features of Greek art closely and accurately. Like the romantic hellenists of later generations, Winckelmann read into the "ruins" which he beheld something that was really within himself.[10] This is obvious from his frequently quoted description of the Laocoon:

The universal, dominant characteristic of Greek masterpieces, finally, is *noble simplicity and serene greatness* in the pose as well as in the expression. The depths of the sea are always calm, however wild and stormy the surface; and in the same way the expression in Greek figures reveals greatness and composure of soul in the throes of whatever passions. This spirit is depicted in Laocoon's face, and not in the face alone, in spite of the most violent sufferings. The pain which is manifest in all the muscles and sinews of the body, and which one almost seems to feel oneself, without aid from the face or other parts, when one contemplates the painful contraction of the abdomen;—this pain, I say, nevertheless does not express itself with any violent motion either in the face, or in the position as a whole. This Laocoon, unlike the hero in Vergil's poem, is raising no dreadful cry. The opening of the mouth

[8] *Ibid.*, p. 45.

[9] Walter Pater, *Greek Studies*, London, 1901.

[10] *Cf.* Lionello Venturi, *op. cit.*, p. 143: "Winckelmann . . . looks at art with the intention of finding in them the reason for his judgments. Or rather, he identifies his judgment with that which he believes to be peculiar to the Greek artists belonging to the 'beautiful style.' "

does not admit of this. It is rather an oppressed and anxious sigh. The pain of the body and the greatness of the soul are equally balanced throughout the composition of the figure, and seem to cancel each other out. Laocoon suffers; but he suffers like Sophocles' Philoctetes; his misery pierces us to the soul; but we should like to be able to bear anguish in the manner of this great man.[11]

Thus, "dazzled by the flash of a great revelation," Winckelmann looks through the Laocoon into his own imagination and produces his thesis of simplicity, serenity, and greatness as the basis of great art. Greatness of soul is best displayed in the condition of rest. Depiction of passion in movement cannot attain the artistic height of serenity and repose. This, he maintains, is true of all art, literary as well as plastic. Art is an organic growth, inseparable from racial, climatic, social, and political conditions. It reaches its zenith in the lost art of antiquity:

The imitation of sensuous beauty in nature and of spiritual beauty in man; the combination of the beautiful and the sublime, of the human and the god-like by means of nobility, simplicity, serenity and greatness; all this could only be attained by studying and imitating the Greeks. This was Winckelmann's aesthetic message to his contemporaries.[12]

After Winckelmann the stream of German romantic hellenism widens rapidly. In 1766, Lessing published his *Laokoon oder über die Grenzen der Malerie und Poesie,* a brilliant critical investigation of aesthetic laws, inspired by Winckelmann's work; in 1776 he began to edit and annotate the *Geschichte der Kunst des Alterthums.* In 1769 appeared Herder's *Sylvae Criticae,* an answer to *Laokoon,* in which there appear many elements of primitivism. Lessing applies principles of sculpture to drama; Herder applies them to poetry. His lyrical dramas, *Philocetes, Admetus and Alcestis,* and *Prometheus Unbound,* show the poetic use of Greek myths to preach humanitarian ideals. The "myth of Laocoon," seen first in Winckelmann in 1755 and 1764, appears throughout the movement, in Lessing in 1766, Herder in 1769, Schiller in 1793, Goethe in 1797, Hölderin in 1790, and in Heine in 1821. The vogue of Greek art and culture in Germany, initiated by

[11] Translated in E. M. Butler, *op. cit.,* p. 46.
[12] *Ibid.,* p. 48.

Winckelmann, was thus destined to develop into one of the central streams of the romantic movement.

The influence of Winckelmann in England, directly and indirectly, does not reach its full force until after 1786.[13] Within the limits of this study, however, it is possible to trace the beginnings of this influence in the series of English translations from Winckelmann's work made in 1765 by his disciple in England, Henry Fuseli or Füssli.[14] Fuseli was born on February 7, 1741, at Zurich, Switzerland, the son of John Caspar Fuessli, a painter. Although he was early intended for the Church, the boy had a strong desire to draw. He attended the Colegium Carolinum at Zurich, where he made lasting friendships with Lavater, Usteri, Tomman, and Jacob and Felix Hess. Here, too, he acquired an extensive knowledge of English, German, French and Italian literature. He was fascinated by Shakespeare, Richardson, and Dante. He early made a translation of Macbeth into German, and attempted verse in the manner of Klopstock and Weiland. In 1761, with Lavater, he took orders. A rich and influential land bailiff named Grebel was, at this time, accused of appropriating to himself property belonging to others. Fuseli, Lavater, and the Hess brothers, influenced by their reading of Rousseau, Voltaire, and other reform literature, interested themselves in this matter, which was to them a glaring instance of social injustice in Zurich, and wrote Grebel an anonymous letter, demanding the restoration of the property to its lawful owners. When this protest proved futile, Fuseli and

[13] Besides the lectures of Fuseli, discussed below, Winckelmann's theories appear clearly in the 10 lectures of John Flaxman, delivered between 1810 and 1826. See John Flaxman, *Lectures on Sculpture as delivered by him before the President and members of the Royal Academy*, London, 1829. Flaxman says, for example: "In the ancient groups we see the sentiment, heroism, beauty, and sublimity of Greece existing before us" (p. 94). "The arts of Greece astonished and delighted the world in their own times, and they have continued to do so through the lapse of many ages; and now in their fragments and mutilations demand the same just homage from the beholder, and afford the same example of excitement, admiration, and instruction to the artist" (p. 291). Further influence of Winckelmann in England comes, of course, with the vogue of Schiller, Herder, and Goethe.

[14] The definitive study of Fuseli's life and work is Arnold Federmann, *Johann Heinrich Füssli, Dichter und Maler, 1741-1825*, Zurich and Leipzig, 1927. This includes a complete list of Fuseli's paintings and poems, as well as extracts from his correspondence. *Cf.* John Knowles, *The Life and Writings of Henry Fuseli, Esq., M.A., R.A.*, London, 1831, 3 Vols.

Lavater published an anonymous pamphlet, *The Unjust Magistrate, or the Complaint of a Patriot,* giving details of the fraud and calling upon the government to make an investigation. The pamphlet, widely circulated, created such a stir that government officials promised action against Grebel if the author would give his name. When Fuseli and Lavater made themselves known, Grebel was forced to flee. He had, however, left behind him members of his family who were politically influential. For this reason the two young men were compelled, at least temporarily, to leave Zurich. In 1763 they went to Leipzig and Berlin in the company of Professor Sulzer.

At Berlin Fuseli and Lavater made many friends for their liberal cause. Fuseli spent six months with Professor Spalding at Barth, studying the classics and fine arts, and then was called back to Berlin by Sulzer to join a group of German and Swiss literati who planned to establish closer literary relationships between those countries and England. Fuseli was to be a most desirable member of this group because of his extensive knowledge of languages. Accordingly, Fuseli, at the close of 1763, went to England with Sir Andrew Mitchell, British minister to the Court of Prussia. In England Sir Andrew introduced Fuseli to such distinquished gentlemen as Dr. Armstrong, Lord Scarsdale, Mr. Coutts the banker, and Andrew Millar and Joseph Johnson, the publishers. With the latter Fuseli's friendship became particularly strong. During this first sojourn in England Fuseli worked for various booksellers, translating French, Italian, and German books into English, and some English books into German. It was while thus employed that he issued a signed translation of Winckelmann's *Gedanken über die Nachahmung der griechischen Wercke in der Mahlerey und Bildhauer-Kunst,* published by Millar in 1765. Two additional translations from Winckelmann, one of them signed, appeared in the *Annual Register* for 1765. Fuseli also visited Falconer and Smollett, for whom he made drawings to illustrate an early edition of *Peregrine Pickle.*

After a year spent as travelling tutor to the young Viscount Chewton, Fuseli returned to England in 1767 and obtained an introduction to Sir Joshua Reynolds, who praised his work highly.

In 1767 he published anonymously his *Remarks on the Writings and Conduct of J. J. Rousseau,* in which he defended his countryman against the attacks of Voltaire and Hume. In 1769 he went to Italy with Dr. Armstrong, visiting Genoa, Milan, Florence, and Rome. In Rome, in 1770, he changed his name to "Fuseli," and for the next eight years devoted himself to an intensive study of art and to the collection of notes later published posthumously as *A History of Art in the Schools of Italy.* Here also he made friends with David and Gambini and reached his conviction of the dominating excellence of Greek art which was to influence his later writings. He also visited Venice and Naples, studying art remains there. Occasionally he sent a picture which he had painted at Rome to the Royal Academy in England for the annual exhibition. In 1778 he returned to London, having visited Zurich, France, Holland, and the Low Countries. The remainder of Fuseli's life was spent in England in the interest of art. In 1781 he finished his most popular painting, *The Nightmare.* In 1786, through the influence of Johnson, the publisher, Fuseli became literary adviser and editor of Cowper's translation of Homer because of his knowledge of Greek. In the same year he executed nine pictures for Boydell's *Shakespeare Gallery.* In May, 1788, he began his critical reviews for his friend Johnson's *Analytical Review.* Before December, 1798, he had written more than eighty articles, reviewing books on the classics, history, belles lettres, physiology, geography, and fine arts. In the same year he was elected an Associate of the Royal Academy. In 1789 he published an English translation of Lavater's *Aphorisms on Man* and began writing his own *Amphorisms on Art.* In 1790, through his connection with Johnson and the *Analytical Review,* he met Mary Wollstonecraft, who fell in love with him. This love was, apparently, not returned, for in 1792 Mary left for France, "heartbroken." In 1790 Fuseli undertook to make the illustrations for Cowper's edition of Milton. In the same year he was elected Royal Academician, precipitating the temporary resignation of Reynolds, who had favored the election of a rival candidate, H. Bonomi. Between 1793 and 1794 Fuseli painted four pictures for Woodmason's *Illustrations of Shakespeare.* In 1799 he was elected Professor of Painting to the

Royal Academy. In 1800 he painted pictures of *The Bard, The Descent of Odin,* and *The Fatal Sisters.* In 1801 he began his series of lectures to the Royal Academy, including the significant one on Ancient Art.[15] In 1805 he edited the new edition of Pilkington's *Dictionary of Painters.* Fuseli had been friendly with William Blake since 1787, and in 1805, he wrote a commendatory opinion of Blake's engravings for Blair's *The Grave.* Early in 1825, having delivered his last series of lectures to the Royal Academy, he died.

The romantic hellenism in the writings of Fuseli himself appears too late to fall within the limits of this study. His significance for us consists in the series of translations from Winckelmann which he published in 1765. The first of these bears on the title-page, *Reflections on the painting and sculpture of the Greeks: With instructions for the Connoisseur, and An Essay on Grace in Works of Art. Translated from the German original of the Abbé Winckelmann, Librarian of the Vatican . . . by Henry Fusseli, A.M. London . . . 1765.* Dedicated to Lord Scarsdale, the book is calculated to stimulate interest in the aesthetics of Greek art. The *Reflections,* occupying pages 1-64, consist of seven parts, the first four of which contain discussions of the general characteristics of Greek sculpture: Nature, Contour, Drapery, and Simplicity

[15] The lectures of Fuseli, delivered between 1801 and 1825 to the Royal Academy, display the romantic hellenism found in Winckelmann. This is particularly true of Lecture I, "Ancient Art," which, according to John Knowles, *op. cit.,* p. 241, was "much canvassed" by artists and antiquaries. To Fuseli Greece is "that happy coast, where, from an arbitrary hieroglyph, the palliative of ignorance, from a tool of despotism, or a ponderous monument of eternal sleep, art emerged into life, motion, and liberty; where situation, climate, national character, religion, manners, and government conspired to raise it on that permanent basis, which after the ruins of the fabric itself, still subsists and bids defiance to the ravages of time; as uniform in the principle as various in its applications, the art of the Greeks possessed in itself and propagated, like its chief object Man, the germs of immortality." (Knowles, Vol. II, pp. 23ff.) Speaking of the Laocoon, he says: "His figure is a class, it characterizes every beauty of virility verging on age; the prince, the priest, the father are visible, but, absorbed in the man, serve only to dignify the victim of *one* great expression; though poised by the artist, for us to apply the compass to the face of the Laocoon, is to measure the wave fluctuating in the storm: this tempestuous front, this contracted nose, the immersion of these eyes, and above all, that long-drawn mouth, are separate and united, seats of convulsion, features of nature struggling within the jaws of death." (Knowles, Vol. II, pp. 71ff.) Knowles reprints the entire lecture in Vol. II, pp. 17-72.

and Grandeur of expression. The fifth part deals with "Workmanship in Sculpture"; the sixth, with "Painting"; the seventh, with "Allegory."

The first significant element of romantic hellenism in the *Reflections* is an enthusiastic idealization of the superiority of Greek art over all others. To Winckelmann the Greeks far outshone all modern artists:

> Let any one, sagacious enough to pierce into the depths of art, compare the whole system of the Greek figures with that of the moderns, by which, as they say, nature alone is imitated; good heaven! what a number of neglected beauties will he not discover.[16]

The Greeks, moreover, bear the wonderful distinction of being original, not imitators:

> An antient Roman statue, compared to a Greek one, will generally appear like Virgil's Diana amidst her Oreads, in comparison of the Nausicae of Homer, whom he imitated.[17]

From this Winckelmann deduces the principle that to be a good artist one must follow the Greeks, not merely by imitation, but by empathy:

> There is but one way for the moderns to become great, and perhaps unequalled; I mean, by imitating the antients. And what we are told of Homer, that whoever understands him well, admires him, we find no less true in matters concerning the antient, especially the Greek arts. But then we must be as familiar with them as with a friend, to find Laocoon as inimitable as Homer.[18]

What, he asks, is it in Greek art that makes the sculpture of the Greeks so magnificent? The answers which he gives are those of the romantic hellenist. One reason is the painstaking care in artistry characteristic of the Greeks:

> The Greek artist . . . adjusted his Contour, in every figure, to the breadth of a single hair, even in the nicest and most tiresome performances, as gems. Consider the Diomedes and Perseus of Dioscorides, Hercules and Iole by Teucer, and admire the inimitable Greeks.[19]

[16] P. 15.
[17] P. 3.
[18] Pp. 2-3.
[19] P. 25.

A more important reason is that the Greeks were able to imitate an ideal supernature:

> It is not only *Nature* which the votaries of the Greeks find in their works, but still more, something superior to nature; ideal beauties, brain-born images, as Proclus says.[20]

This, however, they were able to do because of their wonderful liberty:

> In the most happy times of their freedom, the humanity of the Greeks abhorred bloody games, which even in the Ionick Asia had ceased long before, if, some guess, they had once been usual there. . . .
>
> These frequent occasions of observing Nature, taught the Greeks to go on still farther. They began to form certain general ideas of beauty, with regard to the proportions of the inferiour parts, as well as of the whole frame: these they raised above the reach of mortality, according to the superiour model of some ideal nature.[21]

In addition to their social and political freedom, moreover, the Greeks were blest with the most propitious of climates, in which they could bask in the sun, indulge in athletics, and develop the most beautiful bodies in the world:

> The most beautiful body of ours would perhaps be as much inferior to the most beautiful Greek one, as Iphicles was to his brother Hercules. The forms of the Greeks, prepared to beauty, by the influence of the mildest and purest sky, became perfectly elegant by their early exercises.[22]

Their liberty, their benevolent climate, and their remarkable bodies, together banished disease and produced a blissful Arcadia, where nature herself was free and peaceful:

> Those diseases which are destructive of beauty, were moreover unknown to the Greeks. There is not the least hint of the small-pox, in the writings of their physicians; and Homer, whose portraits are always so truly drawn, mentions not one pitted face. Venereal plagues, and their daughter the English malady, had not yet names.
>
> And must we not then, considering every advantage which nature bestows, or art teaches, for forming, preserving, and improving beauty, enjoyed and applied by the Grecians; must we not then confess, there is the strongest probability that the beauty of their persons excelled all we can have an idea of?

[20] P. 4. [21] Pp. 11-12. [22] P. 4.

Art claims liberty: in vain would nature produce her noblest off-springs, in a country where rigid laws would choak her progressive growth, as in Egypt, that pretended parent of sciences and arts: but in Greece, where, from their earliest youth, the happy inhabitants were devoted to mirth and pleasure, where narrow-spirited formality never restrained the liberty of manners, the artist enjoyed nature without a veil.[23]

Is it any wonder, he asks, that, possessed of such incomparable advantages, the Greeks were able to produce perfect art:

It would be no easy matter, I fancy, for our nature, to produce a frame equal in beauty to that of Antinous; and surely no idea can soar above the more than human proportions of a deity, in the Apollo of the Vatican, which is a compound of the united Force of Nature, Genius, and Art.

Their imitation discovering in the one every beauty diffused through Nature, shewing in the other the pitch to which the most perfect Nature can elevate herself, when soaring above the senses, will quicken the genius of the artist, and shorten his discipleship; he will learn to think and draw with confidence, seeing here the fixed limits of human and divine beauty. . . . The ideas of unity and perfection, which he acquired in meditating on antiquity, will help him to combine, and to ennoble the more scattered and weaker beauties of our Nature.[24]

Indeed, Greek art, through the influence of Greek liberty and Greek climate, is itself Arcadian and peaceful amidst the most passionate of emotions. In its contemplation one may find ecstasy and inspiration:

The last and most eminent characteristic of the Greek works is a noble simplicity and sedate grandeur in Gesture and Expression. As the bottom of the sea lies peaceful beneath a foaming surface, a great soul lies sedate beneath the strife of passions in Greek figures.

'Tis in the face of Laocoon this soul shines with full lustre, not confined however to the face, amidst the most violent sufferings. Pangs piercing every muscle, every labouring nerve; pangs which we almost feel ourselves, while we consider—not the face, nor the most expressive parts—only the belly contracted by excruciating pains: these however, I say, exert not themselves with violence, either in the face or gesture. He pierces not heaven, like the Laocoon of Virgil; his mouth is rather opened to discharge an anxious overloaded groan, as Sadolet says; the struggling body and the supporting mind exert themselves with equal strength, nay balance all the frame.

[23] Pp. 8-9. [24] Pp. 18-19.

Laocoon suffers, but suffers like the Philoctetes of Sophocles: we weeping feel his pains, but wish for the hero's strength to support his misery.

The Expression of so great a soul is beyond the force of mere nature.[25]

Thus Winckelmann, reading into Greek art what is really a desire within himself, contributes to romantic hellenism its fundamental aesthetic tenet: that the perfection of art in Greece was the result of social and political freedom and an Arcadian climate and life pattern. This idea he ultimately passed on to his successors in Germany and to the nineteenth century romanticists in England. The beginnings of its influence in England, however, may here be observed as early as 1765.

The second translation from Winckelmann appeared in the same year in *The Annual Register,*[26] under the title, "A description of the famous marble trunk of Hercules, dug up at Rome, commonly called the Torso of Belvedere; wrought by Apollonius the son of Nestor, and universally allowed to have been made for a statue of Hercules spinning. Translated from the German of the Abbé Winckelmann . . . by Henry Fusle." This is a rhapsodic eulogy of the ruin of Greek sculpture, full of idealizations. He calls it "that celebrated trunk of Hercules, of whose exalted beauties every praise falls short."[27] He finds it "a performance the sublimest in its kind, and the most perfect offspring of art among those that have escaped the havoc of time."[28] In sentimental fashion, he examines with much enthusiaism each part of the trunk: the muscles, the shoulders, the bones, etc.:

Ask those who know the height of mortal beauty, if they have ever seen a side comparable to his left one? The elasticity of the muscles is admirably balanced between rest and motion: by them the body must have been enabled to execute whatever it attempted. As when from the first movings of the sea, a gentle horror glides over its smooth surface, and undulating, as they rise, the waves play, absorbed in each other and again refunded: thus waving, thus softly undulating flows each muscle into the next, and a third that rises between them, dissolves itself amidst their gentle conflict, and, as it were, escapes our eye.[29]

[25] Pp. 30-31.
[26] Vol. VIII (1765), pp. 130-132.
[27] *Ibid.*, p. 130.
[28] *Ibid.*
[29] *Ibid.*, p. 131.

Then he proceeds once more to read into the remains of Greek art some higher "philosophical" idea which is really within himself:

> This eminent and noble form of perfect nature is, we might say, wrapt up in immortality—of which the shape is but the recipient; a higher spirit seems to have occupied the place of the mortal parts; 'tis no longer that frame which still has monsters to face, and fiends to subdue: 'tis that, which on Oeta's brow, purified from the dregs of mortality, has recovered its primitive splendor, the likeness of his supreme father.[30]

> Where the poets ceased, the artists began: they leave him as soon as, matched with the goddess of eternal youth, he mixes with the gods; but the artist shows us his deified form, and, as it were, an immortal frame, in which humanity is only left to make visible that strength and ease, by which the hero had become conqueror of the world.
>
> In the mighty out-lines of this body I see the unsubdued force of him who crushed the giants in the Phlegraean plains, whilst the undulating contour reminds me, at the same time, of that elastic flexibility, that winged haste, from which all the various transformations of Achelous could not escape.[31]

And then he concludes his account with a genuinely romantic rhapsody:

> O could I see this image in that primitive grandeur, that beauty with which it appeared to the artist—to say what he thought—what we should think; my great part after his were then to describe it! but wishes are vain: and as Psyche saw the fatal charms of her lover only to bewail his flight; so I see only the shadow of this Hercules, to bewail him irreparably lost!
>
> Him art bemoans with me: for this work, which she might have opposed to the greatest discoveries of wit or meditation, and proud of whose superior merits she might even now, as in her golden days, have looked down on the homages of mankind; this very work, and perhaps the last, which the united strength of her forces produced—this work she sees now cruelly mangled, and, with many hundred others, almost destroyed. But from these melancholy reflections her genius turns, to teach us, from what remains, the ways that lead to perfection.[32]

Here again, then, is a significant contribution to the rise of romantic hellenism in England.

The third translation from Winckelmann, like the preceding,

[30] *Ibid.*, p. 132. [31] *Ibid.*, p. 130. [32] *Ibid.*, p. 132.

appeared in *The Annual Register* for 1765[33] under the title, "Observations on the influence of the different climates upon the polite arts; taken from A history of the fine arts, by the Abbé Winckelmann, librarian of the Vatican, and antiquary to the Pope." In this further discussion of the fundamental tenet of Winckelmann's aesthetic theory, there is a clear identification of ancient and modern Greece:

> The same may be said of the modern Greeks [i.e., that their government, religion, language, and manners are different from those of the ancient Greeks]: with this difference, that the human face, and the human form, still retain, under that happy climate, a considerable measure of that surpassing beauty which so eminently distinguished the antient Grecians. Neither the change of manners among the modern Greeks, nor their intermarriages with foreigners, have effaced these fair strokes of nature. It would seem as if nature had fixed upon Greece, as the chief region of beauty, and given its climate a peculiar influence on the human form, since the human species seem really to increase in corporeal perfection, in proportion as they approach the Grecian isles. . . . It is in the temperate clime of Ionia, and the islands of the Archipelago, that the *human face divine,* as Milton calls it, is most remarkable for its beauty.[34]

This philosophical idealization of the Greeks found in Winckelmann is echoed in many publications after 1765. In 1767, for example, there appeared an unsigned pamphlet entitled, *An Enquiry into the causes of the Extraordinary Excellency of Ancient Greece in the Arts,*[35] in which the causes are shown to consist largely in the liberal social and political institutions of the Greeks. The perfection of the Greek art is reiterated in *The Elements of Universal Erudition, containing an Analytical Abridgement of the Sciences, Polite Arts, and Belles Lettres, by Baron Bielfeld . . . Translated from the last edition printed at Berlin. By W. Hooper, M.D. London . . . 1770. In Three Volumes.* Chapter XI of Book II of this work, entitled, "Sculpture and Plastics," presents the art of Greece in an extremely favorable light:

> All the Gods of the Pagans were represented by statues. Phidias and Praxiteles carried this art to the most sublime degree of excellence: and

[33] Vol. VIII, pp. 250-253. [34] *Ibid.*, pp. 250-251.
[35] A review of this work appears in *Critical Review,* Vol. XXIV, pp. 75-76.

the statues of Greece, at this day, are in the highest esteem among the connoisseurs, who regard those of Rome, Tuscany, and other parts of Europe, as far inferior both in taste and execution. . . . The Venus of Medicis, which is also called the shameless Venus, the Grecian Shepherdess, the Gladiator, the Peasant, the Hercules, the Milo of Croton, and the Fawn, are yet to be found in Italy, and they are almost all that have escaped devouring time. To these are given, by way of excellence, the name of perfect statues.[36]

More significant than these, however, is the praise bestowed upon the virtues of Greek sculpture in the exceedingly popular *Essays Moral and Literary, by Vicesimus Knox, M.A. A New Edition in Two Volumes. London, 1782.* Vicesimus Knox (1752-1821), a fellow of St. Johns College, Oxford, between 1775 and 1779, had, in 1778, sent a group of essays which he had written to Charles Dilly, the publisher. Dilly consulted Dr. Johnson, who gave him a favorable opinion of them. The essays appeared unsigned in one volume in 1778 and proved so popular that in the second edition, 1779, thirty-nine additional essays were printed in a second volume, and the author's name added to the title page. The popularity of these essays seems to have increased after the publication of the second edition. A twelfth edition had appeared by 1793, a seventeenth by 1815, and more followed. The edition of 1782 contains 179 essays on varied but timely subjects. No. 67 is entitled, "Reflections on the Origin and Effects of Sculpture, With Miscellaneous Remarks on It."[37] No. 68 bears the title, "That the English Possess a fine Taste for Sculpture, and That It Ought To Be Encouraged For Its Moral Effects."[38] In these two essays Knox reflects the tendency already present in the age to read into Greek art that which is really in the beholder:

Just representations of the irrational or inanimate creation, are, indeed, in a great degree pleasing; but the highest delight which the fine arts can bestow, is derived from imitations of human nature. . . . The bloom of the grape, the blush of the peach, and the crimson of the rose, designed by nature to please, may perhaps please yet more when artificially presented to the view by her hand-maiden. . . . To touch the heart with

[36] Vol. II, pp. 385-386.
[37] The essay is in Vol. I, pp. 291-296.
[38] *Ibid.*, pp. 296-299.

sympathy, to excite the nobler affections, and to give a masculine pleasure, man must be the object of imitation. . . .

To represent the attitudes of his actions, and the features of his passions, is the principal business of *Sculpture;* and though a considerable degree of its excellence depends on the delicacy of manual execution, yet has it ever maintained a distinguished place among the arts which require a fine imagination. Nature, indeed, lies open to the inspection of the learned and of the unlearned, of the stupid and of the ingenious; but the man of fine feeling, and of elegant taste, can alone perceive and imitate her more delicate traits, her more captivating, though less obvious, allurements.

The first productions of this art probably owe their origin to religion. . . . The statue that was formed as an object of religious adoration, has, indeed, failed in its original purpose; but it has been viewed with a degree of wonder little less than worship.

And, indeed, it is to be presumed, that few will wish that idolatrous attention, which is at present paid to the statues of the antient deities, forbidden: for whenever they shall cease to be admired, they will cease to be imitated. Such an event every friend to just taste will deprecate, since to renounce the models of the antients, is to renounce the most captivating embellishment of art, an adherence to simplicity and nature. While a *Venus de Medicis,* and an *Apollo Belvedere,* shall continue to be standards of excellence, no one can with reason apprehend, lest the chaste graces of real elegance should be sacrificed to the false glare of Gothic affectation.[39]

The master's hand can give to matter the features of the soul, and impress on the rude block those thoughts and passions, which naturally excite congenial sentiments and sympathetic emotions; and the mind, which, perhaps, could never be sensible of the beauty of virtue from the reasonings of a Plato, or a Socrates, may be captivated with her amiable form when displayed by a Phidias or Praxiteles.

No man of sensibility can walk in the repositories of the illustrious dead, where the forms that moulder beneath his feet are represented in marble on the walls, without feeling, as he treads the solemn aile, the most virtuous sensations. His faculties seem to stretch, and his virtues to expand, in efforts to reach the level of such exalted society. . . . It [sculpture] has, in common with all the fine arts, an invisible effect in softening the temper and humanizing the manners. . . .

Sculpture claims, indeed, the power of exciting virtue, and the privilege of rewarding it.[40]

A similar illustration of the influence of the philosophical aes-

[39] *Ibid.,* pp. 292-293.

[40] *Ibid.,* pp. 298-299.

thetics of Greek art in the age is found in the paper dated February 19, 1783, entitled, "On the Comparative Merit of the Ancients and Moderns, with respect to the Imitative Arts. By Mr. Thomas Kirshaw." The paper was published at Warrington in 1785 in the *Memoirs of the Literary and Philosophical Society of Manchester.*[41] Kirshaw's purpose, he says, is "to point out the excellencies of the ancients in the imitative arts,"[42] and he bases much of his reasoning on the evidence in "the discoveries of Herculaneum."[43] His conclusion recalls Winckelmann in the mind of the reader:

> There is not a doubt, but the ancients possessed a polished taste, and a critical knowledge of the various and exquisite forms of beauty: they knew the arts, could only receive their perfection from ideal beauty, superior to what is ever found, in individual, and imperfect nature. There is no man equal, in strength and proportion to the Farnesian Hercules: nor, any woman comparable, for symmetry of form, to Medicean Venus.
>
> These instances seem to prove, that the authors of the finest remains of antiquity formed to themselves ideas of *perfect* nature, and collected from *various* individuals, what *no one* could supply.[44]

By 1786[45] the philosophical aesthetics found in Winckelmann had, it seems, become sufficiently current to be stated almost as a matter of course in a history of Greece. In that year there appeared the first edition of the popular *History of Ancient Greece, Its Colonies and Conquests, to The Division of the Macedonian Empire; Including the History of Literature, Philosophy, and the Fine Arts. By John Gillies, LL.D., F.A.S. In Two Volumes.* Gillies

[41] Vol. I, pp. 405-413. [42] *Ibid.*, p. 406.
[43] *Ibid.*, p. 408. [44] *Ibid.*, p. 406.
[45] Mention should also be made of the publication, in 1785, of a French work in London which similarly reflected the philosophical aesthetics that we have been tracing. This work was by Pierre François Hugues, called d'Hancarville, and bears the title, *Récherches sur l'origine, l'esprit et les progrès des Arts de la Grèce; sur leurs connections avec les arts et la religion des plus ancients peuples connus.* London, 1785, 2 Vols. Dedicated to Charles Towneley, this is a description and discussion of Greek art as displayed chiefly in medals, gems, urns, and coins, and is adorned with 63 plates. In the preface, d'Hancarville says: "La Sculpture fut restée au point où elle s'arrêta dans l'Egypte et dans l'Asie, si le Genie des Grecs n'eut imaginé de comprendre la Beauté dans le nombre des Attributs ou des Qualités des Dieux. Celle-ci ne pouvant s'exprimer que par l'harmonie des proportions, et la régularité, des formes, il fallut pour les réunir, éloigner d'abord tout ce qui pouvoit leur être contraire. . . . Cette Perfection, à laquelle l'Esprit des Arts les fit arriver en Grece, par le moyen des Statues Divines, n'exista nulle part ailleurs. . . ." (pp. xxii-xxiii.)

(1747-1836)[46] had been tutor to Henry Hope, the second son of John, second Earl of Hopetoun. In the course of his duties he visited various parts of the continent. He was afterwards travelling tutor to the Earl's two younger sons, John and Alexander. A good classical scholar, he received the degree of LL.D. in 1784. He was also a corresponding member of the French Institute and a fellow both of the Royal Society and the Society of Antiquaries. In 1793 Gillies was appointed Royal Historiographer for Scotland, upon the death of Robertson. His *History of Greece* was popular, being translated into French at Basle in 1790 and into German at Vienna in 1825. Other English editions appeared in 1792-3 and 1825.[47]

Gillies' work is highly detailed and scholarly. It consists of forty long chapters, describing in detail the history of Greece during the seven centuries between the settlement of the Ionians in Asia Minor and the establishment of the Macedonian Empire in the East. Chapter 14[48] consists of a discussion of the fine arts among the Greeks which reminds one strongly of Winckelmann in its attribution of the perfection of Greek art to climate and social and political life:

> The testimony . . . of modern travellers confirms the evidence of antiquity, that the shores and islands of the Archipelago produce more elegant and liberal forms, and features more animated and expressive, with fewer individual imperfections, and more of general nature, than can be found in any other divisions of the world. Yet whatever the Greeks owed to their skies and climate, they were probably not less indebted to their active laborious education and way of life, and to the manly spirit of their religious, civil, and military institutions. Long before the invasion of Xerxes, the Grecian sculpture was distinguished by an air of majesty peculiar to itself; and the awful images of the gods, as yet rudely finished, displayed a grandeur and sublimity of expression that delighted and astonished the best judges, in the most refined ages of art.[49]

But it is in the praise which he heaps upon the productions of

[46] A memoir of Gillies appears in the *Gentleman's Magazine,* new series, Vol. V (1836), pp. 436-437.

[47] My quotations are taken from the American edition in one volume, New York, 1852.

[48] Pp. 176-180.

[49] *Ibid.,* p. 176.

Greek sculpture that Gillies' chapter takes on significance in the development of romantic hellenism:

The sculptors Phidias, Polycletus, Scopas, Alcamenes, and Myron . . . softened the asperities of their predecessors, rendered their contours more natural and flowing, and by employing greater address to conceal the mechanism of their art, displayed superior skill to the judgment, and afforded higher delight to the fancy. . . . In the works of those admired artists, the expression was skilfully diffused through every part, without disturbing the harmony of the whole. Pain and sorrow were rather concentrated in the soul than displayed on the countenance; and even the more turbulent passions of indignation, anger, and resentment, were so tempered and ennobled, that the indications of them became consistent with the sublimest grace and beauty.[50]

To Gillies the perfection of the Greeks in fine arts knows no bounds:

Their [the ancient marbles'] authors perfectly understood proportion, anatomy, the art of clothing, without concealing the naked figure, and whatever contributes to the justness and truth of design. The exact knowledge of form is as necessary to the painter or statuary, whose business it is to represent bodies, as that of language to the poet or historian, who undertakes to describe actions. In this particular, it would be unnecessary to institute a comparison between Grecian writers and artists, since they are both allowed as perfect in their respective kinds as the condition of humanity renders possible.[51]

Then, like Winckelmann, Gillies proceeds to this rhapsodic analysis of concrete specimens of Greek sculpture:

The Apollo Belvedere is universally felt and acknowledged to be the sublimest figure that either skill can execute, or imagination conceive. . . . Animated by the noblest conception of heavenly powers, the artist has far outstepped the perfections of humanity, and (if we may speak without irreverence) made the corrupt put on incorruption, and the mortal immortality. His stature is above the human, his attitude majestic; the Elysian spring of youth softens the manly grace of his person, and the bold structure of his limbs. Disdain sits on his lips, and indignation swells his nostrils; but an unalterable serenity invests his front, and the sublime elevation of his aspect aspires at deeds of renown still surpassing the present object of his victory.

The irascible passions are not represented with more dignity in the

[50] *Ibid.*, p. 178. [51] *Ibid.*, p. 179.

Apollo, than are those of fear, terror, and consternation in the Niobe. . . . The excess and suddenness of their disaster, occasioned a degree of amazement and horror, which, suspending the faculties, involved them in that silence and insensibility, which neither breaks out in lamentable shrieks, nor distorts the countenance, but which leaves full play to the artist's skill to represent motion without disorder, or, in other words, to render expression graceful.

The Laocoon may be regarded as the triumph of Grecian sculpture; since bodily pain, the grossest and most ungovernable of all our passions, and that pain united with anguish and torture of mind, are yet expressed with such propriety and dignity, as afford lessons of fortitude superior to any taught in schools of philosophy. The horrible shriek which Virgil's Laocoon emits, is a proper circumstance for poetry, which speaks to the fancy by images and ideas borrowed from all the senses, and has a thousand ways of ennobling its object; but the expression of this shriek would have totally degraded the statue. It is softened, therefore, into a patient sigh, with eyes turned to heaven in search of relief. The intolerable agony of suffering nature is represented in the lower part, and particularly in the extremities, of the body; but the manly breast struggles against calamity. The contention is still more plainly perceived in his furrowed forehead; and his languishing paternal eye demands assistance, less for himself, than for his miserable children, who look up to him for help.

If subjects of this nature are expressed without appearing hideous, shocking, or disgustful, we may well suppose that more temperate passions are represented with the greatest moderation and dignity.[52]

Thus, by 1786 the philosophical aesthetics of Greek art in Winckelmann had begun to be popularized. It would be a mistake, however, to think that this theory was universally accepted. Between 1765 and 1786, in fact, there were at least four presentations of views on Greek art considerably different from those which we have examined. One of these is to be found in the eighth and tenth of Sir Joshua Reynolds' *Discourses Delivered at the Royal Academy*. Reynolds is not quite so appreciative of Greek sculpture as the other aestheticians:

Those works of the ancients, which are in the highest esteem, have something beside mere simplicity to recommend them. The Apollo, the Venus, the Laocoon, the Gladiator, have a certain composition of action, have contrasts sufficient to give grace and energy in a high degree; but it

[52] *Ibid.*, p. 180.

must be confessed, of the many thousand antique statues which we have, that their general characteristic is bordering at least on inanimate insipidity.[53]

With the philosophical meaning of Greek sculpture, Reynolds has no sympathy:

It may be thought, at the first view, that even this form [in sculpture], however perfectly represented, is to be valued and take its rank only for the sake of a still higher object, that of conveying sentiment and character, as they are exhibited by attitude, and expression of the passions: but we are sure, from experience, that the beauty of form alone, without the assistance of any other quality, makes of itself a great work, and justly claims our esteem and admiration.[54]

Though the Laocoon and his two sons have more expression in the countenance than perhaps any other antique statues, yet it is only the general expression of pain; and this passion is still more strongly expressed by the writhing and contortion of the body, than by the features.

It has been observed, in a late publication, that if the attention of the father, in this group, had been occupied more by the distress of his children, than by his own sufferings, it would have raised a much greater interest in the spectator. Though this observation comes from a person whose opinion, in every thing relating to the arts, carries with it the highest authority, yet I cannot but suspect that such refined expression is scarce within the province of this art; and in attempting it, the artist will run great risk of enfeebling expression, and making it less intelligible to the spectator.[55]

A much more vigorous protest against a philosophical hellenic aesthetics appeared in 1775 by James Barry (1741-1806), the English painter.[56] Barry had, in 1763, sent a picture, *The Conversion by St. Patrick of the King of Cashel,* to an exhibition sponsored at Dublin by the Society for the Encouragement of Arts and Manufactures. In this way he had attracted the attention of Burke, who brought him to London in 1764 and introduced him to "Athenian" Stuart and Sir Joshua Reynolds. In 1769 he travelled to Naples, where he became much attached to the an-

[53] Discourse VIII, 1778, in *Discourses on Painting and the Fine Arts, Delivered at the Royal Academy. By Sir Joshua Reynolds, Knt.,* London, 1805, p. 55.

[54] Discourse X, 1780, *ibid.,* p. 65.

[55] *Ibid.,* p. 66.

[56] A memoir of Barry by Edward Fryer is prefixed to *The Works of James Barry,* London, 1825.

tique, but was made irritable by constant quarrels with dilettanti and dealers in antiquities. He seems to have been very quarrelsome by temperament. In Naples he painted his *Philoctetes in the Isle of Lemnos,* which won him election to the Clementine Academy at Bologna. In 1772, having been made a member of the Royal Academy, he proposed to the Academicians that they sponsor a project to decorate St. Paul's with historical pictures. The reason for this proposal was Barry's contempt for the day's fashion in painting what he called "trifles." Historical painting would, he maintained, establish a "solid, manly taste for real art." The Academicians agreed to this proposal in 1773, and selected artists for the purpose, including Barry himself. The proposal was, however, later rejected. In 1774 Barry made a similar proposal to decorate the new room of the Society of Arts in the Adelphi, but without success.[57] Embittered by his defeat, he proceeded to write a vigorous defense of his theory concerning historical painting. This appeared under the title, *An Inquiry Into the Real and Imaginary Obstructions To The Acquisition of the Arts in England. By James Barry, Royal Academician, and Member of the Clementine Academy of Bologna . . . London, 1775.* This is a pamphlet of 227 pages, in twenty chapters, which attempts to demonstrate the validity of Barry's theory by attacking the theories advanced by Winckelmann, the Abbé du Bos, and Montesquieu concerning the effects of climate and social organization upon the production of art. These foreign critics had maintained that England could not reach the perfection of Greek and Italian art because its climate was not conducive to such creation. Barry first states this theory and then vehemently refutes it. Reviewing the history of arts in Greece and Italy, he shows that the perfection of the arts in these countries was the

[57] When, in 1777, Barry offered to execute this project himself, without remuneration, permission was granted him. The result was the now famous series of 6 pictures decorating the room of the Society of Arts in the Adelphi. These are 11 feet 6 inches in height. Two of them are each 42 feet long. Their total length is 140 feet. Their subject is the historical development of human culture. Ultimately, Barry made money by this project. He was not only remunerated by the Society of Arts, but he was granted permission to open the room for public inspection and to sell engravings of the pictures. See S. T. Davenport's account in the *Journal of the Society of Fine Arts,* Vol. XVIII, p. 803.

result not of climate and natural circumstances, but of a combination of moral or accidental causes:

By a gradual and slow progress, . . . the ancient Greeks wrought themselves up to such an exalted perfection, that their works stand as the most glorious monuments of extensive knowledge, grandeur of conception, beauty and graceful propriety, that ever were erected to the honour of the human capacity. When we look upon the remains of their works, and lay aside all considerations of moral causes and gradual progress, it is no wonder if we can bring ourselves to believe them the productions of a people transcending humanity. But after all, facts and experience will have their weight with us; and these shew, that neither were the Greeks above the want of that accidental happy concurrence of moral circumstances and combinations, which must operate in other countries, before the possible extent of men's powers and attainments can display itself. No, quite the contrary; behold the Greeks now, and for many ages past, buried in rust and ignorance; and amongst the lowest and most contemptible people of Europe, even whilst their neighbours, the Italians, have been gathering laurels in every avenue of Parnassus. And further, the histories that give an account of their beginning, shew that, like other people, they also were born in ignorance.[58]

Barry ridicules those

half critics in the arts, who, from a train of shallow ridiculous observation, pretend to deduce the superiority of taste and beauty in the Greek statues and Italian pictures, from a more beautiful system of nature and superior proportions, which they *affect* to discover in the natives of those two countries. Every circumstance of difference, between the Greeks, Italians, and the English . . ., they consider in the first place as advantages, and secondly as permanent advantages, fastened to the climate and nature of the Greeks and Italians. Such reasoners are not worth much attention. . . . As it is absolutely impossible that our philosophers, or indeed any body else, can ever be so furnished with the facts, as to obtain a distinct view of all these ingredients that compose the human character, and to separate and weigh the quantity and degree of each as it is grafted on the original stamina, it is ridiculous to pretend to decide any thing about the original differences (if there be any) between the Greeks, the Italians, the French, and the English.[59]

As a matter of fact, the Greeks worked hard and learned their art from experience. We do not recognize this because we have been prejudiced in their favor:

[58] Pp. 40-41. [59] Pp. 80-84.

The ancient Greeks could find nothing in human nature but rude materials, which it cost them great labour to cultivate and fashion up to national and glorious purposes; their fine shapes and proportions did not (we see) spring up like grass out of the earth, but out of the exercises of the Pentathlon, and out of all the other exercises, studies, and progressive mental and bodily improvements of an education, exceedingly perfect and happily calculated to form the best models of beauty, dignity, and virtue.[60]

There are vast numbers of Greeks and Levantines at Venice, and one is struck at first sight with a certain air of elevated character and picturesque natural beauty about them, that is not seen in the Italians, French, or English; this does not altogether arise either from the novelty of their appearance, or from any prejudices in their favour from our admiration of their ancestors, or from any vanity to shew our own skill and discernment in tracing out long resemblances and family likenesses. These, no doubt, have sometimes their weight, and the fanciful curious discoveries and magnified descriptions of many writers and travellers but too clearly evince it. . . .[61]

Having demolished this theory, Barry turns to the reasons why the English have not perfected their art. The chief of these reasons he finds in the fact that the introduction of superior art into England has been prevented by the monopoly of Rome and the mistaken notions of Virtuosi. Against these he is very bitter:

It is . . . certain that modern taste and art have derived great utility from this estimation in which the celebrated ancients are so generally held. But the absurd abuse of it (and it is more liable to be abused than otherwise) is the disgrace of our country and age, and has been lying a dead weight upon the loins of national improvement.

Artful men, both at home and abroad, have not failed to avail themselves of this passion for ancient art, as it afforded a fine coverlet for imposition, for vending, in the name of those great masters, the old copies, imitations, and studies, of all the obscure artists that have been working in Italy, Flanders, and other places for two hundred years past. These things are to be had in great plenty, and may be (as I have often known at Rome) easily baptized; first thoughts, second thoughts with alterations, duplicates, and what not. The great admiration so deservedly bestowed on some antique statues in the pope's, the duke of Tuscany's, the Borghesi, and other princely collections, is also turned to good account by those dealers. When the Italians, between two and three centuries ago, were digging in the ruins for statues, etc. they only preserved

[60] P. 89. [61] P. 95.

what they thought worth it, the refuse they either threw with the rest of the rubbish back into the cava, or suffered to be dispersed without care. Now as the name of antique is with many passport sufficient, these cavas are opened once more, and all the obscure corners of Rome are raked for old marble (it is indeed for the most part but little more) to sell to such of the rich Inglesi, whose passion for collecting antiques might outrun their knowledge of the merit and value of them. It would be endless to give an account of all the various ways in which our antiquaries and picture dealers, with their whippers in and dependents, both at home and abroad, carry on this business of imposition; let it suffice to say, that it is the most difficult thing in the world for any travelling gentleman who may be inclined to purchase, to avoid the springes and the nets that are so artfully laid for them.

The great models of perfection are in Italy, but these are not now to be purchased. The pope has officers appointed to inspect every picture, statue etc. going out of Rome, and admitting the possibility of bribing these officers, (another source of trick in the dealer) even the third or fourth rate things, are too well known to be moved without making a noise. The state of Venice have also set their seal upon all the pictures they thought worth the keeping; so that this ill fated country of ours is to be crammed with nothing but rubbish from abroad; and our artists at home must necessarily, to avoid risquing the displeasure of their patrons, favour this mockery and cheat that is put upon them. . . . A most excellent writer, David Hume, has well observed before me, that this importation of foreign art, was the real cause why the ancient Romans never were able to produce any thing in the arts that did them honour; however, the case is not in all parts exactly parallel, for the victorious Romans stripped Greece of every thing that was excellent and valuable; and if they buried the genius of their own country, they buried it however under the most consummate monuments of foreign perfection; whereas our importations and numerous sales of pictures can hardly be considered in any other light, than as a common cloaca and sink, through which all the refuse and filth of Europe is emptied into this country.[62]

Thus, since the superiority of Greek art is not the result of any natural superiority of the ancient Greeks, the English can attain to a similar perfection. There is, however, one sure way in which this may be hastened: historical painting:

History painting and sculpture should be the main views of any people desirous of gaining honour by the Arts. These are the tests by which the national character will be tried in after ages, and by which it

[62] Pp. 74-78.

has been, and is now, tried by the natives of other countries. These are the great sources from whence all the rivulets of art flow, and from whence only is derived the vigour and character that truly enobles them.[63]

Moreover, says Barry, if we would find the ultimate secret of the perfection of Greek art, we will discover it in the use by the Greeks of the technique of historical art:

The prime object of study to a history-painter being the entire man, body and mind, he can occasionally confine himself to any part of this subject, and carry a meaning, a dignity, and a propriety into his work, which a mere portrait-painter must be a stranger to, who has generally no ideas of looking further than the likeness and in its moments of still life. . . . Is not the Apollo a sublime figure? and yet all the parts of it are finished with the accuracy of a gem. The Laocoon also is as much made out, in all the component parts, from the head to the foot, as it is possible for a figure to be. This great attention to the particular parts, was the principal reason why the great artists were always fond of making their figures naked, whenever they could do it with propriety; nay, they even sometimes sacrificed propriety to obtain it, as it afforded them an ample field to display the highest abilities, and where a common capacity must certainly loose [*sic*] its way. If you cover with drapery the swelling thorax, and the writhing convulsions of the muscles of the abdomen, and that agony which is diffused all over the parts of the legs and the arm of Laocoon; the attitude, no doubt, still remains, and the story is carried on, but every difficulty (both in the choice and precision of form, and the agitation that is superadded to it) which required superior knowledge and skill to execute, is by this means taken away, and any vulgar artist will be equal to the task of making his agonized foot, if you allow him to put a shoe upon it. All the peculiar graces and beautiful selection of parts in the Apollo vanish if you cover him with a drapery, he will then differ but little from any other tall man. The Hercules and the fighting Gladiator, if they are clad, all is gone that the world has been so long admiring in them.[64]

The agonies of the Laocoon are as discernible in his foot as in his face. This naked nature, or but thinly and partially clad, speaks a universal language, which is understood and valued in all times and countries, when the Grecian dress, language, and manners, are neither regarded or known.[65]

Thus Barry, disagreeing with Winckelmann, nevertheless uses the same aesthetic method; he reads into Greek art what is really

[63] Pp. 132-133. [64] Pp. 133-137.
[65] P. 156.

within himself. In method his work possesses as much significance in the rise of romantic hellenism as Winckelmann's.

A similar expression of a theory of Greek art at variance with that of Winckelmann appears in the English translation of the work of the French jurist, Antoine Yves Goguet, *The Origin of Laws, Arts, and Sciences, And Their Progress Among The Most Ancient Nations. Translated From The French of The President De Goguet. In Three Volumes. Adorned With Cuts. Edinburgh . . . 1775.* This is a treatment of the early history of the Babylonians, Assyrians, Egyptians, Greeks, and others, considering the origin of laws, government, fine arts, manufactures, sciences, commerce, navigation, military arts, manners, and customs. Volume I covers the period from the Deluge to the death of Jacob; Volume II, from the death of Jacob to the establishment of monarchy among the Israelites; Volume III, from the Monarchy among the Israelites to their return from the Babylonian captivity. The period of highest perfection in Greek art under Pericles, it should be noted, is not discussed.

In the preface Goguet states his thesis clearly:

The history of laws, arts, and sciences, is, properly speaking, the history of the human mind. This great and most important subject has often indeed been treated of already; but, in my opinion, sufficient pains have not as yet been taken to discover the real origin, and unfold the gradual improvements of all the various branches of our knowledge. In general, the writers who have engaged in this vast and arduous undertaking, have fallen into great mistakes, by indulging themselves too much in conjectures, by following fancies more than facts, and taking their own imaginations, rather than the lights of history, for their guides. . . . In all nations, the state of the arts and sciences has at all times been intimately connected with, and greatly influenced by the political constitution and form of government. . . . The arts especially, bear so strong an impression of the character of the people by whom they have been cultivated, that an attentive examination of their origin and progress is the most effectual way to discover the genius, the manners, and turn of mind, of the various nations of the world.[66]

Goguet readily admits that Greece raised the arts to a "point of perfection. We owe to Greece . . . all the beauties . . . of which the

[66] Vol. I, p. v.

arts are capable."[67] He insists, however, that this was the result of later times, when their government was not democratic. Because of their early form of government, the Greeks before Pericles were far from the naturally gifted and blessed people we are so prone to think them:

> Although the Athenians, like all the other states of Greece, were originally governed by kings, never any people were more strongly inclined to democracy. The power of their kings, restrained nearly to the mere command of the armies, was nothing in time of peace.[68]

> To explain the constitution of the government of Athens, is to make known its defects. Every state where the people judges and decides, is essentially vitious. How in effect is it possible to debate affairs in assemblies so numerous? How is it possible even to be heard?[69]

> In republics men easily agree to look upon unbounded headlong liberty as the most precious attribute of humanity. They usually make perfect equality consist in unlimited freedom of speech. This sentiment always imprints on republican spirits a certain asperity which must necessarily affect the manners.[70]

> We commonly view the Athenians on their favourable and advantageous side. We are struck with the shining images of the history of Athens, and imposed upon by its lustre. We are dazzled by the battles of Marathon and Salamis, by the pomp of the spectacles, by the taste and magnificence of the public monuments, by that crowd of great men excellent in every way, which will render the name of Athens for ever precious and memorable. Nevertheless, if we would examine the interior state of this republic, very different scenes would present themselves. We should see a state in incessant combustion, assemblies always tumultuous, a people perpetually agitated by brigues and factions, and abandoned to the impetuosity of the vilest haranguer; the most illustrious citizens persecuted, banished, and continually exposed to violence and injustice. Virtue was proscribed at Athens. . . . The history of all the other people of Greece cannot furnish near so many examples of injustice and ingratitude towards the benefactors of the state, as does the single city of Athens.[71]

Because of this bad government, says Goguet, the arts could not flourish and the people were ignorant and coarse:

[67] Vol. II, p. 173.
[68] Vol. III, p. 29.
[69] Vol. III, p. 36.
[70] Vol. III, p. 228.
[71] Vol. III, pp. 37-38.

The riches of these first sovereigns could not be very considerable; it is sufficient, to be convinced of this, to consider, that Greece, in the heroic times, was without trade, without arts, without navigation, destitute, in a word, of all the resources which procure abundance and riches to a country.[72]

The praises which certain authors have thought to heap on the heroic times, are false and unreasonable. . . . The Greeks were at that time as ignorant, and, of consequence, as vitious as . . . could be. There passed many ages before the greatest part of the universe came out of that fatal ignorance, of which the most shameful vices and excesses were the unavoidable consequence.[73]

But Goguet does not leave the matter there. He has his own theory to account for the ultimate perfection of Greek art, and the theory, as might be expected, is anti-republican:

An Athenian was free to feed, clothe, and lodge himself as he would. He was also at liberty to give himself to any art or science that he thought proper. . . . He might pass his time in the manner that appeared to him the most convenient, provided it was not in absolute idleness. . . . Solon . . . had . . . been sensible, that sloth and too much leisure are more to be feared than all the vices that can reign in a state. It was to prevent the introduction of those that he appointed the Areopagus to watch the private conduct of the inhabitants of Athens, and to take cognisance of the means which individuals employed for their subsistence. This legislator had even ordained punishments for those who should pass their lives in entire idleness.

The effect of a policy so wise and so attentive, was the flourishing at Athens of the fine arts, of manufactures, of commerce, of navigation, sciences, eloquence, in short, of all the knowledge which can advantageously distinguish a nation. But at the same time, the great riches introduced into Athens by arts and commerce, produced the same effects that they have always produced amongst all nations. I would say an excessive inclination for pageantry, luxury, and magnificence, joined to an extreme love of pleasure and sensuality. Athens, after Solon's time, very soon became a voluptuous city, and its inhabitants yielded but too readily to the allurements of sensual pleasure.[74]

It is interesting to observe how Goguet concludes his account of the Greeks with evident enjoyment at having lowered them a peg in the estimation of the age:

[72] Vol. II, p. 54. [73] Vol. II, p. 393. [74] Vol. III, pp. 224-225.

To define the Athenians in a few words, they were a mild, humane, and beneficent people, magnanimous, generous, most brave and most warlike, having besides great talents for commerce and sea-affairs; but at the same time light, touchy, and capricious, hot-headed, haughty, and inconstant; polite, moreover, and delicate in point of decorum, the times of which I speak being considered, sensual and voluptuous, taken up with a fine picture, a beautiful statue, passionately fond of spectacles, lovers of the sciences, and fine arts in every kind and branch; curious, in a word, of news, and very talkative, sprightly, humorous, fond of drollery and jests, of quick feelings, and expressing themselves with the most exquisite taste and delicacy; having produced besides many men of wit as brilliant as solid, and many great and sublime geniuses.[75]

But at the same time, says Goguet:

The Greeks were yet very ignorant in the time of Cyrus, the epocha of the third and last part of our work. Near two ages elapsed between those which close our researches, and the times in which the Greeks made most of the discoveries which obtained them that glory and just esteem they yet at present enjoy, and of which nothing can ever rob them. No body has yet surpassed them in poetry, in eloquence, nor in the art of writing history. It is not quite the same thing with the demonstrative sciences, nor even with many parts of the arts. It must be allowed, that, if we except architecture, sculpture, and the engraving of precious stones, no comparison can be made between what the Greeks knew of the objects I have just indicated and what we know of them at present.[76]

Similar to Goguet's account in its use of a theory of Greek art and culture to bolster a social and political theory, is *The History of Greece. By William Mitford, Esq. The First Volume. London, 1784.* Mitford (1744-1827) had met Gibbon, his brother officer, while a colonel in the South Hampshire militia. At Gibbon's suggestion he undertook to write a history of Greece in 1779. While only the first volume appeared within the years to which this study is limited,[77] the completed work was very popular, passing through six editions after 1810. Mitford, an anti-republican, was evidently trying to counteract the visionary ideas concerning the blessings of Greek democracy during the years of the French Revolution. It is this work which Byron had in mind when he said of Mitford:

His great pleasure consists in praising tyrants, abusing Plutarch, spelling

[75] Vol. III, pp. 233-234.
[76] Vol. III, p. 249.
[77] Vol. II appeared in 1790. The fifth and final volume appeared in 1810.

oddly, and writing quaintly; and—what is strange, after all—his is the best modern history of Greece in any language, and he is perhaps the best of all modern historians whatsoever. Having named his sins, it is but fair to state his virtues—learning, labour, research, wrath, and partiality. I call the latter virtues in a writer, because they make him write in earnest.[78]

Volume I of this work treats, in ten chapters, the history of Greece from "the earliest accounts" through the Trojan War, up to "the conclusion of the Persian Invasion" under Xerxes. Chapter III is entitled, "Of the Religion, Government, Jurisprudence, Arts, Commerce, and Manners of the early Greeks."[79] It should be noted that, in the first volume, Mitford, like Goguet, has not yet reached the great period of Greek art. He is, indeed, somewhat mystified by the reasons for its later excellence:

There was more generosity and less cruelty in the Gothic spirit of war than in the Grecian. Whence this arose; what circumstances gave the weaker sex so much more consequence among the Teutonic nations than among the Greeks . . . will probably ever remain equally a mystery in the history of man, as why perfection in the sciences and every elegant art should be confined to the little territory of Greece, and to those nations which have derived it thence.[80]

He is certain, however, that this excellence was not owing to any benevolence in its government, its liberty, its climate, or its social life. The latter, he says, was barbarous. "Murders were so common, that, without peculiar circumstances of enormity, they scarcely left a stain upon the character of the perpetrator."[81] The government of Greece was bad, rather than favorable:

Greece was a country holding out to its possessors every delight of which humanity is capable; but where, through the inefficiency of law, the instability of governments, and the character of the times, happiness was extremely precarious, and the change frequent from the height of bliss to the depth of misery. Hence, rather than from his natural temper, Homer seems to have derived a melancholy tinge widely diffused over his poems.[82]

That age, says Plutarch, produced men of extraordinary dexterity, of extreme swiftness, of unwearied strength; who used these natural advantages for no good purpose, but placed their enjoyment in the com-

[78] *Don Juan,* Canto 12, stanza 19, note.

[79] This appears on pp. 61-122.

[80] P. 122.

[81] P. 110.

[82] Pp. 121-122.

mission of insults, outrage, and cruelty; esteeming the commendations bestowed upon modesty, righteousness, justice, and benevolence, as proceeding from fear to injure, or dread of receiving injury, and little becoming the powerful and the bold. This seems a picture of all countries, where, with a competency of inhabitants, a regular and vigorous government is wanting. Five centuries ago, it would have suited England, France, and all western Europe. This turbulent state of things produced also nearly the same consequences in Greece, as since in western Europe. It is amid anarchy and desolation that great virtues, as well as great vices, have the strongest incentives to exertion, and the most frequent opportunities of becoming conspicuous.[83]

The most striking features in the Homeric manners are that licentiousness, and that hospitality, together with that union, at first view so strange to us, of the highest dignities with the meanest employments, which have prevailed in the East so remarkably through all the ages. These are, however, not the peculiar growth of any soil and climate. The two first are the seldom failing produce of defective government; and the other two will everywhere be found in an unimproved state of society.[84]

Having demolished the theory of the ancient Greek Arcadian government and climate, Mitford advances his own theory, strongly reminiscent of Goguet:

This extensive communication of the rights of hospitality was of powerful effect to humanize a savage people, to excite a relish for elegance in stile of living, and to make the more refined joys of society more eagerly sought, as well as more easily obtained. There was in Homer's time great difference in the possessions of individuals; some had large tracts of land with numerous herds and flocks; others had none. This state of things is generally favorable to the arts; a few, who have a superabundance of wealth, being better able, and generally more willing to encourage them than numbers who have only a competency. The communication of the rights of hospitality would also assist toward the preservation of property to those families which had once acquired it. A sort of association was thus formed, which in some degree supplied the want of a regular administration of law. . . . The wealthy . . . had houses built of freestone, spacious, and with many apartments on different floors.[85]

Thus Mitford, like Goguet and Winckelmann, uses the arts of ancient Greece as the symbol of a political philosophy which he wishes to express. This is, as we have seen, the method of the romantic hellenist.

[83] P. 39. [84] P. 109. [85] Pp. 116-117.

The aesthetic theories of Greek sculpture and fine arts which we have been tracing were, in the latter half of the eighteenth century applied also to poetry, particularly by the writers who discussed the idea of "Genius." Ever since the publication of Young's *Conjectures on Original Composition* in 1759, this idea had been the subject of philosophical investigation. In many of these discussions Greece is used as an illustration of such genius.[86] A typical example is *An Essay on Original Genius; and its various modes of exertion in Philosophy and the Fine Arts, Particularly in Poetry. By William Duff. London, 1767.* Duff (1732-1815) was a Scotch minister of the parishes of Glenbucket, Peterculter, and Foveran, Aberdeenshire. His discussion is divided into two books, the first entitled, "Of the Nature, Properties, and Indications of Genius; and of the various modes of Exertion";[87] the second, "Of that degree of Genius, which is properly denominated Original."[88] While Duff deals with all the fine arts, including painting, sculpture, and architecture, his thesis is "That original Poetic Genius will in general be displayed in its utmost vigour in the early and uncultivated periods of Society, which are peculiarly favorable to it. . . ."[89] As examples of this idea he cites the Greeks and Ossian:

Such a person [the poet in an early period of society] looks round him with wonder; every object is new to him, and has the power to affect him with surprise and pleasure; and as he is not familiarised by previous description to the scenes he contemplates, these strike upon his mind with their full force; and the Imagination, astonished and enraptured with the surveys of the Vast, the Wild, and the Beautiful in nature, conveyed through the medium of sense, spontaneously expresses its vivid ideas in bold and glowing metaphors, in sublime, animated and picturesque description. . . .

We may add, that the productions of the early ages, when they present to us scenes of nature and a state of life we are little acquainted with, and which are very different from those that now subsist, will to us appear original, though they may not be really such if the true originals are lost, of which the works that yet remain are only copies or imitations. Thus the comedies of Terence are valued, because the originals of Menander, which the Roman poet imitated, excepting a few fragments, are lost. Could the works of the latter be recovered, those of the former

[86] *Cf.* Wood's *Essay on the Original Genius and Writings of Homer, supra,* pp. 34ff.

[87] Pp. 1-84.

[88] Pp. 85-296.

[89] Book II, Section V.

would lose much of their reputation. Thus far the superiority of Poetic Genius in those early ages is accidental, and therefore no way meritorious. It is the effect of a particular situation. It is the consequence of antiquity.[90]

The chief reason for the flourishing of Genius in a primitive society, says Duff, is the repose and peace of such a state. Once again he cites the Greeks as an illustration:

Genius naturally shoots forth in the simplicity and tranquillity of uncultivated life. The undisturbed peace, and the innocent rural pleasures of this primeval state, are, if we may so express it, congenial to its nature. A Poet of true Genius delights to contemplate and describe those primitive scenes, which recall to our remembrance the fabulous era of the golden age. Happily exempted from that tormenting ambition, and those vexatious desires, which trouble the current of modern life, he wanders with a serene, contented heart, through walks and groves consecrated to the Muses; or, indulging a sublime, pensive, and sweetly-soothing melancholy, strays with a slow and solemn step, through the unfrequented desert, along the naked beach, or the bleak and barren heath. In such a situation, every theme is a source of inspiration, whether he describes the beauties of nature, which he surveys with transport; or the peaceful innocence of those happy times, which are so wonderfully soothing and pleasing to the imagination. His descriptions therefore will be perfectly vivid and original, because they are the transcript of his own feelings. Such a situation as that we have above represented, is particularly favourable to a pastoral Poet, and is very similar to that enjoyed by Theocritus, which no doubt had a happy influence on his compositions.[91]

Almost an echo of this idea appears in *An Essay on Genius. By Alexander Gerard, D.D. Professor of Divinity in King's College, Aberdeen. London, 1774.* Gerard (1728-1795) had in 1756 won a prize offered by the Edinburgh Society for the Encouragement of Arts, Sciences, Manufactures, and Agriculture for the best essay on taste. This was published in 1759. His investigation of taste later led him to consider the idea of original genius, which he, like Duff, finds best flourishing in primitive states, such as that of ancient Greece:

In Greece, the sciences made rapid progress, and reached a very high degree of improvement. If the Egyptians were the inventors, this proves them to be ingenious; but the Greeks shewed themselves to possess superiour genius, and are acknowledged to have possessed it, for greater

[90] Pp. 267-269. [91] Pp. 271-272.

invention was necessary for the perfection to which they rose. Arts and sciences have been known to the Chinese for many ages, held in the highest veneration, and studied with great ardor; yet they have not gone beyond the elements of most of them. This is an evidence that real genius is not frequent among them.[92]

It is very remarkable that all the fine arts have been cultivated, and even brought to perfection, before the rules of art were investigated or formed into a system: there is not a single instance of any art that has begun to be practised in consequence of rules being prescribed for it. The first performers could not have explained the several rules which the nature of their work made necessary; but their judgment was notwithstanding so exact and vigorous as to prevent their transgressing them. Their correctness is so wonderfully perfect, that critics discovered the rules which they prescribe, only by remarking those laws by which true genius, though uninstructed, had actually governed itself. Aristotle does not invent new rules of composition, but only points out those which Homer had formerly observed in the Epos, Sophocles in the Drama, and many of the Grecian orators in Eloquence. The same observation may be extended to painting, music, and every other art. The great geniuses who invented and improved them, have possessed the acutest judgment, which has faithfully attended them, and carefully guarded their steps in those distant and unfrequented regions which the boldness of their fancy led them to explore. . . .[93]

Perhaps the most interesting of the aesthetic theories of ancient Greek poetry, however, is the essay "On the Imitative Arts," first published as Essay II in *Poems by Sir William Jones, London, 1777*.[94] Jones (1746-1794), a brilliant oriental scholar, had spent ten years at Harrow, where he became a thorough classical scholar and learned French, Italian, Arabic, and Hebrew.[95] One of his amusements was to map out the neighborhood of Harrow into the states of Greece and to act out the events of history with his classical friend, Dr. Pars. In 1765, because of his brilliant reputation, he became tutor to Lord Althorp, the only son of the first Earl Spencer, for five years. This connection brought him the opportunity to travel and to extend his knowledge of

[92] P. 25. [93] P. 72.

[94] This is reprinted in Alexander Chalmers, *The Works of the English Poets from Chaucer to Cowper*, London, 1810, Vol. 18, pp. 508-511, from which my quotations are taken.

[95] A memoir of Jones by Lord Teignmouth appears in Vol. IX of *The Collected Works of Sir William Jones, edited by Lord Teignmouth and Lady Jones*, London, 1804.

languages. In 1770 he translated the biography of Nadir Shah from Persian[96] into French. In 1771 appeared the first edition of Jones' *Grammar of the Persian Language*. In 1772 he was made a member of the Royal Society; in 1773, of Johnson's Literary Club, where he became intimate with Burke and Gibbon. Later in life he became a lawyer and statesman. Between 1783 and 1794 he lived in India. Jones was also the first English scholar to master Sanskrit.

As a literary figure Jones is significant because of his interest in oriental poetry and mythology, attested by "On the Gods of Greece, Italy, and India," 1785, one of the eleven anniversary discourses which he delivered to the Bengal Asiatic Society.[97] The essay which we are considering was written to stimulate appreciation of "Eastern verse," by justifying its beauties aesthetically. The thesis of the essay is that the greatest effect of poetry and music is produced not by imitation but by a different principle, "which must be sought for in the deepest recesses of the human mind."[98] Poetry, he says, is no more than the musical expression of primitive passions, not imitation, as is demonstrated by Greek lyrics:

> Now let us conceive that some vehement passion is expressed in strong words, exactly measured, and pronounced, in a common voice, in just cadence, and with proper accents, such an expression of the passion will be genuine poetry; and the famous ode of Sappho is allowed to be so in the strictest sense; but if the same ode, with all its natural accents, were expressed in a musical voice . . . if it were sung in due time and measure, in a simple and pleasing tune, that added force to the words without stifling them, it would then be pure and original music, not merely soothing to the ear, but affecting to the heart; not an imitation of nature, but the voice of nature itself.[99]
>
> We may define original and native poetry to be the language of the violent passions, expressed in exact measure, with strong accents and significant words; and true music to be no more than poetry, delivered in a succession of harmonious sounds, so disposed as to please the ear. It is in this view only that we must consider the music of the ancient Greeks, or attempt to account for its amazing effects . . .; it was wholly passionate or descriptive, and so closely united to poetry, that it never

[96] This had been brought to England in 1768 by Christian VII of Denmark.

[97] Jones had founded this society in January, 1784.

[98] Chalmers, *op. cit.*, Vol. 18, p. 508.

[99] *Ibid.*, p. 509.

obstructed, but always increased its influence; whereas our boasted harmony, with all its fine accords, and numerous parts, paints nothing, expresses nothing, says nothing to the heart, and consequently can only give more or less pleasure to one of our senses; and no reasonable man will seriously prefer a transitory pleasure, which must soon end in satiety, or even in disgust, to a delight of the soul, arising from sympathy, and founded on the natural passions, always lively, always interesting, always transporting.[100]

The lyric verses of Alcaeus, Alcman, and Ibycus, the hymns of Callimachus, the elegy of Moschus on the death of Bion, are all beautiful pieces of poetry; yet Alcaeus was no imitator of love, Callimachus was no imitator of religious awe, and admiration, Moschus was no imitator of grief at the loss of an amiable friend. . . .

What has been said of poetry, may with equal force be applied to music, which is poetry, dressed to advantage; and even to painting, many sorts of which are poems to the eye, as all poems, merely descriptive, are pictures to the ear; and this way of considering them will set the refinements of modern artists in their true light; for the passions, which were given by nature, never spoke in an unnatural form, and no man, truly affected with love or grief, ever expressed the one in an acrostic, or the other in a fugue. . . .

Thus will each artist gain his end, not by imitating the works of nature, but by assuming her power, and causing the same effect upon the imagination, which her charms produce to the senses: this must be the chief object of a poet, a musician, and a painter, who know that great effects are not produced by minute details, but by the general spirit of the whole piece, and that a gaudy composition may strike the mind for a short time, but that the beauties of simplicity are both more delightful, and more permanent.[101]

Observe once more how Jones, like the other aestheticians whom we have considered, is here using Greek art and culture to bolster a romantic notion.

Thus, by 1786 there had appeared the beginnings of a body of hellenized aesthetics in which ancient Greece was made to be the symbol of primitivism, genius, liberty, and equality, as well as their opposites. These writings strengthened the vogue of the idealization and sentimentalization of ancient Greece as an Arcadia, where life was sublime because it was free and kind. They strengthened, too, the tendency of romantic hellenism to read into the remains of ancient Greece that which was not necessarily there.

[100] *Ibid.*, p. 510. [101] Pp. 510-511.

# V

## ROMANTIC HELLENISM IN ENGLISH POETRY 1735-1786

A study of English poetry that appeared between 1735 and 1786 reveals romantic hellenic strains in the verse of many major, as well as minor, authors. As might be expected, of course, the bulk of such verse was written by poets who have long been cited, in other connections, as "precursors of the romantic movement." Such are Thomson, Gray, Collins, Mason, and the Wartons. But even among poets who have not before been so designated, one can find definite signs of a sentimental attitude toward the ruins and the lost culture of the ancient Greeks which is used by them to produce a poetic mood. Such are Whitehead, Glover, Akenside, and Mickle.

Analysis of this poetry reveals, moreover, the same elements which appear in the hellenic poems of Byron, Shelley, and Keats, elements which we have observed to be the outgrowth of the development of Greek archaeology, travel to Greece, and Greek-inspired aesthetics. There is to be found in this poetry, for example, the conception of ancient Greece as a primitive and blissful Arcadia to which the poets long to return. Again, Greece is used in many of the poems for the purpose of lending color to the action or atmosphere to the mood. More frequently, Greece becomes the symbol of liberty and repose, and the poets use hellenic material to express some political or social theory or simply to launch a protest against tyranny.

Before proceeding to such an analysis, however, it should be noted that there is not necessarily a cause and effect relationship between this poetry and the development of hellenic archaeology, travel, and aesthetics. Unquestionably much of the poetry which we are about to examine was stimulated by the ideas arising from the growth of interest in things Greek. It would be difficult to demonstrate, however, that in every case the poet wrote what he did because of some specific fruit born of the work of antiquarians, travellers, and aestheticians. It is more probable, indeed, that the poetry, like the literature of Greek archaeology, travel, and aesthetics, is a reflection of the current of ideas present in the age. In all four of these reflections, acting and interacting upon each other, is to be found the rise of romantic hellenism in eighteenth century England.

The earliest instance of romantic hellenism in English poetry during the period which we are considering is to be found in the work of James Thomson (1700-1748), whose *The Seasons* has long been studied as an early manifestation of romantic naturalism. Thomson possessed a poetic sensibility not very common in his time, and in his work is to be found clear evidence of a propensity toward the subjectivism so common in the nineteenth century romantic movement.[1] In the autumn of 1730 Thomson had been appointed travelling tutor and companion to Charles Richard Talbot, the son of the future chancellor. This appointment, of course, enabled him to travel extensively on the continent and to react poetically to new stimuli. In December, 1730, he was at Paris, where he saw Voltaire's Brutus declaiming on liberty to a French audience. In November, 1731, he was in Rome, where he beheld the ruins of antiquity. The contrast between the declamation and the ruins, on the one hand, and the state of affairs in modern France and Rome as he observed it, apparently stimulated Thomson's sensibility. The more he saw of foreign countries, the more the patriotic poet was convinced that true liberty was to be found only in England.

The fruit of these travels appeared in print, after the young Talbot had died in 1733, in the didactic poem, *Liberty,* dedicated to Frederick, Prince of Wales. The poem is an "attempt to trace Liberty, from the first ages down to her excellent establishment in Great Britain,"[2] for the patriotic purpose of demonstrating what Thomson learned during his travels. It is divided into five parts, the first three in about 500 lines each, the last two more

[1] See Léon Morel, *James Thomson, Sa Vie et Ses Oevres,* Paris, 1895.
[2] Dedication in *Liberty, a Poem,* London, Millar, 1735, p. 1.

than twice as long. The poem as a whole is cast in the form of a vision that comes to the poet, in which the Goddess of Liberty speaks. The first part, which appeared in 1734, bears the title, "Ancient and Modern Italy Compared." In it the Goddess of Liberty contrasts the magnificence and glory of ancient Italy, particularly republican Rome, with the desolation and ruin of modern times, touching upon sculpture, architecture, painting, and poetry. In Part II, published together with Part III in 1735 and entitled, "Greece," the Goddess traces the origin of Liberty "from the pastoral ages" to its establishment in ancient Greece. In Part III she continues her history in ancient Rome. In Parts IV and V, published together in 1736, the Goddess brings Liberty to Britain and concludes with a long and blissful "Prospect" of the future development of England under her guidance.

Written in Miltonic blank verse, rather stilted and rhetorical, the poem was not very popular despite its patriotic fervor. The second book of the poem, however, has for us a distinct historical value, for in it may be found definite strains of romantic hellenism. After the Goddess has traced her early life in the "woods and tents and cottages of eastern swains," for example, she describes her arrival in Greece with an enthusiastic and sentimental apostrophe which was to be echoed and reechoed by succeeding poets:

> Hail, Nature's utmost boast! unrivalled Greece!
> My fairest reign! where every power benign
> Conspired to blow the flower of human kind,
> And lavished all that genius can inspire.
> Clear sunny climates, by the breezy main,
> Ionian or Aegean, tempered kind;
> Light, airy soils; a country rich, and gay;
> Broke into hills with balmy odors crowned,
> And, bright with purple harvest, joyous vales;
> Mountains, and streams, where verse spontaneous flowed;
> Whence deemed by wondering men the seat of gods,
> And still the mountains and the streams of song.
> All that boon Nature could luxuriant pour
> Of high materials, and my restless Arts
> Frame into finished life.
>
> . . . . . . . .

> Thrice happy land!
> Had not neglected art, with weedy vice
> Confounded, sunk.[3]

Here is an instance of the romantic view of ancient Greece as an Arcadian paradise, where life was easy, free, blissful, and where the sun always shone upon scenes of joy and happiness. The poet is here giving vent to emotions which arise from his longing for such a land. Because he really knows little of ancient Greece factually, he envelops it with a sentimentalized attractiveness, the source of which is within himself. Greece has become, in his hands, a symbol of a spirit and an emotion much broader than the culture which he is describing. In this sense his description is romantic.

This tendency by Thomson to read into ancient Greece what he believes ought to have existed there, is seen even more clearly as he warms to his subject. Thus, after discussing the patience and valor of Sparta, he comes to this rapturous description of Athens:

> Where, with bright marbles big and future pomp,
> Hymettus spread, amid the scented sky,
> His thymy treasures to the labouring bee,
> And to botanic hand the stores of health;
> Wrapt in a soul-attenuating clime,
> Between Ilissus and Cephissus glowed
> This hive of science, shedding sweets divine,
> Of active arts, and animated arms.
> There, passionate for me, an easy-moved,
> A quick, refined, a delicate, humane,
> Enlightened people reigned.[4]

Here, again, is a clear instance of the emotional idealization of Greek antiquity which we have called romantic hellenism.

This Arcadian view of ancient Greece in Thomson is brought about by his use of Greek culture as a symbol of Liberty and its blessings. To this theme, in itself a romantic strain, Thomson constantly reverts:

> Then stood untouched the solid base
> Of Liberty, the liberty of mind;

[3] Part II, ll. 86ff. [4] *Ibid.*, ll. 138ff.

For systems, yet, and soul-enslaving creeds,
Slept with the monsters of succeeding times.
From priestly darkness sprung the enlightening arts
Of fire, and sword, and rage and horrid names.
O Greece! thou sapient nurse of finer arts!
Which to bright science blooming fancy bore;
Be this thy praise, that thou, and thou alone,
In these hast led the way, in these excelled,
Crowned with the laurel of assenting Time.
In thy full language, speaking mighty things;
Like a clear torrent close, or else diffused
A broad majestic stream, and rolling on
Through all the winding harmony of sound:
In it the power of eloquence, at large,
Breathed the persuasive or pathetic soul,
Stilled by degrees the democratic storm,
Or bad it threatening rise, and tyrants shook. . . .[5]

All the beauties and glories and wonders of Greece, then, were the result of Liberty's sojourn in the land. But when all these have been described and eulogized, Thomson sees her ruins and, like succeeding romantic hellenists, he mourns for her loss:

"Where are they now?" I cried, "say, goddess, where?
And what the land, thy darling thus of old?"
"Sunk!" she resumed, "deep in the kindred gloom
Of Superstition, and of Slavery, sunk!
No glory now can touch their hearts, benumbed
By loose dejected sloth and servile fear;
No science pierce the darkness of their minds;
No nobler art the quick ambitious soul
Of imitation in their breast awake.
E'en to supply the needful arts of life,
Mechanic toil denies the hopeless hand.
Scarce any trace remaining, vestige gray,
Or nodding column, on the desert shore,
To point where Corinth, or where Athens stood.
A faithless land of violence, and death!
Where commerce parleys, dubious, on the shore;
And his wild impulse curious search restrains,
Afraid to trust the inhospitable clime.
Neglected nature fails; in the sordid want

[5] *Ibid.*, ll. 247ff.

> Sunk, and debased, their beauty beams no more.
> The sun himself seems, angry, to regard,
> Of light unworthy, the degenerate race;
> And fires them oft with pestilential rays;
> While earth, blue poison steaming on the skies,
> Indignant, shakes them from her troubled sides.
> But as from man to man, Fate's first decree,
> Impartial Death the tide of riches rolls,
> So states must die, and liberty go round."[6]

Observe how in this passage, again like succeeding romantic hellenists, Thomson identifies ancient with modern Greece, the "primitive Arcadians" with the modern "degenerate race." It is clear that the poet is indulging in a sentimental reverie which partakes of the very essence of romanticism:

> Not so the times when, emulation-stung,
> Greece shone in genius, science and in arts.
> . . . . . . . .
> To live was glory then![7]

Such is the view of ancient Greece to Thomson beholding her ruins. The glory of her life, however, exists only in his own longing for an escape from the present. This is precisely the mood of Byron sighing for the isles of Greece and of Keats seeking poor Pan.

Two years after the publication of the second part of Thomson's *Liberty*, there appeared a work by Richard Glover (1712-1785) in which may be observed a similar, if not quite so clear, use of Greece as a poetic symbol of liberty. Glover, a merchant by calling, was fond of poetry and, according to Dr. Warton, "one of the best and most accurate Greek scholars of his time."[8] In 1737 he published his long epic, *Leonidas,* in form a narrative of ancient Greece, but in fact a poetical manifesto in the interests of Walpole's antagonists. More political than poetical, it achieved

[6] *Ibid.,* ll. 394ff.
[7] Part V, ll. 275ff.
[8] An account of the life of Glover by Isaac Reed appeared in the *European Magazine* for January, 1786. The facts in this account are reprinted in the life prefixed to the poetical works of Glover in Alexander Chalmers, *The Works of the English Poets, from Chaucer to Cowper,* London, 1810, Vol. 17, pp. 3-12, from which the above statement is taken. Warton made the statement in his *Essay on the Genius and Writings of Pope.*

great popularity, going through four editions before it was enlarged from nine books to twelve in 1770, and then was printed in two more editions, one in 1798, another in 1804. In 1738 it was translated into French; in 1766, into German.[9] The nature of its appeal to a contemporary reading public is made clear by the praise which it evoked from Lord Lyttleton, in the periodical, *Common Sense:*

> The whole plan and purpose of it is to show the superiority of freedom over slavery; and how much virtue, public spirit, and the love of liberty are preferable both in their nature and effects, to riches, luxury, and the insolence of power.[10]

The story of *Leonidas* is sufficiently simple to have permitted Glover to spend most of his effort on long, bombastic speeches in Miltonic blank verse, full of sentimental idealizations of Greek heroism and devotion to liberty. The events in the poem take place in the fifth century B.C., during the war between Greece and Persia. Xerxes, king of Persia, has been led to make war on Greece by his insatiable desire to vanquish it completely. In this emergency, delegates from the various Greek states meet at Corinth to decide on a mode of defense. While they are deliberating, however, they learn that Xerxes, with a huge army, has passed into Thrace. All eyes now turn to Sparta, the most militaristic of the states, for decisive action in this emergency. But in Sparta there is some dissention. Leutychides, one of the two kings who rule the Spartan state, urges his countrymen not to advance in their war beyond the Isthmus of Corinth. But Leonidas, their other king, realizing that such action would be the equivalent of sacrificing the Lacedemonians to Xerxes, urges that they fight fearlessly and aggressively, without regard to borders. In the meantime a messenger arrives with a report from the Oracle at Delphi, who had been consulted in this crisis. The Oracle has said

[9] Although it appeared too late to fall within the limits of this study, Glover's *Athenaid,* the long epic in thirty books which was published posthumously in 1787 by Glover's daughter, Mrs. Halsey, is further evidence of the continued popularity of the theme. The *Athenaid* is a sequel to *Leonidas,* dealing with the continuation of the war between the Greeks and Xerxes until the final emancipation of their country from his invasions.

[10] Quoted in Alexander Chalmers, *op. cit.,* p. 4.

that one king must lose his life for the safety of the commonwealth. Leonidas immediately volunteers for the role, an army of three hundred Spartans is appointed to accompany him, and after a brave parting from his queen, Leonidas sets out to meet the enemy.

On the way, Leonidas is joined by other generals, with armies from other Greek states, and together they proceed to Thermopylae, where they expect to meet Xerxes. Hundreds of lines of blank verse are devoted by Glover to building up the remarkable heroism and valor of the Spartan king. By his actions, which are described in much detail, by his speech, which is elaborately set down, and by the words of generals, heroes, and enemies of Greece, he is made to appear not only an epic hero, but almost a symbol of the greatness and nobility which Glover attributes to ancient Greece. The enemy tries in vain to intimidate Leonidas and his armies through spies and messengers. The magnificent camp of Xerxes and the tremendous power of his armies are carefully drawn as a contrast to the humbler and smaller power of Leonidas, but only for the purpose of accentuating the victory of the Greeks, in spite of such odds, because of their indomitable love of freedom. Six of the twelve books of the poem are devoted to the depiction of the bravery of the Greeks, especially the Arcadians, in battle. At the end they win the battle after a tempestuous destruction of Xerxes' camp. But Leonidas, worn out by his efforts, dies gloriously, fulfilling the decree of the Oracle. Forever after he is known as "the last of the Grecian commanders."

In his preface to the epic, Glover cites such historians as Herodotus, who was almost contemporary with the events of the poem, Plutarch, and Pausanias, as his sources. While the poem is based on history, however, it is obvious that Glover was attracted to the story because to him it was a symbol of a valor and a love of liberty peculiarly Greek. For this reason he handles the characters and events very freely and imaginatively, coloring, accentuating, and frequently exaggerating them in order to stress what might be termed his thesis:

. . . The fall of Leonidas and his brave companions; so meritorious to their country, and so glorious to themselves, hath attained such a high degree of veneration and applause from past ages that few among the ancient compilers of history have been silent on this amazing instance of magnanimity and zeal for liberty."[11]

That Glover, indeed, was himself aware of his idealization is shown by the painstaking effort which he makes in his preface "to vindicate the subject from the censure of improbability, and to show by the concurring evidence of the best historians, that such distinterested public virtue did once exist. . . ."[12]

It is because of this sentimental idealization of ancient Greece and its zeal for liberty that *Leonidas* may be considered one of the early poems exhibiting romantic hellenism. Such a spirit is observable on almost every page of the epic. Notice, for example, the romantic halo which he places around Greece when, in Book IV, he makes the exiled Spartan king, Demaratus, speak these words to Xerxes:

> Prince, the difference learn
> Between thy warriors and the sons of Greece.
> The flower, the safeguard of thy numerous camp
> Are mercenaries.
>
> . . . . . . . . .
>
> Their watchful eyes
> Observe not how the flocks and heifers feed.
> To them, of wealth, of all possessions void,
> The name of country with an empty sound
> Flies o'er the ear, nor warms their joyless hearts,
> Who share no country . . . with limbs
> Enervated and soft, with minds corrupt,
> From misery, debauchery, and sloth;
> Are these to battle drawn against a foe
> Train'd in gymnastic exercise and arms,
> Inured to hardship, and the child of toil.
> Wont through the freezing shower, the wintry storm,
> O'er his own glebe the tardy ox to goad,
> Or in the sun's impetuous heat to glow
> Beneath the burden of his yellow sheaves;
> Whence on himself, on her whose faithful arms
> Infold him joyful, on a growing race
> Which glad his dwelling, plenty he bestows
> With independence. When to battle call'd,

[11] Preface to *Leonidas, ibid.*, p. 24.

[12] *Ibid.*, p. 22.

For them, his dearest comfort and his care,
And for the harvest promised to his toil,
He lifts the shield, nor shuns unequal force.
Such are the troops of every state in Greece.[13]

Again, when in Book I Leonidas has delivered his brave speech, an old Spartan speaks thus to him:

Thy bright example every heart unites.
From thee her happiest omens Greece derives
Of concord, safety, liberty, and fame.
Go then, O first of mortals! go, impress
Amaze and terror on the barbarous host;
The freeborn Greeks instructing life to deem
Less dear than honour and their country's cause.[14]

This is the spirit of the poetry that surrounds a group of brave, romantic heroic Greeks.

An interesting illustration of the early development of romantic hellenism is to be found in a poem much different from those of Thomson and Glover. This is *The Ruins of Rome,* by John Dyer (1700-1758), which was published in 1740. The poem exhibits the characteristics which we have observed before, yet in Dyer the ideas and emotions expressed are not associated exclusively with Greece, but with all antiquity. The melancholy lyricism of the poetry, though in this work it is not yet isolated from other lost civilizations and made peculiarly Greek, is, nevertheless, the same as later poetry, which has been influenced by Greek archaeology, travel, and æsthetics. It would not be precise to say that *The Ruins of Rome* is a lament over the remains of ancient Rome alone. As a matter of fact, the "moral" which Dyer draws in the last thirteen lines of the poem shows clearly that he is thinking not merely of Rome, but of the ruins which he is beholding as the symbol of the decay of all antiquity:

Vain end of human strength, of human skill,
Conquest, and triumph, and domain, and pomp,
And ease, and luxury! O Luxury,
Bane of elated life, of affluent states,
What dreary change, what ruin is not thine?

. . . . . . . . . . .

[13] *Ibid.*, p. 43.

[14] *Ibid.*, p. 28.

Behind thee gapes
Th' unfathomable gulf where Asher lies
O'erwhelm'd, forgotten; and high-boasting Cham;
And Elam's haughty pomp; and beauteous Greece;
And the great queen of earth, imperial Rome.[15]

It is, then, possible to trace in Dyer's poem early manifestations of romantic hellenism, if we bear in mind that the influences which were to bend this mood toward Greece exclusively had not yet begun to function.

Dyer, educated at Westminster, had studied art under Jonathan Richardson.[16] After a period of years during which he rambled as an itinerant artist through South Wales and its vicinity, he published, in 1727, the little nature poem, *Grongar Hill,* in which his art training produced notably concrete observations of natural scenery. It was this interest in art which led Dyer to visit Italy between 1727 and 1740 for the purpose of studying painting. *The Ruins of Rome,* the fruit of this sojourn in Italy, is, like *Grongar Hill,* realistically descriptive. What is most notable in the six hundred odd lines of Miltonic blank verse, however, is the tendency shown by Dyer to use the ruins of antiquity to produce melancholy moods and romantically colored verse. He climbs the hills of Rome and looks with much melancholy upon the ruins. These he describes and then, recalling their former state, mourns and meditates. The Palatine Hill, the Capitol, the Temple of Concord, the Campus Martius, the Baths of Caracella, the Temple of Romulus and Remus—all arouse in the poet a grief and a loneliness which must have been very pleasurable to him, just as similar grief and loneliness gave pleasure to the romantic poets of the nineteenth century. Observe, for instance, how in the following passage Dyer finds the ruins of antiquity an inspiration for a poetic mood:

Fall'n, fall'n, a silent heap; her heroes all
Sunk in their urns; behold the pride of pomp,
The throne of nations fall'n; obscur'd in dust;

[15] Alexander Chalmers, *op. cit.,* Vol. 13, p. 228.

[16] See Samuel Johnson's account of Dyer in *Lives of the Poets* reprinted in the collection of Dyer's poetical works in Chalmers, *op. cit.,* Vol. 13. *Cf.* the introduction in Edward Thomas, *The Poems of John Dyer,* London, 1903.

E'en yet majestical: the solemn scene
Elates the soul, while now the rising sun
Flames on the ruins in the purer air
Towering aloft, upon the glittering plain,
Like broken rocks, a vast circumference:
Rent palaces, crush'd columns, rifled moles,
Fanes roll'd on fanes, and tombs on buried tombs.
Deep lies in dust the Theban obelisk
Immense along the waste.

. . . . . . . . .

The pilgrim oft
At dead of night, 'mid his oraison hears
Aghast the voice of Time, disparting towers,
Tumbling all precipitate down-dash'd,
Rattling around, loud thundering to the Moon;
While murmurs soothe each awful interval
Of ever-falling waters.

. . . . . . . . .

Deep empty tombs,
And dells, and mouldering shrines, with old decay
Rustic and green, and wide-embowering shades,
Shot from the crooked clefts of nodding towers.
O solemn wilderness! with errour sweet,
I wind the lingering step, where'er the path
Mazy conducts me, which the vulgar foot
O'er sculptures maim'd has made; Anubis, Sphinx,
Idols of antique guise, and horned Pan
Terrific, monstrous shapes! . . .[17]

This mood is painted by Dyer with even greater clarity further on, when he has almost completed his survey of the ruins:

There is a mood,
(I sing not to the vacant and the young)
There is a kindly mood of melancholy,
That wings the soul and points her to the skies;
When tribulation clothes the child of man,
When age descends with sorrow to the grave,
'Tis sweetly-soothing sympathy to pain,
A gently-wakening call to health and ease.
How musical! when all-devouring Time,

[17] Chalmers, *op. cit.*, Vol. 13, p. 226.

Here sitting on his throne of ruins hoar,
While winds and tempests sweep his various lyre,
How sweet thy diapason, Melancholy!
Cool evening comes; the setting Sun displays
His visible great round between yon towers,
As through two shady cliffs. . . .[18]

Here is the authentic mood of the romantic hellenist who finds in the ruins of antiquity an escape from a burdensome reality.

One other characteristic in Dyer's poem which later merges with romantic hellenism should be pointed out before we leave it. Like Thomson and Glover, Dyer finds in the ruins before him a symbol of liberty and repose:

See the tall obelisks from Memphis old,
One stone enormous each, or Thebes convey'd;
. . . . . . . . .
O Liberty,
Parent of Happiness, celestial-born;
When the first man became a living soul,
His sacred genius thou;—be Britain's care;
With her, secure, prolong thy lov'd retreat;
Thence bless mankind. . . .[19]

It is obvious that *The Ruins of Rome* shows almost all the qualities which we have been tracing.

The record of Dyer's romantic experience with the ruins of antiquity may be seen also in his well-known didactic poem, *The Fleece,* which was published in 1757. This is a blank verse poem in four books dealing with the history, growth, manufacture, and sale of wool. In the first two books Dyer touches on the development of sheep-raising in early times. In discussing the contrast between the present state of sheep-raising in Britain and that in other countries long ago, he indulges in this romantic idealization of ancient Greece:

See the swift furies, Famine, Plague and War,
In frequent thunders rage o'er neighboring realms,
And spread their plains with desolation wide:
Yet your mild homesteads, ever-blooming, smile

[18] *Ibid.*, p. 227.
[19] *Ibid.*

Among embracing woods; and waft on high
The breath of plenty, from the ruddy tops
Of chimneys, curling o'er the gloomy trees,
In airy azure ringlets, to the sky.
Nor ye by need are urg'd, as Attic swains,
And Tarentine, with skins to clothe your sheep;
Expensive toil; howe'er expedient found
In fervid climates, while from Phoebus' beams
They fled to rugged woods and tangling brakes.
But those expensive toils are now no more,
Proud tyrrany [*sic*] devours their flocks and herds:
Nor bleat of sheep may now, nor sound of pipe,
Sooth the sad plains of once sweet Arcady,
The shepherd's kingdom: dreary solitude
Spreads o'er Hymettus, and the shaggy vale
Of Athens, which, in solemn silence, sheds
Her venerable ruins to the dust.[20]

Observe how here again ancient Greece has become a blissful Arcadia, where life was peaceful and sweet. It is for this same idealized state that the poet yearns when he observes in a melancholy vein:

Lo the revolving course of mighty Time,
Who loftiness abases, tumbles down
Olympus' brow, and lifts the lowly vale.
Where is the majesty of ancient Rome,
The throng of heroes in her splendid streets,
The snowy vest of peace, or purple robe,
Slow trail'd triumphal? Where the Attic fleece,
And Tarentine, in warmest litter'd cotes,
Or sunny meadows, cloth'd with costly care?
All in the solitude of ruin lost,
War's horrid carnage, vain Ambition's dust.[21]

The qualities observed in the work of Dyer stimulated by antiquity in general arise from an interest in Greek antiquity alone in the poetry of Mark Akenside (1721-1770). This precocious physician had, as early as 1737, when he was only sixteen years old,[22] displayed romantic talents in "The Virtuoso," a poem

[20] Book I, *ibid.*, p. 233.
[21] Book II, *ibid.*, p. 237.
[22] See the memoir of Akenside by the Rev. A. Dyce reprinted in *The Poetical Works of Akenside and Beattie,* Riverside edition, Boston, 1864.

of ten stanzas in imitation of Spenser, which was printed in the *Gentleman's Magazine*. In the following year he began the work for which he is chiefly remembered, *The Pleasures of Imagination*. It was during a visit to Morpeth, he says, within hearing of "the mossy falls of solitary Wensbeck's limpid stream,"[23] that the plan of this long poem originally came to him. Most of the poem was written at Newcastle-on-Tyne in the five years between 1738 and 1743. In the latter year Akenside came to London and offered the poem to Dodsley for 120 pounds. According to Dyce,[24] Pope advised Dodsley to accept the offer, for "this is no everyday writer." The poem was accordingly published by Dodsley in 1744 without the author's name and was well received. A second edition followed in four months, with Akenside's name on the title page. In 1757, because of the favorable reception of his work, Akenside began a revision of the poem which he did not live to complete. The revised version is considerably longer, but not better, than the original, despite Akenside's preoccupation with it for the rest of his life.[25]

The reasons for the popularity of the poem are not difficult to find. *The Pleasures of Imagination,* in its original form, is a conventional eighteenth century didactic poem of about two thousand lines of blank verse in three books. Essentially it is the expression of an attractive prescription by a physician to those who seek fuller happiness in life. The prescription is the simple one of greater indulgence in the wholesome recreation afforded by art, both natural and imitative. This idea is expounded with all the erudition of conventional rationalism, but, at the same time, it is a poetic rationalization of the enjoyment of "enthusiasm" by the very means employed by the neo-classicists. The poem, then, is a timely one, capable of pleasing a variety of tastes and appealing to people of different types.

It is well-known that the philosophical ideas in Akenside's *Pleasures of Imagination* are, for the most part, versified versions

[23] *Ibid.*, p. 124.
[24] *Ibid.*, p. 88.
[25] The dates of composition of the revised portions of the poem are: Book I, 1757; Book II, 1765; Book III, 1770; a fragment of a projected Book IV, 1770.

of the ethical doctrines of Shaftesbury.[26] Shaftesbury's ethical theory revolves about the central idea that the laws of beauty are most fully exemplified not in material objects, but in the spiritual condition of the soul; that is, in the harmony and proportion which regulate man's impulses and keep his passions in equilibrium:

> Harmony is harmony by nature, let men judge ever so ridiculously of music. So is symmetry and proportion founded still in nature, let men's fancy prove ever so barbarous . . . in their architecture, sculpture. . . . 'Tis the same case where life and manners are concerned. Virtue has the same fixed standard. The same numbers, harmony, and proportion will have place in morals, and are discoverable in the characters and affections of mankind; in which are laid the just foundations of an art and science superior to every other of human practice and comprehension.[27]

It is this basic idea that Akenside has in mind when, in explaining the purpose of his poem in the preface to the original version, he says:

> The design of the following poem is to give a view of these [pleasures of imagination], in the largest acceptation of the term; so that whatever our imagination feels from the agreeable appearances of nature, and all the various entertainment we meet with either in poetry, painting, music, or any of the elegant arts, might be deducible from one or other of these principles in the constitution of the human mind which are here established and explained.[28]

Following Addison's analysis,[29] Akenside then reduces the "original forms or properties of being about which the Imagination is conversant" to three: greatness, novelty, and beauty. The

[26] See, for instance, B. Sprague Allen, *op. cit.*, Vol. I, p. 88: "Of the poets who took their cue from Shaftesbury, Akenside is a heavy borrower. The measure of his indebtedness is plain to anyone who has the fortitude to grapple with the *Pleasures of Imagination*, a long poem chiefly distinguished for the absence of the faculty that it eulogizes."

[27] *Characteristics of Men, Manners, Opinions, Times*, 1710. *Soliloquy, or Advice to an Author*, Part III, Section III. *Cf. Miscellaneous Reflections*, 1714, Miscellany III, Chapter II: "Who can admire the outward beauties, and not recur instantly to the inward, which are the most real and essential, the most naturally affecting, and of the highest pleasure, as well as profit and advantage?"

[28] *Poetical Works, op. cit.*, p. 116.

[29] See *Spectator*, Nos. 409 (Thursday, June 19, 1712) and 411 (Saturday, June 21, 1712).

poem is then concerned with a versified explanation, analysis, and illustration of these qualities and of the pleasures to which they give rise.[30] The first book deals with the origin of those intellectual qualities which combine to form the imagination. The enjoyment of the imagination is shown to be caused by the exercise of these qualities in perception and invention. Different degrees of beauty, such as color and shape, are evolved by them in the conduct of life and the study of nature. Thus, different degrees of beauty are present in vegetables, animals, and the mind. The presence of mind produces the highest degree of beauty, for the imagination is intimately associated with the moral faculty. This is best observed in the culture of ancient Greece. In the second book philosophy is shown to have been gradually distinguished from imagination after the Greeks, to the detriment of beauty. There follows an enumeration of the accidental pleasures which enhance the imagination, and the action of the passions upon the imagination is described in a long allegorical vision. The third book discourses on the pleasures arising from the observation of the manners of mankind, such as ridicule. It then inquires into the origin of vice and describes the action of the mind when engaged in producing works of imagination. The pleasures of imitation are shown to be secondary, while the pleasures arising from objects which excite them are primary and an indication of the benevolent order of the world. The poem concludes with a discussion of the nature of Taste and an enumeration of the natural

[30] It is interesting to observe that 13 years later, in 1757, Akenside shows greater influence by the growing forces of the romantic movement. In his preface to the revised version of Book I (*Works,* pp. 200ff.), his ideas are expressed with greater clarity and simplicity. Notice also how his aim now is not merely to rationalize the appreciation of beauty, but to form a romantic taste: "The pleasures of the imagination proceed either from natural objects, as from a flourishing grove, a clear and murmuring fountain, a calm sea by moonlight; or from works of art, such as a noble edifice, a musical tune, a statue, a picture, a poem. In treating of these pleasures, we must begin with the former class, they being original to the other; and nothing more being necessary, in order to explain them, than a view of our natural inclination toward greatness and beauty, and of those appearances, in the world around us, to which that inclination is adapted. . . . There are certain particular men, whose imagination is endowed with powers, and susceptible of pleasures, which the generality of mankind never participate. These are the men of genius, destined by nature to excel in one or other of the arts already mentioned. It is proposed . . . to delineate that genius which in some degree appears common to them all. . . ."

and moral advantages resulting from a well-formed imagination.

It is obvious from Book I that Akenside looks upon ancient Greece as the symbol of the highest beauty, and for this reason the poem is studded with hellenic references. The romantic use made by Akenside of this Greek material is the most striking quality of *The Pleasures of Imagination* for this study. Thus, at the end of Book I, after the poet has described the highest type of beauty, comes this striking apostrophe:

> Genius of ancient Greece! whose faithful steps
> Well pleas'd I follow through the sacred paths
> Of Nature and of Science; nurse divine
> Of all heroic deeds and fair desires!
> O! let the breath of thy extended praise
> Inspire my kindling bosom to the height
> Of this untempted theme. Nor be my thoughts
> Presumptuous counted, if, amid the calm
> That soothes this vernal evening into smiles,
> I steal impatient from the sordid haunts
> Of Strife and low Ambition, to attend
> Thy sacred presence in the sylvan shade,
> By their malignant footsteps ne'er profan'd.
> Descend propitious! to my favour'd eye;
> Such in thy mien, thy warm, exalted air,
> As when the Persian tyrant, foil'd and stung
> With shame and desperation, gnash'd his teeth
> To see thee rend the pageants of his throne;
> And at the lightning of thy lifted spear
> Crouch'd like a slave. Bring all thy martial spoils,
> Thy palms, thy laurels, thy triumphal songs,
> Thy smiling band of art, thy godlike sires
> Of civil wisdom, thy heroic youth
> Warm from the schools of glory. Guide my way
> Through fair Lyceum's walk, the green retreats
> Of Academus, and the thymy vale,
> Where oft enchanted with Socratic sounds,
> Ilissus pure devolv'd his tuneful stream
> In gentler murmurs. From the blooming store
> Of these auspicious fields, may I unblamed
> Transplant some living blossoms to adorn
> My native clime: while, far above the flight
> Of Fancy's plume aspiring, I unlock
> The springs of ancient wisdom; while I join

> Thy name, thrice honour'd! with the immortal praise
> Of Nature; while to my compatriot youth
> I point the high example of thy sons,
> And tune to Attic themes the British lyre.[31]

Here are the essential characteristics of romantic hellenism: the yearning for a happy, Arcadian Greece, where living was simple, beautiful, calm, and unsophisticated; the idealization of an antique culture by making it the symbol of the poet's own aspirations; the attempt to couple ancient Greece with modern England; the mingling of hellenic elements with "evening" and "sylvan shade."

A similar instance of romantic hellenism occurs when the poet is describing the pleasures arising from beautiful poetry:

> Or wilt thou rather stoop thy vagrant plume,
> Where, gliding thro' his daughter's honour'd shades
> The smooth Peneus from his glassy flood
> Reflects purpureal Tempe's pleasant scene?
> Fair Tempe! haunt belov'd of sylvan Powers,
> Of Nymphs and Fauns; where in the golden age
> They play'd in secret on the shady brink
> With ancient Pan; while round their choral steps
> Young Hours and genial Gales with constant hand
> Shower'd blossoms, odours, shower'd ambrosial dews
> And spring's Elysian bloom.[32]

In the revised version this passage is more striking:

> Or wilt thou that Thessalian landscape trace,
> Where slow Peneus his clear glassy tide
> Draws smooth along, between the winding cliffs
> Of Ossa and the pathless woods unshorn
> That wave o'er huge Olympus? Down the stream,
> Look how the mountains with their double range
> Embrace the vale of Tempe; from each side
> Ascending steep to heaven, a rocky mound
> Cover'd with ivy and the laurel boughs
> That crown'd young Phoebus for the Python slain.
> Fair Tempe! on whose primrose banks the morn
> Awoke most fragrant, and the noon repos'd

[31] *Poetical Works, op. cit.,* Book I, ll. 567-604, pp. 138-9.
[32] *Ibid.,* ll. 295-305, p. 129.

In pomp of lights and shadows most sublime;
Whose lawns, whose glades, ere human footsteps yet
Had trac'd an entrance, where the hallow'd haunt
Of silvan powers immortal; where they sate
Oft in the golden age, the Nymphs and Fauns,
Beneath some arbour branching o'er the flood,
And leaning round hung on the instructive lips
Of hoary Pan, or o'er some open dale
Danc'd in light measures to his sevenfold pipe,
While Zephyr's wanton hand along their path
Flung showers of painted blossoms, fertile dews,
And one perpetual spring.[33]

Here, again, are the primitivism and the yearning for the ancient culture characteristic of romantic hellenism.

In Akenside, as in Thomson, Glover, and Dyer, the idealization of ancient Greece results in the identification of hellenism with liberty. At the end of Book II, for example, as Akenside expresses his admiration for the life of antiquity, occurs a passage in which he contrasts the freedom of the Greeks with modern servitude:

Ask thy own heart, when, at the midnight hour,
Slow through that studious gloom thy pausing eye,
Led by the glimmering taper, moves around
The sacred volumes of the dead, the songs
Of Grecian bards, and records writ by Fame
For Grecian heroes, where the present power
Of heaven and earth surveys the immortal page,
Even as a father blessing, while he reads
The praises of his son. If then thy soul,
Spurning the yoke of these inglorious days,
Mix in their deeds, and kindle with their flame;
Say, when the prospect blackens on thy view,
When rooted from the base, heroic states
Mourn in the dust, and tremble at the frown
Of curst ambition; when the pious band
Of youths, who fought for freedom and their sires,
Lie side by side in gore; when ruffian pride
Usurps the throne of Justice, turns the pomp
Of public power, the majesty of rule,
The sword, the laurel, and the purple robe,
To slavish, empty pageants, to adorn

[33] *Ibid.*, ll. 813-836, p. 213.

> A tyrant's walk, and glitter in the eyes
> Of such as bow the knee; when honor'd urns
> Of patriots and of chiefs, the awful bust
> And storied arch, to glut the coward rage
> Of regal envy, strew the public way
> With hallow'd ruins;
>
> . . . . . . . . .
>
> Till Desolation o'er the grass-grown street
> Expands his raven wings, and up the wall,
> Where senates once the price of monarchs doom'd,
> Hisses the gliding snake through hoary weeds
> That clasp the mouldering column; thus defac'd,
> Thus widely mournful when the prospect thrills
> Thy beating bosom, when the patriot's tear
> Starts from thine eye, and thy extended arm
> In fancy hurls the thunderbolt of Jove
> To fire the impious wreath on Philip's brow,
> Or dash Octavius from the trophied car;
> Say, does thy secret soul repine to taste
> The big distress?[34]

Here, once more, is a typical characteristic of romantic hellenism. Greece is here an inspiration for action, moods, poetry.

A similar illustration of Akenside's use of hellenic material as a symbol of individualism and the passionate love of freedom is to be found in the unfinished revision of Book III.[35] This consists of 540 lines, 510 of which are devoted to the fragmentary story of the rebellion of Pisistratus in Athens when Solon, absent in Egypt, is an old, "silver-haired" man. In the absence of Solon, Pisistratus, by his remarkable talents of demagoguery, has played upon the feelings of the people until he has won over enough adherents to establish tyranny in Athens. When Solon returns ready to lead an army heroically against the tyrant, the Athenians, shaking their heads in mistrust because of his age, refuse to support him.

Solon goes home sad and grieving. But early the next morning four patriotic Athenians, each stemming from noble and heroic ancestry, come to visit him. These are Megacles, son of Alcmaeon, Clisthenes, son of Megacles, Miltiades, descendant of Aeacus, and

[34] *Ibid.*, Book II, ll. 712-771, pp. 164-6.
[35] Dated 1770. See *ibid.*, pp. 251-269.

the valorous Cimon, his half-brother. As Solon tells them the story of his career, with much sentimental emphasis on his passionate love of liberty and his sorrow at finding the Athenians mistrustful of his prowess, the book is cut short. It is clear that the book would have ended with the celebration of virtue and freedom triumphing over evil and tyranny. What is interesting to observe, however, is that here is the use of a Greek narrative exclusively as the symbol of romantic courage and valor in the cause of liberty and equality. Such a spirit is obvious, for example, in Solon's speech to the four Athenians. He is telling them how he came from Egypt to Greece, particularly to the city of Minos. The thought of Greece evokes from him this rapturous outburst:

> O ye gods,
> Who taught the leaders of the simpler time
> By written words to curb the untoward will
> Of mortals, how within that generous isle
> Have ye the triumphs of your power display'd
> Munificent! Those splendid merchants, lords
> Of traffic and the sea, with what delight
> I saw them at their public meal, like sons
> Of the same household, join the plainer sort
> Whose wealth was only freedom! whence to these
> Vile envy, and to those fantastic pride,
> Alike was strange; but noble concord still
> Cherish'd the strength untam'd, the rustic faith,
> Of their first fathers.[36]

This is the same mood that we have observed before; Greece is here the inspiration for poetry.

Akenside's romantic hellenism is not limited to *The Pleasures of Imagination,* for a similar idealization of ancient Greece is to be found in some of his less known poems. Thus, in his "Ode to the Right Hon. Francis Earl of Huntington, 1747," first published in 1748,[37] Akenside urges the Earl to continue to exert himself in the cause of liberty by encouraging poets. To justify this idea he cites the example of Greece:

> Such as when Greece to her immortal shell
> Rejoicing listen'd, godlike sounds to hear;

[36] *Ibid.,* ll. 443-456.

[37] See *ibid.,* p. 453, note 11.

To hear the sweet instructress tell
(While men and heroes throng'd around)
How life its noblest use may find,
How well for freedom be resign'd;
And how, by glory, virtue shall be crown'd

. . . . . . . . .

O noblest, happiest age!
When Aristides rul'd and Cimon fought;
When all the generous fruits of Homer's page
Exulting Pindar saw to full perfection brought.
O Pindar, oft shall thou be hail'd of me:
Not that Apollo fed thee from his shrine;
Nor that thy lips drank sweetness from the bee;
Nor yet that, studious of thy notes divine,
Pan danc'd their measure with the sylvan throng;
But that thy song
Was proud to unfold
What thy base rulers trembled to behold;
Amid corrupted Thebes was proud to tell
The deeds of Athens and the Persian shame:
Hence on thy head their impious vengeance fell.
But thou, O faithful to thy fame,
The Muse's law didst rightly know;
That who would animate his lays,
And other minds to virtue raise,
Must feel his own with all her spirit glow.[38]

Perhaps the most striking example of romantic hellenism in Akenside's poetry, however, is his "Inscription No. VIII," first printed by Dyson in his edition of Akenside in 1772.[39] This little lyric is an almost perfect instance of the poetic mood inspired by the idealization of ancient Greece. Observe how the poem blends hellenism gracefully with other romantic elements—loneliness, solitude, repose, natural scenery, a bird's song, a yearning for the infinite. Yet all of these are made to be secondary in influence to the spirit of ancient Greece. One cannot help but be reminded of Shelley when he reads such lines as these:

Ye powers unseen, to whom the bards of Greece
Erected altars; ye who to the mind
More lofty views unfold, and prompt the heart

[38] *Ibid.*, pp. 327-336.

[39] See *ibid.*, pp. 97-101.

With more divine emotions; if ere while
Not quite unpleasing have my votive rites
Of you been deem'd, when oft this lonely seat
To you I consecrated; then vouchsafe
Here with your instant energy to crown
Happy solitude. It is the hour
When most I love to invoke you, and have felt
Most frequent your glad ministry divine.
The air is calm: the sun's unveiled orb
Shines in the middle heaven. The harvest round
Stands quiet, and among the golden sheaves
The reapers lie reclin'd. The neighbouring groves
Are mute; nor even a linnet's random strain
Echoeth amid the silence. Let me feel
Your influence, ye kind powers. Aloft in heaven,
Abide ye? or on those transparent clouds
Pass ye from hill to hill? or on the shades
Which yonder elms cast o'er the lake below
Do you converse retir'd? From what lov'd haunt
Shall I expect you? Let me once more feel
Your influence, O ye kind inspiring powers:
And I will guard it well; nor shall a thought
Rise in my mind, nor shall a passion move
Across my bosom unobserv'd, unstor'd
By faithful memory. And then at some
More active moment, will I call them forth
Anew; and join them in majestic forms,
And give them utterance in harmonious strains;
That all mankind shall wonder at your sway.[40]

A similar illustration of hellenism occurring in a poem which contains other notable romantic elements is to be found in Joseph Warton's (1722-1800) well-known "Ode to Fancy," which appeared in his volume of *Odes on Various Subjects* in 1746. Joseph, brother of Thomas Warton the younger, a profound Greek scholar and a schoolfellow of Gilbert White and William Collins, had already expressed admiration for ancient Greece[41] in the "Ode to

[40] *Ibid.*, pp. 406-7.

[41] Warton's hellenic interest is adequately attested by his announcement in 1784 that two quarto volumes of a history of Grecian, as well as other, poetry were about to be published by him. The volumes, however, never appeared. See the memoir of Joseph Warton by Eric Partridge in *The Three Wartons, a Choice of Their Verse,* London, 1927. Similar indications of a hellenic devotion may be

Mr. West on his Translation of Pindar," published in a volume containing Warton's best known poem, "The Enthusiast," in 1744. In the fifth stanza of the Ode to West, for example, occurs this rapturous passage:

> O parent of the lyre,
> Let me forever thy sweet sons admire;
> O ancient Greece, but chief the bard whose lays
> The matchless tale of Troy divine emblaze;
> And next Euripides, soft Pity's priest,
> Who melts in useful woes the bleeding breast;
> And him, who paints th' incestuous king,
> Whose soul amaze and horrour wring;
> Teach me to taste their charms refin'd,
> The richest banquet of th' enraptur'd mind.[42]

Warton's "Ode to Fancy" is a celebration of the simple pleasures of a lover of imaginative literature and of the poetic inspiration to be found in such pleasures. Written in the lilting meter of "L'Allegro," the poem describes in rapid succession the joys of watching "deep and pathless vales," "hoary mountains," "fall of waters," "broken rocks and forests dark," where one can hear "the woodman's stroke" and "where never human art appear'd." The poet calls upon Fancy to "lay me by the haunted stream, rapt in some wild, poetic dream." There he will conjure up visions of Spenserian beauties in a fairy grove which will afford him infinite enjoyment. Later Fancy will lead him to Melancholy. Together they will go, with silent footsteps,

> To charnels and the house of woe,
> To Gothic churches, vaults, and tombs,
> Where each sad night, some virgin comes
> With throbbing breast, and faded cheek,
> Her promis'd bridegroom's urn to seek. . . .[43]

Then, when Warton has described additional romantic pleasures, he concludes with this invocation to Fancy:

> O queen of numbers, once again
> Animate some chosen swain,
> Who, fill'd with unexhausted fire,

---

found in the many references to Greek culture in his *Essay on the Genius and Writings of Pope*, 1757, *passim*.

[42] Chalmers, *op. cit.*, Vol. 18, p. 169.

[43] *Ibid.*, p. 164.

May boldly smite the sounding lyre,
Who with some new unequall'd song,
May rise above the rhyming throng,
O'er all our list'ning passions reign,
O'erwhelm our souls with joy and pain,
With terrour shake, and pity move,
Rouse with revenge, or melt with love,
O deign t' attend his evening walk,
With him in groves and grottos talk;
Teach him to scorn with frigid art
Feebly to touch th' unraptur'd heart;
Like lightning, let his mighty verse
The bosom's inmost folding's pierce;
With native beauties win applause
Beyond cold critics' studied laws;
O let each Muse's fame increase,
O bid Britannia rival Greece.[44]

Here, then, as in Akenside's "Inscription," the devotion to Greece is blended with other romantic elements, while the Greek muse is made to hover above all other pleasures. What is even more interesting to observe in this passage, however, is the isolation of Greece from all other antiquity and the attribution to her of "native beauties . . . beyond cold critics' studied laws." Presumably the romantic poet is going beyond the neo-classicist's authoritarian worship of Roman antiquity; Greece seems to symbolize for him the antithesis of the neo-classic.

Another aspect of romantic hellenism appears in Warton's "Ode to a Gentleman on His Travels," 1746, in which the poet expresses thinly-veiled envy of the opportunity the "Gentleman" will have to meditate among the ruins of antiquity. Here occurs the sad but pleasurable lament over what was so beautiful in the past which we have observed in other similar poems:

Oft to those mossy mould'ring walls,
Those caverns dark and silent halls,
Let me repair by midnight's paly fires;
There muse on empire's fallen state,
And frail ambition's hapless fate,
While more than mortal thoughts the solemn scene inspires.
What lust of pow'r from the cold north

[44] *Ibid.*

Could tempt those Vandal-robbers forth,
Fair Italy, thy vine-clad vales to waste;
Whose hands profane, with hostile blade,
Thy story'd temples dar'd invade,
And all thy Parian seats of Attic art defac'd;

They weeping Art in fetters bound,
And gor'd her breast with many a wound,
And veil'd her charms in clouds of thickest night;
Sad Poesy, much injur'd maid,
They drove to some dim convent's shade,
And quench'd in gloomy mist her lamp's resplendent light.[45]

In the same month and year which saw the publication of Joseph Warton's Odes, there appeared the more successful volume, *Odes on Several Descriptive and Allegoric Subjects,* by William Collins.[46] Warton and Collins (1721-1759) seem to have been subject to similar literary influences. They were schoolfellows at Winchester until 1740, and the friendship formed here lasted throughout Collins' life. In 1741 Collins was elected to a demyship at Magdalene College, while Warton was at Oriel College with Gilbert White, who made the third member of an intimate trio.[47] Sharing their antiquarian interests,[48] Collins displays romantic hellenism which is considerably more subtle than that of his contemporaries other than Gray. Professor Courthope has said:

An ardent admirer of the Greek tragic poets . . . his [Collins'] verse is filled with glowing, though often despondent, aspirations for the recovery of their departed music. . . . With Collins the inspiration of the Renais-

[45] *Ibid.*, p. 165.

[46] "London, A. Millar, 1747" appears on the title-page. Comparison with contemporary literary registers long ago revealed that this date is an error, and that the correct date is December, 1746. See Chalmers, *op. cit.*, Vol. 18, p. 146. *Cf.* the memoir of Collins by Christopher Stone prefixed to his *Poems of William Collins,* London, 1907.

[47] See the recollections of Collins by Gilbert White in a letter to the *Gentleman's Magazine* for 1781, p. 11.

[48] Thomas Warton refers to Collins' library at Chichester, where he had collected some curious old books. See Thomas Warton, *History of English Poetry,* London, 1840, Vol. III, pp. 80, 244, 386. In 1751, moreover, Collins wrote a letter to Dr. Hayes from Chichester mentioning an "Ode on the Music of the Grecian Theater," which, if written, is now lost. See William Seward's *Supplement to the Anecdotes of Distinguished Persons, Chiefly of the Present and 2 Preceding Centuries,* London, 1798, p. 123.

sance naturally shaped itself into Greek forms. His fancy, like that of Shelley, roamed freely through all the varieties of spiritual polytheism. . . . Amidst the profuse abundance of his impersonations, he aimed always at preserving the purity of Grecian outline. As he says in his "Ode to Simplicity":

> Thou who, with hermit heart,
> Disdainst the wealth of art,
> And gauds, and pageant weeds, and trailing pall,
> But com'st a decent maid,
> In *Attic robe* arrayed,
> O chaste, unboastful nymph, to thee I call!

Even in his diction the influence of Greek models is apparent; especially in his frequent practice of accumulating epithets without conjunctions. . . .[49]

The romantic hellenism of Collins, because of its subtle nature, is much less outspoken than that of other poets. Very frequently, however, the reader can detect clearly a passionate longing for the sublimity of ancient Greek culture, its music, its poetry, its love of liberty, its wonderful power to stimulate strange moods. In the epode to his "Ode to Fear," for instance, Collins is the romantic hellenist who reads into Greece what is really within himself:

> In earliest Greece to Thee with partial Choice,
> The Grief-full Muse addrest her infant Tongue;
> The Maids and Matrons, on her Awful Voice,
> Silent and pale in wild Amazement hung.
> . . . . . . . . .
>
> O Fear, I know thee by my throbbing Heart,
> Thy with'ring Pow'r inspir'd each mournful Line,
> Tho' gentle Pity claim her mingled Part,
> Yet all the Thunders of the Scene are thine![50]

Here Greece is a symbol of a poetic mood. In the strophe of the "Ode to Liberty," on the other hand, Greece becomes to Collins, as to so many other poets, a symbol of freedom:

> Who shall awake the Spartan Fife,
> And call in solemn Sounds to Life,

[49] W. J. Courthope, *A History of English Poetry,* London, 1911, Vol. V, p. 397.
[50] Christopher Stone, *op. cit.,* p. 32.

The Youths, whose Locks divinely spreading,
Like vernal Hyacinths in sullen Hue,
At once the Breath of Fear and Virtue shedding,
Applauding Freedom lov'd of old to view?
What new Alcaeus, Fancy-blest
Shall sing the Sword, in Myrtles drest,
At Widsom's Shrine a-while its Flame concealing,
(What Place so fit to seal a Deed renown'd?)
Till she her brightest Lightnings round revealing,
It leap'd in Glory forth, and dealt her prompted Sound![51]

The power of music in "early Greece" is, in part, the theme of Collins' "The Passions. An Ode for Music." The poet personifies various moods—Fear, Anger, Despair, Hope, Revenge, Pity, Jealousy, Melancholy, Joy, and Love—and shows how each of them is held in thrall by Music. After he has done this, however, he arrives at what is really the point of the poem, in the last twenty-four lines:

O Music, Sphere-descended Maid,
Friend of Pleasure, Wisdom's Aid,
Why, Goddess, why, to us deny'd?
Lay'st Thou thy antient Lyre aside?
As in that lov'd Athenian Bow'r,
You learn'd an all-commanding Pow'r.
Thy mimic Soul, O Nymph endear'd,
Can well recall what then it heard.
Where is thy native simple Heart,
Devote to Virtue, Fancy, Art?
Arise as in that elder Time,
Warm, Energic, Chaste, Sublime!
Thy Wonders in that God-like Age,
Fill thy recording Sister's Page—
'Tis said, and I believe the Tale,
Thy humblest Reed could more prevail,
Had more of Strength, diviner Rage,
Than all which charms this laggard Age,
E'en all at once together found,
Coecilia's mingled World of Sound—
O bid our vain Endeavors cease,
Revive the just Designs of Greece,

[51] *Ibid.*, p. 42.

Return in all thy simple State!
Confirm the Tales Her Sons relate![52]

This is the same yearning for the beauties of hellenic culture which runs through the poetry of Shelley and Byron.

The romantic hellenism of Joseph Warton and Collins is largely the result of an antiquarian interest in Greece. Hellenism of a similar nature appears in the poetry of Thomas Warton the younger (1728-1790), a college don most of his life and after 1757, like his father before him, professor of poetry at Oxford. His interest in Greek is indicated by his publication, in 1766, of a collection of Greek inscriptions known as Cephalas' *Anthologia Graeca,* with an original Latin preface, and by his edition of Theocritus, which appeared in 1770.[53] In 1771, moreover, he became a fellow in the London Society of Antiquaries.

The earliest of Thomas Warton's poems which show romantic hellenism is his well-known *Pleasures of Melancholy,* published in 1747. Here, again, is a poem frequently cited for its romantic elements, such as "howling winds and beating rains," "pale Cynthia" overlooking "midnight haunts" where "the lone screech-owl's note" is heard among "ruined abbeys." In celebrating the pleasures which such melancholy scenes produce, the poet describes the sad enjoyment of reading tragedies and meditating upon the vanity of "the splendours of the gaudy court" and of "pageant pomps." This leads him to thoughts of Greece:

Thus seen by shepherd from Hymettus' brow,
What daedal landscapes smile! here palmy groves,
Resounding once with Plato's voice, arise,
Amid whose umbrage green her silver head
Th' unfading olive lifts; here vine-clad hills
Lay forth their purple store, and sunny vales
In prospect vast their level laps expand,
Amid whose beauties glistering Athens tow'rs.
Tho' thro' the blissful scenes Ilissus roll

[52] *Ibid.,* p. 60.

[53] See Clarissa Rinaker, *Thomas Warton, a Bibliographical and Critical Study,* in *University of Illinois Studies in Language and Literature,* Vol. II, No. 1 (Feb., 1916). The romantic hellenism of Thomas Warton, like that of Gray, is highly significant because of the widespread popularity of his poetry. When his collected poems appeared in 1777, four editions had to be printed by 1789.

His sage-inspiring flood, whose winding marge
The thick-wove laurel shades; tho' roseate Morn
Pour all her splendours on th' empurpled scene;
Yet feels the hoary hermit truer joys,
As from the cliff that o'er his cavern hangs,
He views the piles of fall'n Persepolis
In deep arrangement hide the darksome plain.
Unbounded waste! the mould'ring obelisk
Here, like a blasted oak, ascends the clouds;
Here Parian domes their vaulted halls disclose
Horrid with thorn, where lurks th' unpitying thief,
Whence flits the twilight-loving bat at eve,
And the deaf adder wreathes her spotted train,
The dwellings once of elegance and art.
Here temples rise, amid whose hallow'd bounds
Spires the black pine, while thro' the naked street,
Once haunt of tradeful merchants, springs the grass:
Here columns heap'd on prostrate columns, torn
From their firm base, increase the mould'ring mass.
Far as the sight can pierce, appear the spoils
Of sunk magnificence! a blended scene
Of moles, fanes, arches, domes, and palaces,
Where, with his brother Horrour, Ruin sits.[54]

Observe how Warton has here found poetic inspiration in Greek ruins and how, in his lament over the lost magnificence of Greece, he has blended other stock romantic elements with hellenism.

In *Newmarket. A Satire,* published in 1751, Warton, writing a less sentimental poem, is much clearer in the expression of his idealization of Greece. Notice, in this passage, how, like Byron, he identifies ancient with modern Greece and how he finds in it a symbol, again, of liberty. Above all, observe the rapturous admiration in the eleventh and twelfth lines:

How are the Therons of these modern days
Chang'd from those chiefs who toil'd for Grecian bays;
Who, fir'd with genuine glory's sacred lust,
Whirl'd the swift axle through the Pythian dust!
Theirs was the Pisan olive's blooming spray,
Theirs was the Theban bard's recording lay.
What though the grooms of Greece ne'er took the odds?

[54] Chalmers, *op. cit.,* Vol. 18, p. 97.

They won no bets,—but then they soar'd to gods;
And more an Hiero's palm, a Pindar's ode,
Than all th' united plates of George bestow'd.
  Greece! how I kindle at thy magic name,
Feel all thy warmth, and catch the kindred flame.
Thy scenes sublime and visions awful rise
In ancient pride before my musing eyes.
Here Sparta's sons in mute attention hang,
While just Lycurgus pours the mild harangue;
There Xerxes' hosts, all pale with deadly fear,
Shrink at her fated hero's flashing spear.
Here hung with many a lyre of silver string,
The laureate alleys of Ilissus spring;
And lo, where rapt in beauty's heavenly dream
Hoar Plato walks his oliv'd Academe.—
  Yet ah! no more the land of arts and arms
Delights with wisdom, or with virtue warms.
Lo! the stern Turk, with more than Vandal rage,
Has blasted all the wreaths of ancient age:
No more her groves by Fancy's feet are trod,
Each Attic grace has left the lov'd abode.
Fall'n is fair Greece! by Luxury's pleasing bane
Seduc'd, she drags a barbarous foreign chain.[55]

Elsewhere in Thomas Warton's poems one can find similar strains of romantic hellenism, always expressive of the same admiration for the perfect culture that was Greece. Thus, in his Miltonic "Ode on the Approach of Summer," 1753, he calls upon the Goddess of Summer to lay him in a cool cavern,

Or bear me to yon antique wood,
Dim temple of sage Solitude!
There within a nook most dark,
Where none my musing mood may mark,
Let me in many a whisper'd rite
The genius old of Greece invite,
With that fair wreath my brows to bind,
Which for his chosen imps he twin'd,
Well nurtur'd in Pierian lore,
On clear Ilissus' laureate shore.
Till high on waving nest reclin'd,
The raven wakes my tranced mind![56]

[55] *Ibid.*, p. 121.

[56] *Ibid.*, p. 107.

Or in his poem, "On the Death of King George the Second. To Mr. Secretary Pitt," he reminds Pitt of the glory of poetry long ago in Greece,

> For such the tribute of ingenuous praise
> Her harp dispens'd in Grecia's golden days;
> Such were the palms, in isles of old renown,
> She cull'd, to deck the guiltless monarch's crown;
> When virtuous Pindar told, with Tuscan gore,
> How scepter'd Hiero stain'd Sicilia's shore.[57]

Again, when Warton succeeded William Whitehead as Poet Laureate in 1785, his first "Ode on His Majesty's Birth-Day, June 4th, 1785" praises the monarch because under his influence

> Sculpture, licentious now no more,
> From Greece her great example takes,
> With Nature's warmth the marble wakes,
> And spurns the toys of modern lore;
> In native beauty simply plann'd,
> Corinth, thy tufted shafts ascend.[58]

And the following year in his "Ode for his Majesty's Birth-Day, June 4th, 1786," Warton, seeking a theme, looks longingly back at antiquity,

> When Freedom nurs'd her native fire
> In ancient Greece, and rul'd the lyre;
>
> . . . . . . . . .
>
> 'Twas thus Alcaeus smote the manly chord;
> And Pindar on the Persian lord
> His notes of indignation hurl'd,
> And spurn'd the minstrel slaves of eastern sway,
> From trembling Thebes extorting conscious shame;
>
> . . . . . . . . .
>
> And he, sweet master of the Doric oat,
> Theocritus, forsook awhile
> The graces of his pastoral isle,
>
> . . . . . . .
>
> And caught the bold Homeric note
> In stately sounds exalting high,
>
> . . . . . . .

[57] *Ibid.*, p. 92.

[58] *Ibid.*, p. 113.

To deck with honour due this festal day,
O for a strain from these sublimer bards!

. . . . . . . .

For peerless bards like these alone,
The bards of Greece might best adorn,
With seemly song, the monarch's natal morn;
Who, thron'd in the magnificence of peace,
Rivals their richest regal theme:
Who rules a people like their own,
In arms, in polish'd arts supreme;
Who bids his Britain vie with Greece![59]

By 1786 Greece had become a source of inspiration even for a king's birthday ode.

Equally significant with the Warton brothers and Collins in the rise of romantic hellenism in English poetry is the figure of Thomas Gray (1716-1771). Sensitive and introvertive, Gray did not produce much poetry, but, as has been recently shown,[60] his very sterility in creative literature is accounted for by the fact that he spent his productive years in long research on antiquities and historical curiosities, making himself an authority, but never publishing the fruits of his studies. Jones has printed[61] the hitherto unpublished catalogue of Gray's books in the Pierpont Morgan Library and the bibliography which he kept of his classical studies. A study of these compilations, together with Gray's manuscript commonplace book[62] and various autograph notebooks and notes which Jones lists in his register,[63] reveals that Gray was very much interested in Greece. It has, of course, long been observed that Gray diplayed eager curiosity about painting, architecture, and antiquities,[64] but Jones' study reveals clearly that this curiosity

[59] *Ibid.*, p. 114.

[60] William Powell Jones, *Thomas Gray, Scholar: The True Tragedy of an Eighteenth-Century Gentleman,* Harvard University Press, 1937.

[61] *Ibid.*, pp. 151-163.

[62] Now in 3 Vols. folio in Pembroke College, Cambridge.

[63] Pp. 175-181.

[64] See the introduction to *The Correspondence of Thomas Gray,* ed. Paget Toynbee and Leonard Whibley, 3 Vols., Oxford, 1935. *Cf.* Roger Martin, *Essai sur Thomas Gray,* Oxford University Press, 1934. The Rev. William J. Temple, writing in the *London Magazine* for March, 1772, said concerning Gray: "Perhaps he was the most learned man in Europe. . . . He knew every branch of history, both natural and civil; had read all the original historians of England, France, and Italy; and was

was a good deal more scholarly than has been supposed. Between 1746 and 1748 Gray was engaged in research on Greek geography, Greek antiquities, and Greek history, as his bibliography amply demonstrates. In the fall of 1746 he constructed certain tables of Greek history, three columns of which were devoted to political events, six columns to literature illustrative of manners, education, social customs, and ideas.[65] After 1748 he continued to study Diogenes Laertius, Athenaeus, Pausanias, Lysias, Isocrates, Pindar, Aristophanes, Thucydides, Xenophon, Sophocles, and Plato.[66] Moreover, from 1744 to 1756, along with his study of classical civilization, he read widely in Greek, as well as oriental, travel literature, including the accounts of Shaw, Wheeler, Pococke, and Roe. The catalogue of his books reveals a wide acquaintance with treatises on architecture, sculpture, painting, and antiquities, while his notes include references to "Fabricii Bibliotheca Graecae" and the "Mémoires de l'Académie des Inscriptions et des Belles-Lettres."

It has been observed of Gray in another connection[67] that his real significance in a literary movement lay not so much in his published work as in his influence, through conversation or correspondence, on his friends and on younger poets, and this observation is probably applicable also to his hellenism. Yet even in the slender body of poetry which he produced there are indications of the romantic hellenism that a student of his notes might expect. As in Collins, this side of Gray is best reflected in his odes:

> Understanding by sympathy the spiritual significance of Pindar's style, they [Gray and Collins] endeavour to preserve the Greek structure of the Ode, as far as it is compatible with English traditions. They well

a great antiquarian. Criticism, metaphysics, morals, politics made a principal part of his plan of study; voyages and travels of all sorts were his favourite amusement; and he had a fine taste in painting, prints, architecture, and gardening." (Quoted in Jones, *op. cit.*, p. 10.)

[65] These tables are no longer extant, though Gray refers to them frequently. According to Jones, *op. cit.*, p. 55 note, a fragment of two sheets is in a copy of *Designs by Mr. R. Bentley for Six Poems of Mr. T. Gray,* 1753. Two loose leaves were recently in the possession of Dr. A. S. W. Rosenbach.

[66] For full discussion of Gray's study of these authors, see Jones, Chapter III.

[67] Edward D. Snyder, *The Celtic Revival in English Literature, 1760-1800,* Harvard University Press, 1923, pp. 30ff.

knew that the greatness of a nation's art depends upon the state of its freedom and morals. Hence the enthusiastic patriotism that constantly breaks through their most classical strains.[68]

Certainly, there is a clear instance of romantic hellenism in the second epode of "The Progress of Poesy. A Pindaric Ode," first published in 1753:[69]

> Woods that wave o'er Delphi's steep,
> Isles that crown th' Aegean deep,
> Fields that cool Ilissus laves,
> Or where Maeander's amber waves
> In lingering lab'rinths creep,
> How do your tuneful echoes languish,
> Mute, but to the voice of Anguish!
> Where each old poetic mountain
> Inspiration breath'd around,
> Every shade and hallow'd fountain
> Murmur'd deep a solemn sound,
> Till the sad Nine, in Greece's evil hour,
> Left their Parnassus for the Latian plains.
> Alike they scorn the pomp of tyrant Power
> And coward Vice, that revels in her chains.[70]

Here is the characteristic idealization of Greece, with the accompanying strain of nostalgia for the glory of the past, the identification of Greece with liberty, and the poetic inspiration afforded by hellenic culture.

A testimony to Gray's hellenism is contained in the epitaph written by his friend, literary executor, and biographer, William Mason (1724-1797), when Gray died in 1771:

> No more the Grecian Muse unrivall'd reigns,
> To Britain let the nations homage pay;
> She felt a Homer's fire in Milton's strains,
> A Pindar's rapture from the lyre of Gray.[71]

Mason, probably influenced partly by Gray,[72] displays similar

[68] W. J. Courthope, *op. cit.,* Vol. V, pp. 395-6.

[69] By Dodsley in *Designs by Mr. R. Bentley for Six Poems by Mr. T. Gray,* London, 1753.

[70] Ll. 66-80.

[71] Chalmers, *op. cit.,* Vol. 18, p. 338.

[72] See John W. Draper, *William Mason: A Study in Eighteenth Century Culture,* New York University Press, 1924.

romantic hellenism in his own poetry. In his early patriotic vision poem, *Isis,* published in 1748, for example, occurs this lament by the goddess:

> Ilissus! roll thy fam'd Athenian tide;
> Tho' Plato's steps oft mark'd thy neighb'ring glade,
> Tho' fair Lyceum lent its awful shade,
> Tho' ev'ry academic green imprest
> Its image full on thy reflecting breast,
> Yet my pure stream shall boast as proud a name,
> And Britain's Isis flow with Attic fame.
> Alas! how chang'd! where now that Attic boast?
> See! Gothic license rage o'er all my coast.
> See! Hydra faction spread its impious reign,
> Poison each breast, and madden ev'ry brain.
> Hence frontless crowd that, not content to fright
> The blushing Cynthia from her throne of might,
> Blast the fair face of day; and madly bold
> To freedom's foes infernal orgies hold;
> To freedom's foes, ah! see the goblet crown'd!
> Hear plausive shouts to freedom's foes resound!
> The horrid notes my refluent waters daunt,
> The Echoes groan, the Dryads quit their haunt;
> Learning, that once to all diffused her beam,
> Now sheds by stealth a partial private gleam
> In some lone cloister's melancholy shade,
> Where a firm few support her sickly head;
> Despis'd, insulted by the barb'rous train,
> Who scour like Thracia's moon-struck rout the plain,
> Sworn foes like them to all the Muse approves,
> All Phoebus favors, or Minerva loves.[73]

To this view of Greece as the symbol of liberty should be added the admiration for ancient Greek drama which Mason displayed in his well-known poetical dramas, *Elfrida,* 1751, and *Caractacus,* 1759. In both of these Mason employed material from England's mythical history for the express purpose of producing drama "written on the model of the ancient Greek tragedy."[74] In each of these plays are included several Pindaric Odes which, in their straining for majestic sound, attempt to reproduce the effects of a Greek chorus. In the five letters prefixed to the printed version of

[73] Chalmers, Vol. 18, p. 326.

[74] As stated on the respective title-pages.

*Elfrida* in 1751,[75] Mason expresses sincere regret for the paucity of Greek imitation:

> Whatever these play-makers may have gained by rejecting the Chorus, the true poet has lost considerably by it. For he has lost a graceful and natural resource to the embellishments of picturesque description, sublime allegory, and whatever else comes under the denomination of pure poetry.[76]

This admiration he expressed poetically in 1759, in his "Elegy. To The Rev. Mr. Hurd," prefixed to the printed version of *Caractacus:*

> How oft I cry'd, "Oh come, thou tragic queen!
> March from thy Greece with firm majestic tread!
> Such as when Athens saw thee fill her scene,
> When Sophocles thy choral Graces led:
> Saw thy proud pall its purple length devolve;
> Saw thee uplift the glittering dagger high;
> Ponder with fixed brow thy deep resolve,
> Prepar'd to strike, to triumph, and to die.
> Bring then to Britain's plain that choral throng;
> Display thy buskin'd pomp, thy golden lyre;
> Give her historic forms the soul of song,
> And mingle Attic art with Shakespear's fire.[77]

While Mason did not by any means approach "Shakespear's fire," it is noteworthy that he attempted to emulate "Attic art." The significance of this attempt has been thus summarized by his most recent biographer and critic:

> Dramatically, he [Mason] occupies a position very like Shelley, or Byron: only they were great poets, and he was not. Even so, one must give him a certain credit for paving the way for their advent and helping to prepare English poetry and the English public for what they did.
>
> For the scholar of today, perhaps the chief interest in the dramas of Mason lies in the illustration they give of the taste of the ordinary intellect of the eighteenth century . . .; *Elfrida* is no mean document to point eighteenth-century appreciation of Hellenic culture. Just as the age admired the tense emotion of the Elizabethans and reproduced it in rant, so it reverenced the formal simplicity of the Greeks, and reproduced it in stiff conventionality: in both cases it overlooked or at

[75] Reprinted in Chalmers, Vol. 18, pp. 338-342.
[76] *Ibid.*, p. 340. [77] *Ibid.*, p. 336.

least could not imitate the essential greatness. Artistically, the times were out of joint. The age was fascinated with the idea of a rococo combination of what it regarded as the virtues of types and schools that were really in essential opposition. It was an unhappy effort at a new aesthetic synthesis; and Mason, with his Celtic-Greek drama and his Greek-Italian opera, is interesting as one of those who tried by reaction and experiment to evolve something better and new.[78]

Much different from the antiquarian romantic hellenism of Gray and Mason, however, is that which appears in the chief poem of William Falconer (1732-1769), *The Shipwreck*, a colorful narrative poem first published in 1762. The popularity of the poem was considerable, for three editions appeared by 1769. Falconer, primarily a seaman, possessed some degree of literary knowledge and ability.[79] By 1761 he had become second mate on a ship engaged in trade with the Levant. On a voyage from Alexandria to Venice this ship was wrecked, only three of the crew being saved. It is upon this experience that *The Shipwreck* is founded. Dedicated to the Duke of York, then rear admiral, the poem is in three cantos. The setting is the far-away, romantic modern island of Candia, in Greece. Into this colorful background is introduced the figure of the young lover, Palemon, who, because of his love for Anna, daughter of the ship's master, Albert, has met with the disapproving frown of an unsympathetic father. To Candia Palemon has been driven, as if in exile. He is now on board the ship that is to carry him there. On the way Palemon becomes friendly with the young, mysterious Arion, the second mate, to whom he tells his story and from whom he receives tender sympathy. But as the ship approaches its destination, it is caught in a terrific storm and, amid tempestuous cracking and howling, it is wrecked almost on the shores of beautiful Candia. When the dead bodies of Palemon and Arion are washed up on the shore, the tragedy is complete.

It is obvious from this summary that Falconer's interest in the poem is the description of the shipwreck. The love story is introduced only as a sentimental plot around which the depiction

[78] John W. Draper, *op. cit.*, p. 202.

[79] See the memoir of Falconer by Robert Carruthers, prefixed to *The Shipwreck, a Poem, in Three Cantos*, London, 1858.

of the shipwreck may be drawn. What is most striking in the poem for the purposes of this study, however, is the use which Falconer makes of the exotic setting in order to heighten the pathos of his narrative. It is for this reason that the poem is studded with long, rhapsodic descriptions of the beauties of Grecian shores. In order to make these beauties more sentimental, moreover, the poet proceeds to identify them with those of ancient Greece, anticipating *Childe Harolde's Pilgrimage* and *Don Juan.* Such an attitude may be seen in this passage from Canto I:

> Thus time elapsed, while o'er the pathless tide
> Their ship through Grecian seas the pilots guide.
> Occasion call'd to touch at Candia's shore,
> Which bless'd with favouring winds, they soon explore;
> The haven enter, borne before the gale,
> Dispatch their commerce, and prepare to sail.
> Eternal powers! what ruins from afar
> Mark the fell track of desolating war:
> Here arts and commerce with auspicious reign
> Once breathed sweet influence on the happy plain;
> While o'er the lawn, with dance and festive song,
> Young Pleasure led the jocund Hours along.
> In gay luxuriance Ceres too was seen
> To crown the vallies with eternal green;
> For wealth, for valour, courted and revered,
> What Albion is, fair Candia then appear'd.—
> Ah! who the flight of ages can revoke?
> The free-born spirit of her sons is broke,
> They bow to Ottoman's imperious yoke.
> No longer fame the drooping heart inspires,
> For stern oppression quenched its genial fires,
> Though still her fields, with golden harvests crown'd,
> Supply the barren shores of Greece around,
> Sharp penury afflicts these wretched isles,
> There hope ne'er dawns, and pleasure never smiles.
> The vassal wretch contented drags his chain,
> And hears his famish'd babes lament in vain.
> These eyes have seen the dull reluctant soil
> A seventh year mock the weary labourer's toil.
> No blooming Venus, on the desert shore,
> Now views with triumph captive gods adore;
> No lovely Helens now with fatal charms

Excite the' avenging chiefs of Greece to arms;
No fair Penelopes enchant the eye,
For whom contending kings were proud to die;
Here sullen beauty sheds a twilight ray,
While sorrow bids her vernal bloom decay:
Those charms, so long renown'd in classic strains,
Had dimly shone on Albion's happier plains![80]

During the fatal storm in Canto II, Albert gives directions for abandoning the ship. Observe, in what he says, the glorification of the idyllic primitivism of *modern* Greece which is here confused with the perfection of the ancient Greeks:

I know among you some have oft beheld
A blood-hound train, by rapine's lust impell'd,
On England's cruel coast impatient stand,
To rob the wanderers wreck'd upon their strand;
These, while their savage office they pursue,
Oft wound to death the helpless plunder'd crew,
Who, 'scaped from every horror of the main,
Implored their mercy, but implored in vain!
Yet dread not this, a crime to Greece unknown,
Such blood-hounds all her circling shores disown;
Who, though by barbarous tyranny oppress'd,
Can share affliction with the wretch distress'd:
Their hearts, by cruel fate inured to grief,
Oft to the friendless stranger yield relief.[81]

But the most striking instance of romantic hellenism in *The Shipwreck* occurs in Canto III, almost one third of which is devoted to a romantic description, almost a lament and a dirge, of Grecian shores:

Say, Memory! thou from whose unerring tongue
Instructive flows the animated song,
What regions now the scudding ship surround?
Regions of old through all the world renoun'd;
That, once the poet's theme, the muse's boast,
Now lies in ruins, in oblivion lost!

. . . . . . . . . . . . . . .

Immortal Athens first, in ruin spread,
Contiguous lies at port Liono's head;

. . . . . . . . . . . . . . .

[80] *The Shipwreck, A Poem,* by William Falconer, London, 1808, Canto I, ll. 47-85.
[81] *Ibid.*, p. 76.

Of all her towering structures, now alone,
Some columns stand, with mantling weeds o'ergrown;
The wandering stranger near the port descries
A milk-white lion of stupendous size,
Of antique marble; hence the haven's name,
Unknown to modern natives whence it came.
  Next in the gulf of Eugia, Corinth lies,
Whose gorgeous fabrics seem'd to strike the skies;
Whom, though by tyrant victors oft subdued,
Greece, Egypt, Rome, with admiration view'd:
Her name, for architecture long renoun'd,
Spread like the foliage which her pillars crown'd;
But now, in fatal desolation laid,
Oblivion o'er it draws a dismal shade.

. . . . . . . . . .

Ah! who unmoved with secret woe, can tell
That here great Lacedaemon's glory fell;
Here once she flourish'd, at whose trumpet's sound
War burst his chains, and nations shook around;

. . . . . . . . . .

But ah! how low that free-born spirit now!
Thy abject sons to haughty tyrants bow;
A false, degenerate, superstitious race
Invest thy region, and its name disgrace.
  Not distant far, Arcadia's bless'd domains
Peloponnesus' circling shore contains:
Thrice happy soil! Where, still serenely gay,
Indulgent Flora breathed perpetual May;
Where buxom Ceres bade each fertile field
Spontaneous gifts in rich profusion yield!
Then, with some rural nymph supremely bless'd,
While transport glow'd in each enamour'd breast,
Each faithful shepherd told his tender pain,
And sung of sylvan sports in artless strain;
Soft as the happy swain's enchanting lay
That pipes among the shades of Endermay:
Now, sad reverse! Oppression's iron hand
Enslaves her natives, and despoils her land;
In lawless rapine bred, a sanguine train
With midnight ravage scour the' uncultured plain.

. . . . . . . . . .

Delos! through all the Aegean seas renown'd,
Whose coast the rocky Cyclades surround;
By Phoebus honour'd, and by Greece revered,
Her hallow'd groves even distant Persia fear'd:
But now a desert unfrequented land,
No human footstep marks the trackless sand.

. . . . . . . . . .

Achaian marble form'd the gorgeous pile,
August the fabric! elegant its style!
On brazen hinges turn'd the silver doors,
And chequer'd marble paved the polish'd floors;
The roof, where storied tableture appear'd,
On columns of Corinthian mould was rear'd;
Of shining porphyry the shafts were framed,
And round the hollow dome bright jewels flam'd:
Apollo's priests before the holy shrine
Suppliant pour'd forth their orisons divine;
To front the sun's declining ray 'twas placed,
With golden harps and branching laurels graced:
Around the fane, engraved by Vulcan's hand,
The Sciences and Arts were seen to stand;
Here Aesculapius' snake display'd his crest,
And burning glories sparkled on his breast;
While from his eyes' insufferable light,
Disease and death recoil'd in headlong flight:
Of this great temple, through all time renown'd,
Sunk in oblivion, no remains are found.

. . . . . . . . . .

Adieu, ye flowery vales and fragrant scenes,
Delightful bowers and ever-vernal greens!
Adieu, ye streams! that o'er enchanted ground
In lucid maze the' Aonian hill surround;
Ye fairy scenes! where fancy loves to dwell,
And young delight; forever, oh, farewell!
The soul with tender luxury you fill,
And o'er the sense Lethean dews distil.[82]

Here are all the characteristics of romantic hellenism which we have observed before, but in this instance they are especially notable because they are used to lend color and atmosphere to a romantic narrative.

[82] *Ibid.*

By 1770 one can find evidence of the combination of romantic hellenism with escapism. This appears clearly in a poem published in Dodsley's collection for that year by "Dr. D."[83] to his friend, "Dr. T." Amid talk of war and want, politics, commerce, and similar troubled and dull matters, the poet invites his friend away from it all to his country seat, where everything is calm and soothing in the evening. Here they will sit and talk. But their conversation will not be on war and politics, but rather on "books" and "taste" and ancient wisdom, such as that in Thebes,

> Nursing her daughter arts, majestic stood,
> And pour'd forth knowledge from an hundred gates.
> There first the marble learn'd to mimic form;
> The pillar'd temple rose; and pyramids,
> Whose undecaying grandeur laughs at Time.
> Birth-place of letters! where the sun was shewn
> His radiant way, and heav'ns were taught to roll.

Then the poet proceeds to eulogize Greece. In Greece the Muses dwelt; there was nothing but Liberty. The Greeks were always singing and dancing. Everything was beautiful—Religion, Polity, and all of life; witness Pindar and Sappho and Homer:

> Happy Greece!
> Bless'd in her offspring! Seat of eloquence,
> Of arms and reason; patriot-virtue's seat!
> Did the sun thither dart uncommon rays!
> Did some presiding genius hover o'er
> That animated soil with brooding wings!
> The sad reverse might start a gentle tear.
> Go, search for Athens; her deserted ports
> Enter, a noiseless solitary shore,
> Where commerce crowded the Piraean strand.
> Trace her dark streets, her wall-embarrass'd shrines;[84]
> And pensive wonder, where her glories beam'd.
> Where are her orators, her sages, now?—
> Shatter'd her mould'ring arcs, her tow'rs in dust,—
> But far less ruin'd, than her soul decay'd.

[83] *A Collection of Poems in Six Volumes by Several Hands,* London, J. Dodsley, 1770, Vol. VI, pp. 142-148.

[84] A note at the foot of the page says: "*Wheeler's Travels,* page 346, 347, 380, 300."

The stone inscrib'd to Socrates, debas'd
To prop a reeling cot.—Minerva's dome
Possess'd by those, who never kiss'd her shield.
Upon the mount where old Musaeus sung,
Sits the gruff turban'd captain, and exacts
Harsh tribute!—In the grove, where Plato taught
His polish'd strain sublime, a stupid Turk
Is preaching ignorance and Mahomet.

A similar strain frequently runs through the poetry of William Whitehead (1715-1785), Poet Laureate from 1757 to 1785. In his *Hymn to the Nymph of Bristol Spring*, 1751, for example, occurs the following romantic longing for the peace and beauty of ancient Greece:

Happy the man whom these amusive walks,
These waking dreams delight! no cares molest
His vacant bosom: Solitude itself
But opens to his keener view new worlds,
Worlds of his own: from every genuine scene
Of Nature's varying hand his active mind
Takes fire at once, and his full soul o'erflows
With Heaven's own bounteous joy; he too creates,
And with new beings peoples earth and air,
And ocean's deep domain. The bards of old,
The godlike Grecian bards, from such fair founts
Drank inspiration. Hence on airy clifts
Light satyrs danc'd, along the woodland shade
Pan's mystic pipe resounded, and each rill
Confess'd its tutelary power, like thine.
But not like thine, bright deity, their urns
Pour'd health's rare treasures; on their grassy sides
The panting swain reclin'd with his tir'd flock
At sultry noon-tide, or at evening led
His unyok'd heifers to the common stream.[85]

This early romantic hellenism in Whitehead[86] was intensified by a visit to Italy during 1755 and 1756, made in the company of the Viscount Villiers, son of the Earl of Jersey, to whom Whitehead

[85] Chalmers, *op. cit.*, Vol. 17, pp. 211-212.

[86] If we are to believe Whitehead's own words, such an attitude was his from youth. *Cf.* "To the Honourable Charles Townsend," first published in Whitehead's collected poems in 1774 and reprinted by Chalmers, Vol. 17, p. 221:

We are not now beside that osier'd stream
Where erst we wander'd, thoughtless of the way;

was private tutor.[87] In the poetry written as a result of this journey, there are indications of poetic stimulation afforded by the observation of ruins:

> Alas! is this the boasted scene,
> This dreary, wide, uncultivated plain,
> Where sick'ning Nature wears a fainter green,
> And Desolation spreads her torpid reign?
> Is this the scene where Freedom breath'd,
> Her copious horn where Plenty wreath'd,
> And Health at opening day
> Bade all her roseate breezes fly,
> To wake the sons of industry,
> And make their fields more gay?
>
> Where is the villa's rural pride,
> The swelling dome's imperial gleam,
> Which lov'd to grace thy verdant side,
> And tremble in thy golden stream?
> Where are the bold, the busy throngs,
> That rush'd impatient to the war,
> Or tun'd to peace triumphal songs,
> And hail'd the passing car?[88]

After he had become Poet Laureate, Whitehead used a similar theme in his "Ode for His Majesty's Birth-Day, June 4, 1769." After lauding the monarch for encouraging the importation into England of Greek antiquities, the poet concludes with this expression of the value of such monuments:

> And shall each sacred seat,
> The vales of Arno, and the Tuscan stream,
> No more be visited with pilgrim feet?
> No more on sweet Hymettus' summits dream
> The sons of Albion? or below,
> Where Ilyssus' waters flow,
> Trace with awe the dear remains
> Of mould'ring urns, and mutilated fanes?

---

> We do not now of distant ages dream,
> And cheat in converse half the ling'ring day;
> No fancied heroes rise at our command,
> And no Timoleon weeps, and bleeds no Theban band.

[87] See the life prefixed to Chalmers' collection of Whitehead's poetry, Vol. 17, pp. 189-197.

[88] "Ode to the Tiber. On Entering the Campania of Rome, 1755" in Chalmers, Vol. 17, p. 226.

Far be the thought. Each sacred seat,
Each monument of ancient fame,
Shall still be visited with pilgrim feet,
And Albion gladly own from whence she caught the flame.
Still shall her studious youth repair,
Beneath their king's protecting care,
To every clime which art has known;
And rich with spoils from every coast
Return, till Albion learn to boast
An Athens of her own.[89]

In addition to the poems of Whitehead, romantic hellenism appears also in the poetry of John Scott (1730-83), the Quaker poet who was the friend of Beattie and Johnson. In 1770 Scott had taken a house at Amwell with which he was so pleased that he wrote a long, appreciative poem, *Amwell: A Descriptive Poem,* published in 1776. In describing the beauties of Amwell, he compares the panorama with ancient Greece:

How beautiful, how various, is the view
Of these sweet pastoral landscapes! fair, perhaps,
As those renown'd of old, from Tabor's height,
Or Carmel seen; or those, the pride of Greece,
Tempe or Arcady; or those that grac'd
The banks of clear Elorus, or the skirts
Of thymy Hybla, where Sicilia's isle
Smiles on the azure main; there once was heard
The Muse's lofty lay.[90]

Again, in Scott's "Ode After Reading Akenside's Poems," 1782, appears this emotional outburst:

What mean those crystal rocks serene,
Those laureate groves forever green,
Those Parian domes?—Sublime retreats,
Of Freedom's sons the happy seats!—
There dwell the few who dar'd disdain
The lust of power and lust of gain;
The patriot names of old renown'd,
And those in later ages found;
The Athenian, Spartan, Roman boast,
The pride of Britain's sea-girt coast!
But, oh! what darkness intervenes!

[89] *Ibid.*, p. 260.

[90] *Ibid.*, p. 465.

But, oh! beneath what diff'rent scenes!
What matron she, to grief resign'd,
Beside that ruin'd arch reclin'd?
Her sons, who once so well could wield
The warrior-spear, the warrior-shield,
A turban'd ruffian's scourge constrains
To toil on desolated plains!
And she who leans that column nigh,
Where trampled arms and eagles lie;
Whose veil essays her blush to hide,
Who checks the tear that hastens to glide?
A mitred priest's oppressive sway
She sees her drooping race obey:
Their vines unprun'd, their fields untill'd,
Their streets with want and mis'ry fill'd.[91]

Still other instances of romantic hellenism in the ninth decade of the eighteenth century may be found in the "Ode Written in Spring," 1781, by John Logan (1748-1788), a preacher who had distinguished himself by proficiency in the classics while at the University of Edinburgh. In this poem Logan addresses the goddess of Spring and calls upon her to lead him out among the beauties of nature:

Where hills by storied streams ascend,
My dreams and waking wishes tend
  Poetic ease to woo;
Where Fairy fingers curl the grove,
Where Grecian spirits round me rove,
Alone enamour'd with the love
  Of Nature and of you![92]

A similar strain appears in a poem by William Julius Mickle (1734-1788), *Almada Hill. An Epistle from Lisbon,* published in 1781. Mickle had been appointed corrector to the Clarendon Press, Oxford, in 1765, and in 1775 he translated the *Lusiad* of Camoens into English.[93] In 1779 Commodore George Johnstone appointed him his secretary on the Romney man-of-war, sailing with a squadron to Portugal. *Almada Hill* was stimulated by certain ruins among which the author was wandering at Lisbon. One

[91] *Ibid.,* pp. 486-7. [92] *Ibid.,* Vol. 18, p. 56.
[93] See Sister Eustace Taylor, *William Julius Mickle (1734-1788), A Critical Study,* Washington, D.C., Catholic University, 1937.

of the thoughts which come to him gives rise to this passage:

> Alas! how waste Ionia's landscapes mourn;
> And thine, O beauteous Greece, amid the towers
> Where dreadful still the Turkish banner lowers;
> Beneath whose gloom, unconscious of the stain
> That dims his soul, the peasant hugs his chain.
> And whence these woes debasing human kind?
> Eunuchs in heart, in polish'd sloth reclin'd,
> Thy sons, degenerate Greece, ignobly bled,
> And fair Byzantium bow'd th' imperial head,
>
> . . . . . . . . .
>
> Alas, my friend, how vain the fairest boast
> Of human pride! how soon is empire lost!
> The pile by ages rear'd to awe the world,
> By one degenerate race to ruin hurl'd!
> And shall the Briton view that downward race
> With eye unmov'd, and no sad likeness trace?
> Ah, heaven! in ev'ry scene, by mem'ry brought,
> My fading country rushes on my thought.[94]

Thus, between 1735 and 1786 one can trace a distinct strain of romantic hellenism in much of the poetry published chiefly by authors cited as "unconventional" in other literary ways.[95] This body of verse reveals almost all the characteristics observable in the poetry of the nineteenth century romanticists: the use of Greece as a symbol of freedom; the identification of ancient with modern Greece; the nostalgia for the Arcadian life that was ancient Greece; and the inspiration of Greek ruins and other remains to poetry, moods, and action. A study of this poetry indicates that the sentimental idealization of antiquity characteristic of this view arose, apparently, about the same time as the growth of interest in archaeology and travel. This idealization of antiquity in general seems gradually to have been centered about Greece alone, chiefly because the growth of Greek archaeology, travel to Greece, and Greek-inspired æsthetics hellenized the current of ideas in the age.

[94] *Ibid.*, pp. 537-8.

[95] Thomson, Akenside, and the Wartons, for example, are frequently analyzed for their interest in nature. See Myra Reynolds, *op. cit.* Gray and Mason are major figures in the Celtic revival. See Edward D. Snyder, *op. cit.* Similarly, most of the poets whom we have considered belong at least in some ways to the sentimental "school of melancholy." See R. D. Havens, *The Influence of Milton on English Poetry,* Harvard University Press, 1922.

# VI

## CONCLUSION

From what has been said in the preceding chapters, it is clear that by 1786 the idea of romantic hellenism has been definitely established in English literature. 1787 is the date of publication of the second volume of Stuart and Revett's *Antiquities of Athens*. After its appearance, there is a marked increase in the vogue of "Grecian gusto." There is a similar increase, after that date, in the number of scientific Greek archaeologists, antiquaries, and collectors of marbles, such as Thomas Hope, the Marquis of Lansdowne, the Earl of Bristol, and Lord Elgin. Travellers, such as Dodwell and Colonel Leake, became more and more interested in Greece. The influence of Winckelmann becomes more pronounced, while there arise new aestheticians and poets, such as Flaxman and Richard Payne Knight. By 1806 Oxford University awards a prize to John Wilson of Magdalen College for a poem on "Grecian and Roman Architecture, Sculpture, and Painting."[1]

In the study of the rise of romantic hellenism prior to 1786, the student may observe an interesting literary phenomenon. Romanticism is seen to transmute the neo-classical worship of the ancients into a bulwark for the "radical" ideas of genius, primitivism, liberty, and equality. Stimulated in embryo by Rome, this romantic attitude is directed toward Greece primarily by the growth of scientific archaeology under the auspices of the Society of Dilettanti and independent antiquaries and collectors. To this scientific approach to Greece, travel literature adds such sentimental elements as the idealization of ancient Greek life and culture, rhapsodies over the beauties of modern Greece, and lamentations over the decay of the Arcadia that was the Greece of long ago and the slavery to which it has been subjected by the Turks.

[1] See *Oxford Prize Poems: Being a Collection of such English Poems as have at various times obtained prizes in the University of Oxford,* Oxford, 1807 (2nd ed.).

Aestheticians such as Winckelmann and Jones add to these a further romantic element by reading into ancient Greek art what the travellers have read into the islands of modern Greece. Finally, the elements thus created are steeped in emotion by the early romantic poets, who eagerly seize upon the new conception of Greece and make it the symbol of liberty, repose, beauty, and poetic inspiration. Thus, romantic hellenism, like romantic naturalism and humanitarianism, finds its origin within the neo-classical period itself.

When the results of this study are borne in mind, the reader of *Prometheus Unbound, Childe Harolde's Pilgrimage,* and *Don Juan* will possess a deeper understanding and find a keener pleasure in the ideas which these poems express. Certainly, the *Ode on a Grecian Urn* should have for him an enriched and more profound meaning, for it is the product of a long and interesting development.

# BIBLIOGRAPHY

## PRIMARY SOURCES

Academia Ercolanese. Le Antichita di Ercolano. Naples, 1757.

Adam, Robert. Ruins of the Palace of the Emperor Diocletian at Spalatro in Dalmatia. [London], 1763.

[Addison, Joseph]. *The Spectator*. Nos. 409, 411. 1712.

Anonymous. A Journey from Aleppo to Damascus; To Which is Added, An Account of the Maronites Inhabiting Mount-Lebanon. London, 1736.

Anonymous. A Letter to his Excellency Count—on poetry, painting, and Sculpture. London, 1768.

Anonymous. An Enquiry into the Causes of the Extraordinary Excellency of Ancient Greece in the Arts. London, 1767.

Anonymous. Lettres sur l'état actuel de la ville souterraine d'Héraclée. Dijon, 1750.

Anonymous. Review of The Ruins of Balbec. *Monthly Review*. Vol. XVII, pp. 59-66. 1758.

Anonymous. *The Adventurer*. No. 139. Tuesday, March 5, 1754.

Anonymous. *The World*. No. 63. Thursday, March 14, 1754.

Baltimore, F[rederick] Lord. A Tour to the East, in the Years 1763 and 1764. With Remarks on the City of Constantinople and the Turks. With Select Pieces of Oriental Wit, Poetry and Wisdom. London, 1767.

Barry, James. An Inquiry Into the Real and Imaginary Obstructions To The Acquisition of the Arts in England. London, 1775.

Barthélémy, Abbé de. Les Voyages du Jeune Anacharsis. Paris, 1789.

Bielfeld, Baron. The Elements of Universal Erudition, containing an Analytical Abridgement of the Sciences, Polite Arts, and Belles Lettres. . . . Translated from the last edition printed at Berlin. By W. Hooper, M.D. London, 1770. 3 Vols.

Bos, Lambert. Antiquities of Greece. Translated from the original Latin by Percival Stockdale. London, 1772.

Browne, Lyde. Catalogo dei piu scelti e preziosi marmi, che si conservano nella Galleria del Sigr. Lyde Browne, Cavaliere Inglese, a Wimbledon, nella Contea di Surry, raccolti con gran spesa nel corso de trent'anni, molti dei quali si ammiravano prima nelle piu celebri Gallerie di Roma. London, 1779.

Browne, Lyde. Catalogus veteris aevi varii generis monumentorum, quae Cimeliarchio Lyde Browne Arm. apud Wimbledon asservantur. London, 1768.

Brydone, P[atrick]. A Tour through Sicily and Malta. In a Series of Letters to William Beckford, Esq. of Somerly in Suffolk. London, 1773.

Caylus, Anne-Claude-Philippe de Tubières, etc., Comte de. Mémoir sur la peinture à l'encaustique et sur la peinture et de sculpture. Paris, 1755.

Caylus, Anne-Claude-Philippe de Tubières, etc., Comte de. Receuil d'Antiquités égyptiennes, étrusques, grecques, et romaines. Paris, 1752-1767. 7 Vols.

Chalmers, Alexander. The Works of the English Poets from Chaucer to Cowper. London, 1810. Vols. 17-18.

Chandler, Richard. Elegiaca Graeca. Oxford, 1759.

Chandler, Richard. History of Ilium or Troy. London, 1802.

Chandler, Richard. Inscriptiones Antiquae, pleraeque nondum editae: in Asia Minori et Graecia praesertim Athenis, collectae. Cum appendice. Oxford, 1774.

Chandler, Richard. Marmora Oxoniensiae. Oxonii. E Typographeo Clarendoniano. Impensia Academiae. 1763.

Chandler, Richard. Travels in Asia Minor. London, 1775.

Chandler, Richard. Travels in Greece; or, An Account of a Tour Made at the Expense of the Society of Dilettanti. Dublin, 1776.

Chandler, R., Revett, N., and Pars, W. Ionian Antiquities. Published with Permission of the Society of Dilettanti. London, 1769. Vol. I.

Charlemont, Earl of. The Manuscripts and Correspondence of James, First Earl of Charlemont. Historical Manuscripts Commission. 12th Report. Part X. Vol. 28. London, 1891.

Chatterton, Lady. Memorials, personal and historical, of Admiral Lord Gambier. London, 1861.

Chishull, Edmund. Antiquates Asiaticae, Etc. London, 1728.

Chishull, Edmund. Inscriptio Sigea Antiquissima. London, 1721.

Chishull, Edmund. Travels in Turkey and Back to England. London, 1747.

Choiseul-Gouffier, Marie Gabriel Auguste Florent, Comte de. Voyage Pittoresque de la Grèce. Paris, 1782.

Climenson, Emily J. Elizabeth Montague, the Queen of the Blue-Stockings. Her Correspondence from 1720 to 1761. London, 1906. 2 Vols.

Cochin, C. N., et Bellicard, J. C. Observations sur les antiquités d'Herculanum, avec quelque réflexions sur la peinture et la sculpture des anciens. Paris, 1754.

Cockerell, C. R., Kinnard, W., et al. Antiquities of Athens and Other Places in Greece, Sicily, Etc. Supplementary to the Antiquities of Athens by James Stuart . . . and Nicholas Revett. London, 1830.

Coleridge, Ernest Hartley. The Works of Lord Byron. London, 1918. 13 Vols.

Collins, William. Odes on Several Descriptive and Allegoric Subjects. London, 1747. [Really 1746.]

Cornelio Magni of Parma. Relazione della Citta d'Athene colle Provincie dell'Attica, Focia, Beozia, Etc. nei Tempi Che furono passeggiate da Cornelio Magni, Parmegiano, l'anno 1674, e dallo stresso publicato l'anno 1688.

Dallaway, James. Anecdotes of the Arts in England, or Comparative Remarks on Architecture, Sculpture, and Painting, chiefly illustrated by Specimens at Oxford. London, 1800.

Dallaway, James. Statuary and Sculpture Among the Ancients, with some Account of Specimens Preserved in England. London, 1816.

Dalton, Richard. Antiquatum Graecorum. ?1752.

Dalton, Richard. Antiquities and Views in Greece and Egypt, with the Manners and Customs of the Inhabitants. London, 1752.

Dalton, Richard. [A series of engravings representing views of places, buildings, antiquities, etc. in Sicily, Greece, Asia Minor, and Egypt. London, 1751-2. 52 plates.]

David, J. Antiquités d'Herculanum. Paris, 1754.

Dodsley, J. A Collection of Poems in Six Volumes by Several Hands. London, 1755. 4th Ed.

Dodsley, J. A Collection of Poems in Six Volumes by Several Hands. London, 1770.

Dodwell, Edward. A Classical and Topographical Tour through Greece, During the Years, 1801, 1805, and 1806. London, 1819. 2 Vols.

Drummond, Alexander. Travels through Different Cities of Germany, Italy, Greece, and Several Parts of Asia, as far as the Banks of the Euphrates; In a series of letters. Containing an Account of what is most Remarkable in their present State, as well as in their Monuments of Antiquity. London, 1754.

Duff, William. An Essay on Original Genius; and its various modes of Exertion in Philosophy and the Fine Arts, Particularly in Poetry. London, 1767.

Dyce, Rev. A. The Poetical Works of Akenside and Beattie. Boston, 1864.

Dyer, John. The Ruins of Rome. London, 1740.

Falconer, William. The Shipwreck. A Poem. London, 1808.

Flaxman, John. Lectures on Sculpture as delivered by him before the President and members of the Royal Academy. London, 1829.

Forman, H. Buxton. The Poetical Works of John Keats. Oxford University Press, 1920.

Fuseli, Henry. Lectures on Painting, delivered at the Royal Academy. London, 1830.

[Fuseli, Henry.] Remarks on the Writings and Conduct of J. J. Rousseau. London, 1767.
Gerard, Alexander. An Essay on Genius. London, 1774.
Gillies, John. History of Ancient Greece, Its Colonies and Conquests, to The Division of the Macedonian Empire; Including the History of Literature, Philosophy, and the Fine Arts. London, 1786. 2 Vols.
Glover, Richard. Leonidas. An Epic. London, 1737.
Goguet, [Antoine Yves]. The Origin of Laws, Arts, and Sciences, And Their Progress Among the Most Ancient Nations. Translated from the French of the President De Goguet. Edinburgh, 1775. 3 Vols.
Gray, T[homas]. Designs by Mr. R. Bentley for Six Poems of Mr. T. Gray. London, 1753.
Guys, M. Voyage Littéraire de la Grèce, ou lettres sur les Grecs anciennes et modernes avec un parallèlle de leurs moeurs. Paris, 1783.
Hancarville, Pierre François Hugues, Called D'. Récherches sur l'origine, l'esprit et les progrès des Arts de la Grèce; sur leurs connections avec les arts et la réligion des plus anciens peuples connus. London, 1785. 2 Vols.
Hasselquist, Frederick. Voyages and Travels in the Levant; In the Years 1749, 50, 51, 52. Containing observations in Natural History, Physick, Agriculture, and Commerce: Particularly on the Holy Land, and the Natural History of the Scriptures. Written originally in the Swedish Language. . . . Published, by order of her Present Majesty the Queen of Sweden, by Charles Linnaeus, Physician to the King of Sweden, Professor of Botany at Upsal, and Member of all the Learned Societies in Europe. London, 1766.
Hill, Aaron. A Just Account of the Ottoman Empire. London, 1709.
Hogarth, William. Analysis of Beauty. Written with a view to fixing the fluctuating Ideas of Taste. London, 1753.
Irwin, Eyles. A Series of Adventures in the Course of a Voyage up the Red-Sea, on the coasts of Arabia and Egypt; and of a route through the Desarts of Thebais, in the Year 1777. In Letters to a Lady. London, 1780.
Irwin, Eyles. A Series of Adventures in the Course of a Voyage up the Red-Sea . . . Together with a Supplement of a Voyage from Venice to Latichea; and of a route through the Desarts of Arabia, By Aleppo, Bagdad, and the Tygris, to Busrah in the Years 1780 and 1781. London, 1787.
Jones, Sir William. Poems. London, 1777.
Kirshaw, Thomas. On the Comparative Merit of the Ancient and Mod-

erns, with respect to the Imitative Arts. Read Feb. 19, 1783. *Memoirs of the Literary and Philosophical Society of Manchester.* Vol. I, pp. 405-413. Warrington, 1785.

Knowles, John. The Life and Writings of Henry Fuseli, Esq., M.A., R.A. London, 1831.

Knox, Vicesimus. Essays Moral and Literary. London, 1782. 2 Vols.

Le Roy, Julien David. Les Ruines des Plus Beaux Monuments de la Grèce, considérées du côté de l'histoire et du côté de l'architecture. Paris, 1758 and 1770.

Lessing, Gotthold Ephraim. Laokoon. Berlin, 1766.

Mason, William. Caractacus. London, 1759.

Mason, William. Elfrida. London, 1751.

Maundrell, Henry. A Journey from Aleppo to Jerusalem. Oxford, 1703.

McIntosh. Travels in Europe, Asia, and Africa, from 1777 to 1781. London, 1782.

Mickle, William Julius. Almada Hill. An Epistle from Lisbon. Oxford, 1781.

Mitford, William. The History of Greece. The First Volume. London, 1784.

M[ontague], Lady M[ar]y W[ortle]y. Letters of Lady M--y W---y M----. London, 1763. 3 Vols.

Montague, Lady Mary Wortley. Letters . . . Written during her Travels in Europe, Asia, and Africa. Which Contain, Among other curious Relations, Accounts of the Policy and Manners of the Turks; Drawn From Sources That Have Been Inaccessible To Other Travellers. A New Edition. Paris, 1793. 2 Vols.

Muentz, J. H. Encaustic: or Count Caylus's method of painting in the manner of the ancients. London, 1760.

Nichols, John. Anecdotes of the Eighteenth Century. London, 1812-1816. Vol. II.

Norton, Charles Eliot. Letter to F. A. Tupper, 1885. *Harvard Alumni Bulletin,* p. 258. 1927.

Oxford University. Oxford Prize Poems. Being a Collection of such English Poems as have at various times obtained prizes in the University of Oxford. Oxford, 1807.

Paciaudi, P. Lettres au Comte de Caylus. Paris, 1802.

Perry, Charles. A View of the Levant: Particularly of Constantinople, Syria, Egypt, and Greece. In Which Their Antiquities, Government, Politics, Maxims, Manners, and Customs (With Many Other Circumstances and Contingencies) Are Attempted To Be Described and Treated On. London, 1743.

Pinkerton, John. A General Collection of the Best and Most Interesting Voyages and Travels in All Parts of the World. London, 1814. 17 Vols.

Pococke, Richard. A Description of the East, And Some Other Countries. Volume II. London, 1745.

Pococke, Richard. Inscriptionum Antiquarum Graec. et Lat. liber. Accedit numismatum . . . in Aegypto cursorum . . . Catalogus, Etc. [London], 1752.

Potter, John. Archaeologia Graeca, or the Antiquities of Greece . . . To which is added an Appendix, containing a concise history of the Grecian states, and a short account of the lives and writings of the most celebrated authors. London, 1751. 7th Ed.

Price, Joseph. Some Observations and Remarks on the Late Publication, entitled "Travels in Europe, Asia, and Africa." London, 1782.

Reveley, Willey. The Antiquities of Athens. Measured and Delineated. Volume III. London, 1794.

Reynolds, Sir Joshua. Discourses on Painting and the Fine Arts, Delivered at the Royal Academy. London, 1805.

Riedesel zu Eisenbach, Johann Hermann. Reise durch Sicilien und Grossgriechenland. Zurich, 1771.

[Riedesel zu Eisenbach, Johann Hermann]. Travels through Sicily and That Part of Italy formerly called Magna Graecia. And A Tour through Egypt. Translated by J. R. Forster. London, 1773.

Russell. The Natural History of Aleppo, and Ports Adjacent; Containing a Description of the City and the Principal Natural Productions in its Neighborhood. London, 1756.

Rycant, Paul. The Present State of the Ottoman Empire. London, 1668.

Sayer, Robert. The Ruins of Athens. London, 1749.

Scott, John. Amwell: A Descriptive Poem. London, 1776.

Selden, John. Marmora Arundelliana. 1628.

Seward, William. Supplement to the Anecdotes of Distinguished Persons, Chiefly of the Present and 2 Preceding Centuries. London, 1798.

Shaftesbury, Anthony Ashley Cooper, Third Earl of. Characteristics of Men, Manners, Opinions, Times. London, 1710.

Smythe, Sir Sidney Stafford. The Trial of Frederick Calvert, Esq., Baron of Baltimore . . . for a Rape on the Body of Sarah Woodcock, and of Eliz. Griffinburg, and Ann Harvey, otherwise Darby, as Accessaries before the Fact . . . at the Assizes held at Kingston, for the County of Surry, on Saturday, the 26th of March, 1768, before the Hon. Sir Sydney Stafford Smythe. London, 1768.

Spence, Joseph. Polymetis. Or an Enquiry concerning the Agreement between the works of the Roman Poets and the Remains of the Ancient Artists. Being an Attempt to illustrate them mutually from each other. London, 1747.

Stuart, Elizabeth. The Antiquities of Athens. Measured and Delineated. Volume II. London, 1787.

Stuart, James, and Revett, Nicholas. Proposals for Publishing an Accurate Description of the Antiquities of Athens. Rome, 1748.

Stuart, James, and Revett, Nicholas. Proposals for Publishing an Accurate Description of the Antiquities of Athens. London, 1750.

Stuart, James, and Revett, Nicholas. The Antiquities of Athens. Measured and Delineated by James Stuart F.R.S. and F.S.A. and Nicholas Revett, Painters and Architects. Volume I. London, 1762.

Teignmouth, Lord. Memoir of Sir William Jones in The Collected Works of Sir William Jones, edited by Lord Teignmouth and Lady Jones. London, 1804.

"Thompson, Charles." The Travels of the Late Charles Thompson, Esq., containing His Observations on France, Italy, Turkey in Europe, The Holy Land, Arabia, Egypt, and many other parts of the World: Giving a particular and faithful account of what is most remarkable in the Manners, Religion, Polity, Antiquities, and Natural History of those countries: With a curious description of Jerusalem, as it now appears, and other places mentioned in the Holy Scriptures. The whole forming a compleat View of the ancient and modern state of great part of Europe, Asia, and Africa: Publish'd from the Author's original Manuscript, interspers'd with the Remarks of Several other Modern Travellers, and Illustrated with Historical, Geographical, and Miscellaneous Notes by the Editor. Adorn'd with Maps and Prints. Reading, 1744. 3 Vols.

Thomson, James. Liberty. A Poem. London, 1735.

Toynbee, Mrs. Paget. Letters of Horace Walpole. London, 1903. 2 Vols.

Toynbee, Paget, and Whibley, Leonard. The Correspondence of Thomas Gray. Oxford, 1935. 3 Vols.

Turnbull, George. A Treatise on Ancient Painting. Containing Observations on the Rise, Progress, and Decline of that Art amongst the Greeks and Romans. London, 1740.

Van Egmont, J. Aegidius, and Heyman, John. Travels Through Part of Europe, Asia Minor, The Islands of the Archipelago; Syria, Palestine, Egypt, Mount Sinai, Etc. Giving a particular account of the most remarkable Places, Structures, Ruins, Inscriptions, Etc. in these Countries. Together with the Customs, Manners, Religion, Trade, Commerce, Tempers, and Manner of Living of the Inhabitants . . . Translated from the Low Dutch. London, 1759. 2 Vols.

Veryard, Ellis. An Account of Divers Choice Remarks, as Well Geographical, as Historical, Political, Mathematical, Physical, and Moral; Taken in A Journey Through the Low Countries . . . As Also a Voyage to the Levant. Exeter, 1701.

Walpole, Horatio. Aedes Walpolianae. 1747.

Warton, Joseph. Essay on the Genius and Writings of Pope. London, 1757.

Warton, Thomas. History of English Poetry. London, 1840. Vol. III.

Warton, Thomas. Newmarket. A Satire. London, 1751.

Wheler, George. A Journey into Greece in Company with Dr. Spon. London, 1682.

White, Gilbert. Recollections of William Collins. *Gentleman's Magazine.* Vol. LI, p. 11. 1781.

Winckelmann, Johann Joachim. Abstract of a Letter concerning Herculaneum. *Annual Register.* Vol. 8, pp. 182-189. 1765.

Winckelmann, [Johann Joachim]. A description of the famous marble trunk of Hercules, dug up at Rome, commonly called the Torso of Belvedere; wrought by Apollonius the son of Nestor, and universally allowed to have been made for a statue of Hercules spinning. Translated from the German of the Abbé Winckelmann . . . By Henry Fusle. *Annual Register.* Vol. 8, pp. 130-132. 1765.

Winckelmann, Johann Joachim. Geschichte der Kunst des Alterthums. Dresden, 1764.

Winckelmann, [Johann Joachim]. Observations on the influence of the different climates upon the polite arts; taken from A history of the fine arts, by the Abbé Wincklemann, librarian of the Vatican, and antiquary to the Pope. *Annual Register.* Vol. 8, pp. 250-253. 1765.

Winckelmann, Johann Joachim. Gedancken über die Nachahmung der griechischen Wercke in der Mahlerey und Bildhauer-Kunst. Friedrichstadt, 1755.

Winckelmann, [Johann Joachim]. Reflections on the Painting and Sculpture of the Greeks: With Instructions for the Connoisseur, and An Essay on Grace in Works of Art. Translated from the German original of the Abbé Winckelmann, Librarian of the Vatican, by Henry Fusseli. London, 1765.

Wood, Robert. A Comparative View of the Antient and Present State of the Troade. To which is prefixed an Essay on the Original Genius of Homer. London, 1767.

Wood, Robert. An Essay on the Original Genius of Homer. London, 1769.

Wood, Robert. An Essay on the Original Genius and Writings of Homer. With a Comparative View of the Antient and Present State of the Troade. Edited by Jacob Bryant. London, 1775.

Wood, Robert. The Ruins of Balbec, Otherwise Heliopolis in Collosyria. London, 1757.

[Wood, Robert]. The Ruins of Palmyra, Otherwise Tedmor, in the Desart. London, 1753.

Woodberry, George E. The Complete Works of Percy Bysshe Shelley. New York, 1901.
Woods, Joseph. The Antiquities of Athens. Measured and Delineated. Volume IV. London, 1816.
Young, Edward. Conjectures on Original Composition. In a Letter to the Author of Sir Charles Grandison. London, 1759.

SECONDARY SOURCES

Allen, B. Sprague. Tides in English Taste (1619-1800). A Background for the Study of Literature. Harvard University Press, 1937. 2 Vols.
Babbitt, Irving. Rousseau and Romanticism. Boston and New York, 1919.
Badolle, Maurice. L'Abbé Jean Jacques Barthélémy et l'héllénisme en France dans la seconde miotié du XVIIIme siècle. Paris, 1926.
Beers, Henry A. A History of English Romanticism in the Eighteenth Century. New York, 1910.
Bertrand, Louis. La fin du Classicisme et le retour à l'Antique dans la seconde moitié du XVIIIme siècle. Paris, 1897.
Bikelas, D. La Grèce Byzantine et Moderne. Paris, 1893.
Blomefield, Francis. History of the County of Norfolk. London, 1805-1810. 4 Vols.
Butler, E. M. The Tyranny of Greece over Germany. New York, 1935.
Carruthers, Robert. Memoir of William Falconer in The Shipwreck. A Poem. In Three Cantos. London, 1858.
Chambers, Frank P. The History of Taste: An Account of the Revolutions of Art Criticism and Theory in Europe. Columbia Univerversity Press, 1932.
Chapman, R. W. Contributors to Dodsley's Collections of Poems. Oxford Bibliographical Society. Proceedings and Papers. Vol. III. 1931-1933.
Chichester, Henry Manners. Alexander Drummond. *Dictionary of National Biography*. Vol. 17, p. 61. 1921-1922.
Chislett, William. The Classical Influence in English Literature in the Nineteenth Century. Boston, 1918.
Churton, Ralph. Memoir of Richard Chandler in Travels in Asia Minor and Greece. With Corrections and Remarks by Nicholas Revett, Esq. Oxford, 1825. 2 Vols.
Clark, Kenneth. The Gothic Revival. New York, 1929.
Collins, John C. Greek Influence on English Poetry. London, 1910.
Conant, Martha P. The Oriental Tale in England in the Eighteenth Century. Columbia University Press, 1908.
Courthope, W. J. A History of English Poetry. London, 1911. Vol. V.

Cust, Lionel H. James Stuart. *Dictionary of National Biography.* Vol. 19, p. 87. 1921.

Cust, Lionel, and Colvin, Sidney. History of the Society of Dilettanti. London, 1914. 2nd Ed.

Davenport, S. T. Biography of James Barry, R.A. *Journal of the Society of Fine Arts.* Vol. XVIII, pp. 803-805. Aug. 26, 1870.

Draper, John W. Eighteenth Century Aesthetics. A Bibliography. *Anglistische Forschungen,* Heft 71. Heidelburg, 1931.

Draper, John W. The Funeral Elegy and the Rise of English Romanticism. New York, 1929.

Draper, John W. William Mason: A Study in Eighteenth Century Culture. New York University Press, 1924.

Federmann, Arnold. Johann Heinrich Füssli, Dichter und Maler, 1741-1825. Zurich and Leipzig, 1927.

Fontaine, André. Comte de Caylus' Vies d'Artistes du XVIIIme siècle. Discours sur la Peinture et la Sculpture. Paris, 1910.

Foster, Joseph. Alumni Oxonienses. Oxford and London, 1888.

Frantz, R. W. The English Traveller and the Movement of Ideas, 1660-1732. University of Nebraska Studies. Vol. 32/33. 1932-1933.

Fryer, Edward. Memoir of James Barry in The Works of James Barry. London, 1825.

Gillies, John. Memoir in *Gentleman's Magazine,* New Series. Vol. V, pp. 436-437. 1836.

Hamilton, W. R. Extract from The Historical Notices of the Society of Dilettanti. *Edinburgh Review.* Vol. CV, pp. 493-517. 1857.

Hamilton, W. R. Historical Notices of the Society of Dilettanti. Printed for private circulation only. London, 1855.

Havens, R. D. The Influence of Milton on English Poetry. Harvard University Press, 1922.

Hussey, Christopher. The Picturesque; Studies in a Point of View. London, 1927.

Irwin, Eyles. Memoir in *European Magazine.* Vol. XV, pp. 179-181. 1789. Vol. LXXII, p. 277. 1817.

Isambert, G. L'Indépendance Grecque et L'Europe. Paris, 1900.

Jones, William Powell. Thomas Gray, Scholar: The True Tragedy of an Eighteenth-Century Gentleman. Harvard University Press, 1937.

Levin, Harry. The Broken Column; A Study in Romantic Hellenism. Bowdoin Undergraduate Prize Essay. Harvard University Press, 1931.

Lewis, C. S. The Allegory of Love. Oxford University Press, 1936.

Lognon, J. Quatre siècles de philhélénisme français. *Revue de France.* Vol. I, No. 6, pp. 512-542. 1921.

Maar, Harko G. de. A History of Modern English Romanticism. Oxford University Press, 1924. Vol. I.

Malakis, Emile. French Travellers in Greece (1770-1820). An Early Phase of French Philhellenism. Philadelphia, 1925.

Marshall, Roderick. Italy in English Literature, 1755-1815. Columbia University Press, 1934.

Martin, Roger. Essai sur Thomas Gray. Oxford University Press, 1934.

Maskelyne, Story. The Marlborough Gems. London, 1870.

Mead, William Edward. The Grand Tour in the Eighteenth Century. Boston and New York, 1914.

Michaelis, Adolf. A Century of Archaeological Discovery. London, 1908.

Michaelis, Adolf. Ancient Marbles in Great Britain. Cambridge [Eng.], 1882.

Miller, William. The English in Athens Before 1821. A Lecture delivered before the Anglo-Hellenic League in Athens February 10, 1926. Published by the Anglo-Hellenic League, 53 and 54 Chancery Lane W. C. 2. 1926.

Miller, William. The Turkish Restoration in Greece, 1718-1797. London, 1921.

Morel, Léon, James Thomson, Sa Vie et Ses Oevres. Paris, 1895.

Partridge, Eric. The Three Wartons. A Choice of Their Verse. London, 1927.

Pater, Walter. Greek Studies. London, 1901.

Phelps, William Lyon. The Beginnings of the English Romantic Movement. Boston, 1893.

Pierce, Frederick E. The Hellenic Current in English 19th Century Poetry. *Journal of English and Germanic Philology*. Vol. XVI, p. 103 (1917).

Popp, Hermann. Die Architektur der Barock- und Rokoko-zeit in Deutschland und der Schweiz. Stuttgart, 1913.

Reed, Amy L. The Background of Gray's Elegy. Columbia University Press, 1924.

Reynolds, Myra. The Treatment of Nature in English Poetry Between Pope and Wordsworth. Chicago, 1909. 2nd Ed.

Rinaker, Clarissa. Thomas Warton. A Biographical and Critical Study. University of Illinois Studies in Language and Literature. Vol. II, No. 1. 1916.

Sickels, Eleanor M. The Gloomy Egoist. Columbia University Press, 1932.

Sitwell, Sacheverell. German Baroque Art. New York, 1928.

Snyder, Edward D. The Celtic Revival in English Literature, 1760-1800. Harvard University Press, 1923.

Stokoe, F. W. German Influence in the English Romantic Period, 1788-1815. Cambridge University Press, 1926.

Stone, Christopher. The Poems of William Collins. London, 1907.

Taylor, Sister Eustace. William Julius Mickle (1734-1788). A Critical Study. Washington, D.C., 1937.

Templeman, William D. Contributions to the Bibliography of Eighteenth Century Aesthetics. *Modern Philology*. Vol. XXX, pp. 309-316. 1932-1933.

Thomas, Edward. The Poems of John Dyer. London, 1903.

Thomas, W. Moy. Memoir of Lady Mary Wortley Montague in The Letters and Works of Lady Mary Wortley Montague; edited by her great grandson, Lord Wharncliffe. London, 1887.

Tinker, Chauncey B. Nature's Simple Plan. A Phase of Radical Thought in the Mid-Eighteenth Century. The Louis Clark Vanuxem Lectures. Princeton University Press, 1922.

Venturi, Lionello. History of Art Criticism. Translated from the Italian by Charles Marriott. New York, 1936.

# INDEX

[To be used in conjunction with the Bibliography]